Bibliographies for Biblical Research

New Testament Series

in Twenty-One Volumes

General Editor

Watson E. Mills

Bibliographies for Biblical Research

New Testament Series

in Twenty-One Volumes

Volume VII

1 Corinthians

Compiled by

Watson E. Mills

MELLEN BIBLICAL PRESS
Lewiston/Queenston/Lampeter

Library of Congress Cataloging-in-Publication Data

Bibliographies for biblical research.

    Includes index.
    Contents: v. 1. The Gospel of Matthew / compiled by
Watson E. Mills --   -- v. 4. The Gospel of John.
    1. Bible. N.T.--Criticism, interpretation, etc.--
Bibliography. I. Mills, Watson E.
Z7772.L1B4 1993 [BS2341.2]   016.2262'06   93-30864

ISBN 0-7734-2347-8 (v. 1) Matthew ISBN 0-7734-2349-4 (v. 2) Mark
ISBN 0-7734-2385-0 (v. 3) Luke   ISBN 0-7734-2357-5 (v. 4) John
ISBN 0-7734-2432-6 (v. 5) Acts   ISBN 0-7734-2418-0 (v. 6) Romans
ISBN 0-7734-2419-9 (v. 7) 1 Corinthians

> This is volume 7 in the continuing series
> Bibliographies for Biblical Research
> New Testament Series
> Volume 7 ISBN 0-7734-2419-9
> Series ISBN 0-7734-9345-X

A CIP catalog record for this book is available from the British Library.

Copyright © 1996 The Edwin Mellen Press

The Edwin Mellen Press
Box 450
Lewiston, New York
USA 14092

The Edwin Mellen Press
Box 67
Queenston, Ontario
CANADA L0S 1L0

Edwin Mellen Press, Ltd.
Lampeter, Dyfed, Wales
UNITED KINGDOM SA48 7DY

Printed in the United States of America

Dedication

To Susan Ellis
in celebration of her courage
and with much affection

Contents

Introduction to the Series

This volume is the seventh in a series of bibliographies on the books of the Hebrew and Christian Bibles as well as the deutero-canonicals. This ambitious series calls for some 35-40 volumes over the next 3-5 years complied by practicing scholars from various traditions.

Each author (compiler) of these volumes is working within the general framework adopted for the series, i.e., citations are to works published within the twentieth century that make important contributions to the understanding of the text and backgrounds of the various books.

Obviously the former criterion is more easily quantifiable than the latter, and it is precisely at this point that an individual compiler makes her/his specific contribution. We are not intending to be comprehensive in the sense of definitive, but where resources are available, as many listings as possible have been included.

The arrangement for the entries, in most volumes in the series, consists of three divisions: scriptural citations; subject citations; commentaries. In some cases the first two categories may duplicate each other to some degree. Multiple citations by scriptural citation are also included where relevant.

Those who utilize these volumes are invited to assist the compilers by noting textual errors as well as obvious omissions that ought to be taken into account in subsequent printings. Perfection is nowhere more elusive than in the citation of bibliographic materials. We would welcome your assistance at this point.

We hope that these bibliographies will contribute to the discussions and research going on in the field among faculty as well as students. They should serve a significant role as reference works in both research and public libraries.

I wish to thank the staff and editors of the Edwin Mellen Press, and especially Professor Herbert Richardson, for the gracious support of this series.

Watson E. Mills, Series Editor
Mercer University
Macon GA 31207
December 1994

Preface

This Bibliography on 1 Corinthians provides an index to the journal articles, essays in collected works, books and monographs, dissertations, commentaries, and various encyclopedia and dictionary articles published in the twentieth century through 1995 (a few titles for the early months of 1996 are included when these were available for verification). Technical works of scholarship, from many differing traditions constitute the bulk of the citations though I have included some selected works that intend to reinterpret this research to a wider audience.

Again, I have relied upon the work of Paul-Émile Langevin (*Bibliographie biblique* (Les Presses de l'Université Laval, 1972, 1978, 1985). This massive work is heavily slanted toward Catholic publications but particularly the third volume begins to move toward a more balanced perspective. Langevin's work is very heavy in citations to French literature, but is meticulously indexed by scriptural citation as well as subject and contains detailed indexes.

Building the database necessary for a work of this magnitude was a tedious and time-consuming task. I acknowledge the administration of Mercer University for granting me a sabbatical leave during the 1992 academic year. Also, I acknowledge with gratitude the Education Commission of the Southern Baptist Convention which provided funds for travel to overseas libraries during the summers of 1994, 1995, and 1996. Also, the Edwin Mellen Press has supported and encouraged this work from its inception. Most recently the Press has agreed to publish the entire work, when completed, on CD-ROM with annual updated disks to be provided. The initial publication on CD-ROM will be provided without charge to all who have subscribed to the individuals volumes in the collection. The CD-ROM bonus together with the half price subscription rate offered to all subscribers, make this the most economical and simplest way to obtain all of the volumes in the series.

I want to express my gratitude to the staff librarians at the following institutions: Baptist Theological Seminary (Rüschlikon, Switzerland); Oxford University (Oxford, UK); Emory University (Atlanta, GA); Duke University (Durham, NC); University of Zürich (Zürich, Switzerland); Southern Baptist Theological Seminary (Louisville, KY); Harvard Theological Library (Cambridge, MA).

Watson E. Mills
Mercer University
Macon GA 31207
August 1996

Abbreviations

ABQ	*American Baptist Quarterly* (Valley Forge, PA)
ABR	*Australian Biblical Review* (Melbourne)
Affirm	*Affirmation* (Richmond, VA)
AfTJ	*African Theological Journal* (Tanzania)
AJBI	*Annual of the Japanese Biblical Institute* (Tokyo)
AmER	*American Ecclesiastical Review* (Washington, DC)
AnaCra	*Analecta Cracoviensia: Studia philosophico-theologica* (Cracow)
Anima	*Anima: The Journal of Human Experience* (Chambersburg PA)
Ant	*Antonianum* (Rome)
AsSeign	*Assemblees du Seigneur* (Brugge; Paris)
ATR	*Anglican Theological Review* (New York)
Aug	*Augustinianum* (Rome)
AUSS	*Andrews University Seminary Studies* (Berrien Springs, MI)
BA	*Biblical Archaeologist* (New Haven, CN)
BAR	*Biblical Archaeology Review* (Washington, DC)
BB	*Bible Bhashyam: An Indian Biblical Quarterly* (Vadavathoor)
Bib	*Biblica* (Rome)
BibInt	*Biblical Interpretation* (Leiden)
BibO	*Bibbia e Oriente* (Milan)
BibView	*Biblical Viewpoint* (Greenville SC)
Bij	*Bijdragen* (Nijmegen)
BJRL	*Bulletin of the John Rylands University Library* (Manchester)
BK	*Bibel und Kirche* (Stuttgart)
BL	*Bibel und Liturgie* (Vienna)
BLE	*Bulletin de Littérature Eccleésiastique* (Toulouse)
BRev	*Bible Review* (Washington)
BZ	*Biblische Zeitschrift* (Paderborn)
CANZTR	*Colloquium: The Australian and New Zealand Theological Review* (Auchland)
Cath	*Catholica: Vierteljahresschrift füur ökumenische Theologie* (Münster)

CBQ	*Catholic Biblical Quarterly* (Washington, DC)
CBTJ	*Calvary Baptist Theological Journal* (Lansdale, PA)
CC	*Christian Century* (Chicago)
CCER	*Cahiers du cercle Ernest Renan pour libres recherches d'historie du christianisme* (Paris)
Ch	*Churchman: A Journal of Anglican Theology* (London)
Chr	*Christus* (Paris)
ChrLit	*Christianity and Literature* (Seattle)
ChS	*Church and Society* (New York)
CICR	*Communio: International Catholic Review* (Spokane, WA)
CJ	*Concordia Journal* (St. Louis, MO)
Coll	*Colloquium: The Australian and New Zealand Theological Society* (Adelaide)
Communio	*Communio: Commentarii internationales de ecclesia et theologia* (Seville)
Conci	*Concilium* (London)
CrSoc	*Cristianesimo y Sociedad* (Buenos Aires)
Crux	*Crux* (Vancouver)
CS	*Chicago Studies* (Chicago)
CSR	*Christian Scholar's Review* (Grand Rapids, MI)
CStud	*Christian Studies* (Austin TX)
CT	*Christianity Today* (Washington, DC)
CThM	*Currents in Theology and Mission* (St. Louis, MO)
CTJ	*Calvin Theological Journal* (Grand Rapids, MI)
CTM	*Concordia Theological Monthly* (St. Louis, MO)
CTQ	*Concordia Theological Quarterly* (Fort Wayne, IN)
CTR	*Criswell Theological Review* (Dallas)
CVia	*Communio Viatorum* (Prague)
DBM	*Deltío Biblikôn Meletôn* (Athens)
Dia	*Dialog* (Minneapolis, MN)
Dir	*Direction* (Fresno CA)
DR	*Downside Review* (Bath)
DTT	*Dansk Teologisk Tidsskrift* (Cophenhagen)
E-I	*Eretz-Israel* (Jerusalem)
EAJT	*East Asia Journal of Theology* (Singapore)
EB	*Estudios Bíblicos* (Madrid)
EcumRev	*Ecumenical Review* (Geneva)
ED	*Euntes docet* (Rome)
EE	*Estudios Eclesiásticos* (Madrid)
EGLMBS	*Eastern Great Lakes and Midwest Biblical Society*
ÉgT	*Église et théologie* (Ottawa)
EMQ	*Evangelical Missions Quarterly* (Washington, DC)
Enc	*Encounter* (Indianapolis, IN)

EphL	*Ephemerides liturgicae* (Rome)
EPTA	*The Journal of the European Pentecostal Theological Association* (Nantwich UK)
EQ	*Evangelical Quarterly* (London)
ERT	*Evangelical Review of Theology* (Exeter)
EstFr	*Estudios franciscanos* (Barcelona)
EstT	*Estudios Teológicos* (Guatemala City)
ET	*Expository Times* (Edinburgh)
ETL	*Ephemerides Theologicae Lovanienses* (Louvain)
EvJ	*Evangelical Journal* (Myerstown, NJ)
EvT	*Evangelische Theologie* (Munich)
ExA	*Ex Auditu* (Princeton)
FilN	*Filologia Neotestamentaria* (Cordoba)
FM	*Faith and Mission* (Wake Forest, NC)
Found	*Foundations* (Rochester, NY)
FP	*Faith and Philosophy: Journal of the Society of Christian Philosophers* (Wimore KY)
FundJ	*Fundamentalist Journal* (Lynchburg, VA)
FV	*Foi et Vie* (Paris)
GeistL	*Geist und Leben* (Würzburg)
Greg	*Gregorianum* (Rome)
GTJ	*Grace Theological Journal* (Winona Lake, IN)
GTT	*Gereformeered Theologisch Tijdschrift* (Aalten)
HAR	*Hebrew Annual Review* (Columbus OH)
HBT	*Horizons in Biblical Theology* (Pittsburg, PA)
HeyJ	*Heythrop Journal* (Oxford)
Horizons	*Horizons* (Villanova PA)
HTR	*Harvard Theological Review* (Cambridge, MA)
HTS	*Hervormde Teologiese Studies* (Pretoria)
IBS	*Irish Biblical Studies* (London)
IEJ	*Israel Exploration Journal* (Jerusalem)
IJT	*Indian Journal of Theology* (Serampore)
Int	*Interpretation* (Richmond, VA)
IRM	*International Review of Mission* (London)
ITQ	*Irish Theological Quarterly* (Maynooth)
JAAR	*Journal of the American Academy of Religion* (Atlanta)
JBL	*Journal of Biblical Literature* (Atlanta, GA)
JBR	*Journal of Bible and Religion* (Boston)
JETS	*Journal of the Evangelical Theological Society* (Wheaton, IL)
JITC	*Journal of the Interdenominational Theological Center* (Atlanta)
JITS	*Journal of the Interdenominational Theological Seminary* (Atlanta)
JLR	*Journal of Law and Religion* (St. Paul, MN)
JPC	*Journal of Pastoral Care* (New York)

JPsyC	*Journal of Psychology and Christianity* (Farmington Hills, MI)
JPT	*Journal of Psychology and Theology* (La Mirada, CA)
JR	*Journal of Religion* (Chicago, IL)
JRE	*The Journal of Religious Ethics* (Atlanta)
JREth	*Journal of Religious Ethics* (Atlanta)
JSNT	*Journal for the Study of the New Testament* (Sheffield)
JTS	*Journal of Theological Studies* (Oxford)
JTSA	*Journal of Theology for Southern Africa* (Rondebosch)
JWR	*Journal of Women and Religion* (Berkeley, CA)
KD	*Kerygma and Dogma* (Göttingen)
KingsTR	*King's Theological Review* (London)
LB	*Linguistica Biblica* (Bonn)
Levant	*Levant* (London)
LO	*Living Orthodoxy* (Liberty TN)
LouvS	*Louvain Studies* (Louvain)
LQ	*Lutheran Quarterly* (Milwaukee, WI)
LTJ	*Lutheran Theological Journal* (Adelaide)
Luther	*Luther: Vierteljahrsschrift* (Berlin)
LV	*Lumen Vitae* (Washington, DC)
MC	*Modern Churchman* (Herefordshire, England)
McMJT	*McMaster Journal of Theology* (Hamilton, Ontario)
MeliT	*Melita Theologia* (La Valetta)
Miss	*Missiology: An International Review* (Scottsdale, PA)
Missionalia	*Missionalia* (Menlo Park, South Africa)
MSJ	*The Master's Seminary Journal* (Sun Valley CA)
NBlack	*New Blackfriars* (London)
Neo	*Neotestamentica* (Pretoria)
NovT	*Novum Testamentum* (Leiden)
NRT	*La Nouvelle revue théologique* (Louvain)
NTheoR	*New Theology Review* (Collegeville, MN)
NTS	*New Testament Studies* (Cambridge)
NTT	*Norsk teologisk tidsskrift* (Oslo)
OC	*One in Christ* (Turvey, Bedfordshire)
OCP	*Orientalia christiana periodica* (Rome)
Pacifica	*Pacifica: Australian Theological Studies* (Brunswick East, Victoria, Australia)
Para	*Paraclete* (Louisville KY)
Pneuma	*Pneuma: The Journal of the Society for Pentecostal Studies* (Chicago, IL)
PPsy	*Pastoral Psychology* (New York)
Pres	*Presbyterion* (St. Louis)
PRS	*Perspectives in Religious Studies* (Macon, GA)
QR	*Quarterly Review* (Nashville, TN)

RevB	*Revista Biblica* (Buenos Aires)
RevExp	*Review and Expositor* (Louisville, KY)
RevSR	*Revue des Sciences religieuses* (Strasbourg)
RHPR	*Revue d'historie et de philosophie religieuses* (Paris)
Risk	*Risk* (Geneva)
RivBib	*Rivista Biblica* (Brescia)
RoczTK	*Roczniki Teologiczno-Kanoniczne* (Lublin)
RQ	*Restoration Quarterly* (Austin, TX)
RR	*Reformed Review* (Holland, MI)
RSPT	*Revue des Sciences Philosophiques et Thélogiques* (Paris)
RStud	*Religious Studies* (Cambridge)
RTAM	*Recherches de théeologie Ancienne et Médiévale* (Louvain)
RTL	*Revue théologique de Louvain* (Louvain)
RTP	*Revue de théologie et de philosophie* (Geneva)
RTR	*Reformed Theological Review* (Melbourne)
SémBib	*Sémiotique et Bible* (Lyon)
Salm	*Salmanticensis* (Salamanca)
SBLSP	*Society of Biblical Literature Seminar Papers* (Atlanta, GA)
SCIRSR	*Social Compass: International Review of Sociology of Religion* (London)
Scr	*Scripture: Quarterly of the Catholic Biblical Association* (Edinburgh)
ScripT	*Scripta theologia* (Pamplona, Spain)
SE	*Sciences Ecclésiastiques* (Bruges)
SEÅ	*Svensk Exegetisk Årsbok* (Lund)
Semeia	*Semeia* (Atlanta)
SJOT	*Scandinavian Journal of the Old Testament* (Copenhagen)
SJT	*Scottish Journal of Theology* (Edinburgh)
SM	*Studia Missionalia* (Rome)
SMR	*Saint Mark's Review* (Canberra)
SNTU-A	*Studien zum NT und seiner Umwelt* (Linz)
SouJT	*Southwestern Journal of Theology* (Fort Worth, TX)
SR	*Studies in Religion/Sciences religieuses* (Waterloo, Ont)
StTh	*Studia theologica: Scandinavian Journal of Theology* (Lund)
StTheol	*Studia Theologica* (Copenhagen)
TBe	*Theologische Beiträge* (Tübingen)
TD	*Theology Digest* (St. Mary's, KN)
TGl	*Theologie und Glaube* (Paderborn, Germany)
Theology	*Theology* (London)
ThEv	*Theologia evangelica* (Pretoria)
Thomist	*Thomist* (Washington, DC)
Thought	*Thought: A Review of Culture and Ideas* (New York)
TJT	*Toronto Journal of Theology* (Toronto)

TLZ	*Theologische Literaturzeitung* (Leipzig)
TQ	*Theologische Quartalschift* (Tübingen)
TR	*Theologische Rundschau* (Tübingen)
TRev	*Theological Review* (Beruit)
TriJ	*Trinity Journal* (Deerfield, IL)
TS	*Theological Studies* (New York)
TSFB	*Theological Students' Fellowship Bulletin*
TT	*Theology Today* (Princeton, NJ)
TTZ	*Trierer Theologische Zeitschrift* (Trier)
TynB	*Tyndale Bulletin* (Cambridge)
TZ	*Theologische Zeitschrift* (Basel)
USQR	*Union Seminary Quarterly Review* (New York)
VC	*Vigiliae Christianae* Leiden)
VD	*Verbum Domini* (Rome)
VoxE	*Vox evangelica* (London)
VS	*La vie spirituelle* (Paris)
Worship	*Worship* (Collegeville, MN)
WTJ	*Westminster Theology Journal* (Philadelphia)
WuW	*Wissenschaft und Weisheit* (Freiburg)
WW	*Word and World* (St. Paul, MN)
ZEE	*Zeitschrift für Evangelische Ethik* (Gütersloh)
ZKG	*Zeitschrift für Kirchengeschichte* (Stuttgart)
ZKT	*Zeitschrift für Katholische Theologie* (Innsbruck)
ZNW	*Zeitschrift für die neutestamentliche Wissenschaft* (Berlin)
ZTK	*Zeitschrift für Theologie und Kirche* (Tübingen)

PART ONE

Citations by Chapter and Verse

<u>1:1-6:20</u>

0001 I. Fransen, "Le champ du Seigneur," *BVC* 44 (1962): 31-38.

<u>1-4</u>

0002 Glen O. Peterman, "Equipping God's People for Ministry in 1 Corinthians 1-4," *RR* 21 (1967): 56-64.

0003 Gerhard Sellin, "Das 'Geheimins' der Weisheit und das Ra;uatsel der 'Christtuspartei'," *ZNW* 73/1-2 (1982): 69-96.

0004 John Polhill, "The Wisdom of God and Factionalism: 1 Corinthians 1-4," *RevExp* 80/3 (1983): 325-39.

0005 L. L. Welborn, "On the Discord in Corinth: 1 Corinthians 1-4 and Ancient Politics," *JBL* 106/1 (1987): 85-111.

0006 David M. Hay, "Job and the Problem of Doubt in Paul," in John T. Carroll, et al., eds., *Faith and History* (festschrift for Paul W. Meyer). Atlanta: Scholars Press, 1990. Pp. 208-22.

0007 Peter Lampe, "Theological Wisdom and the 'Word about the Cross': The Rhetorical Scheme in 1 Corinthians 1-4," *Int* 44 (1990): 117-31.

0008 Stanley K. Stanley, "Paul on the Use and Abuse of Reason," in David L. Balch, et al., eds., *Greeks, Romans, and Christians* (festschrift for Abraham J. Malherbe). Minneapolis: Fortress Press, 1990. Pp. 253-86.

0009 E. Borghi, "Il tema σόφια in 1 Cor 1-4," *RivBib* 40/4 (1992): 421-58.

0010 T. Söding, "Kreuzestheologie und Rechtfertigungslehre. Zur Verbindung von Christologie und Soteriologie im Ersten Korintherbrief und im Galaterbrief," *Cath* 46/1 (1992): 31-60.

0011 Duane Litfin, *St. Paul's Theology of Proclamation: 1 Corinthians 1-4*. SNTSMS #79. Cambridge: University Press, 1994.

<u>1-3</u>

0012 Wilhelm Wuellner, "Haggadic Homily Genre in 1 Corinthians 1-3," *JBL* 89/2 (1970): 199-204.

0013 Vincent P. Branick, "Source and Redaction Analysis of 1 Corinthians 1-3," *JBL* 101/2 (1982): 251-69.

0014   Michael D. Goulder, "Σόφια in 1 Corinthians," *NTS* 37/4 (1991): 516-34.

1:1-3:4

0015   R. Baumann, *Mitte und Norm des Christlichen. Eine Auslegung von 1 Korinther 1:1-3:4.* Munster: Aschendorff, 1968.

1-2

0016   Otto Betz, "Der gekreuzigte Christus: unsere Weisheit und Gerechtigkeit (der alttestamentliche Hintergrund von 1 Kor 1-2)," in Gerald F. Hawthorne and Otto Betz, eds., *Tradition and Interpretation in the New Testament* (festschrift for E. Earle Ellis). Grand Rapids: Eerdmans, 1987. Pp. 195-215.

0017   Niels Hyldahl, "The Corinthian 'Parties' and the Corinthian Crisis," *StTh* 45/1 (1991): 19-32.

0018   Jerome Murphy-O'Connor, "Christ and Ministry," *Pacifica* 4/2 (1991): 121-36.

1

0019   Markus Barth, "A Chapter on the Church—The Body of Christ," *Int* 12 (1958): 131-56.

0020   E. Earle Ellis, "Christ and Spirit in 1 Corinthians," *Prophecy and Hermeneutic in Early Christianity. WUNT.* Tübingen: Mohr, 1978. Pp. 63-71.

0021   E. Earle Ellis, "A Note on 1 Corinthians," *Prophecy and Hermeneutic in Early Christianity. WUNT.* Tübingen: Mohr, 1978. Pp. 63-71. Pp. 209-12.

0022   Paul Ellingworth, "Translating 1 Corinthians," *BT* 31/2 (1980): 234-38.

0023   Halvor Moxnes, "Paulus og den norske vaerematen: 'skam' og 'aere' i Romerbrevet," *NTT* 86/3 (1985): 129-40.

1:1-9

0024   É. Beaucamp, "Grâce et fidélité," *BVC* 15 (1956): 58-65.

0026 Max A. Chevallier, "L'unité plurielle de l'église d'après le Nouveau Testament," *RHPR* 66 (1986): 3-20.

0027 Ronald Byars, "Sectarian Division and the Wisdom of the Cross: Preaching from First Corinthians," *QR* 9/4 (1989): 65-97.

1:2-16

0028 E. Elizabeth Johnson, "The Wisdom of God as Apocalyptic Power," in John T. Carroll, et al., eds., *Faith and History* (festschrift for Paul W. Meyer). Atlanta: Scholars Press, 1990. Pp. 137-48.

1:2

0029 Cullen I. K. Story, "The Nature of Paul's Stewardship with Special Reference to 1 and 2 Corinthians," *EQ* 48/4 (1976): 212-29.

0030 P.-É. Langevin, "Ceux qui invoquent le nom du Seigneur," *SE* 19 (1967): 393-407; 21 (1969): 71-122.

0031 M. Guerra, "Los 'epikaloümenoi' de 1 Cor 1:2 directores y sacerdotes dc la comunidad cristiana en Corinto," *ScripT* 17 (1985): 11-72.

0032 Gordon D. Fee, "Textual-Exegetical Observations on 1 Corinthians 1:2, 2:1, and 2:10," in David A. Black, ed., *Scribes and Scripture* (festschrift for J. Harold Greenlee). Winona Lake INL Eisenbrauns, 1993. Pp. 1-15

1:4-9

0033 George W. MacRae, "A Note on 1 Corinthians 1:4-9," *E-I* 16 (1982): 171-175.

0034 F. S. Malan, "Die Funksie en boodskap van die 'voorword' in 1 Korintiërs," *HTS* 49 (1993): 561-75.

1:4-8

0035 F. Ogara, "In omnibus divites facti estis in illo, in omni verbo et in omni scientia," *VD* 16 (1936): 225-32.

0036 J. L. Lilly, "Missal Epistles from 1 Corinthians," *CBQ* 13 (1951): 79-85.

0037 R. Feuillet, "Une comment comb lee des richesses divines," *AsSeign* 73 (1962): 18-33.

<u>1:4-7</u>

0038 H. von Lips, "Der Apostolat des Paulus - en Charisma: semantische Aspekte zu charis-charisma und anderen Wortpaaren im Sprachgebrauch des Paulus," *Bib* 66/3 (1985): 305-43.

<u>1:5-10</u>

0039 M. L. Barré, "To Marry or to Burn: Purousthai in 1 Cor. 7:9," *CBQ* 36/2 (1974): 193-202.

<u>1:5</u>

0040 Hans D. Betz, "The Problem of Rhetoric and Theology according to the Apostle Paul," in Albert Vanhoye, ed., *L'Apôtre Paul: personnalité, style et conception du ministre*. Louvain: Peeters, 1986. Pp. 16-48.

<u>1:7-9</u>

0041 P. von der Osten-Sacken, "Gottes treue bis zur Parusie: Formgeschichtliche Beobachtungen zu 1 Kor. 1:7b-9," *ZNW* 68/3-4 (1977): 176-99.

<u>1:7</u>

0042 Norbert Baumert, "Charisma und Amt bei Paulus," in Albert Vanhoye, ed., *L'Apôtre Paul: personnalité, style et conception du ministre*. Louvain: Peeters, 1986. Pp. 203-28.

0043 John J. Kilgallen, "Reflections on Charisma(ta) in the New Testament," *SM* 41 (1992): 289-323.

<u>1:3-9</u>

0044 R. Feuillet, "Action de grâces pour les dons de Dieu," *AsSeign* N.S. 5 (1969): 37-43.

<u>1:10-4:21</u>

0045 Victor P. Furnish, "Belonging to Christ: A Paradigm for Ethics in First Corinthians," *Int* 44/2 (1990): 145-57.

<u>1:10-2:5</u>

0046 D. L. Gragg, "Discourse Ananlysis of 1 Corinthians 1:10-2:5," *LB* 65 (1991): 37-57.

1:10-17
> **0047** William B. Badke, "Baptised into Moses-Baptised into Christ: A Study in Doctrinal Development," *EQ* 60/1 (1988): 23-29.

1:10
> **0048** F. Ogara, "Ut id ipsum dicatis omnes et non sint in vobis schismata," *VD* 16 (1936): 257-66, 289-94, 321-29.

> **0049** Thomas Wieser, "Community-Its Unity, Diversity, And Universality," *Semeia* 33 (1985): 83-95.

1:12-7:16
> **0050** Craig Blumberg, "The Structure of 2 Corinthians 1-7," *CTR* 4 (1989): 3-20.

1:12
> **0051** W. O. Fitch, "Paul, Apollos, Cephas, Christ," *Theology* 74/607 (1971): 18-24.

> **0052** Phillip Vielhauer, "Paulus und die Kephaspartei in Korinth," *NTS* 21/3 (1974): 341-52.

> **0053** Jean Marc Laporte, "Kenosis and Koinonia: The Path Ahead for Anglican-Roman Catholic Dialogue," *OC* 21/2 (1985): 102-20.

1:12-27
> **0054** Dennis Ormseth, "Showing the Body: Reflections on 1 Corinthians 12-13 for Epiphany," *WW* 6 (1986): 97-103.

1:13
> **0055** R. Schnackenburg, "Die Übereignungsformel εἰς τὸ ὄνομα," in *Das Heilsgeschehen bei der Taufe nach dem Apostel Paulus.* München: Zink, 1950. Pp. 15-18.

1:14-26
> **0056** A. C. Wire, "Theological and Biblical Perspective: Liberation for Women Calls for a Liberated World," *ChS* 76 (1986): 7-17.

1:16
> **0057** C. Burchard, "Ei nach einem Ausdruck des Wissens oder Nichtwissens Joh 9:25, Act 19:2, 1 Cor 1:16, 7:16," *ZNW* 52/1-2 (1961): 73-82.

0058 Gerhard Delling, "Zur Taufe von 'Hausern' im Urchristentum,"
NovT 7 (1965): 285-311.

1:17-3:4
0059 Terrance Callan, "Competition and Boasting: Toward a
Psychological Portrait of Paul," *StTheol* 40 (1986): 137-56.

1:17-2:16
0060 Maurice Sachot, "Comment le christianisme est-il devenu religio,"
RevSR 59 (1985): 95-118.

0061 Barry W. Henaut, "Matthew 11:27 - The Thunderbolt in Corinth?"
TJT 3 (1987): 282-300.

1:17
0062 Kenneth E. Bailey, "Recovering the Poetic Structure of
1 Corinthians 1:17," *NovT* 17/4 (1975): 265-96.

0063 Marie Hendrickx, "Sagesse de la parole (1 Cor 1, 17) selon saint
Thomas d'Aquinas," *NRT* 110/3 (1988): 336-50.

0064 N. M. Watson, " 'The Philosopher Should Bathe and Brush His
Teeth'—Congruence between Word and Deed in Graeco-Roman
Philosophy and Paul's Letters to the Corinthians," *ABR* 42 (1994):
1-16.

1:17-25
0065 J. L. Lilly, "Missal Epistles from 1 Corinthians," *CBQ* 13 (1951):
199-207.

0066 E. L Bode, "La follia della Croce," *BibO* 12 (1970): 257-63.

1:18-3:23
0067 L. Cerfaux, "Vestiges d'un florilège dans 1 Cor. 1:18-3:23?" in
Recueil Lucien Cerfaux (festschrift for L. Cerfaux). 3 vols.
Gembloux: Duculot, 1954-1962. 2:319-32.

0068 Hans D. Betz, "The Problem of Rhetoric and Theology according
to the Apostle Paul," in Albert Vanhoye, ed., *L'Apôtre Paul:
personnalité, style et conception du ministre.* Louvain: Peeters,
1986. Pp. 16-48.

1:18-3:4

0069   Victor P. Furnish, "Theology in 1 Corinthians: Initial Soundings," *SBLSP* 28 (1989): 246-64.

1:18-2:5

0070   Benjamin Fiore, " 'Covert Allusion' in 1 Corinthians 1-4," *CBQ* 47/1 (1985): 85-102.

1:18

0071   Luis F. Ladaria, "Presente y futuro en la escatología cristiana," *EE* 60 (1985): 351-59.

0072   J. Louis Martyn, "Paul and His Jewish-Christian Interpreters," *USQR* 42/1-2 (1988): 1-15.

1:18-31

0073   Gail P. Corrington, "Paul and the two wisdoms: 1 Corinthians 1:18-31 and the hellenistic mission," *EGLMBS* 6 (1986): 72-84.

0074   Alan Padgett, "Feminism in First Corinthians: A Dialogue with Elisabeth Schüssler Fiorenza," *EQ* 58/2 (1986): 121-32.

0075   Molly T. Marshall, "1 Corinthians 1:18-31," *RevExp* 85/4 (1988): 683-86.

0076   Ronald Byars, "Sectarian Division and the Wisdom of the Cross: Preaching from First Corinthians," *QR* 9/4 (1989): 65-97.

0077   Molly T. Marshall, "Forsaking a Theology of Glory: 1 Corinthians 1:18-31," *ExA* 7 (1991): 101-104.

0078   John B. Trotti, "1 Corinthians 1:18-31," *Int* 45 (1991): 63-66.

0079   Francis Watson, "Christ, Community, and the Critique of Ideology: A Theological Reading of 1 Cor 1:18-31," *NTT* 46/2 (1992): 132-49.

1:18-29

0080   John V. Taylor, "Weep Not for Me: Meditations on the Cross and the Resurrection," *Risk* 27 (1986): 1-46.

1:18-25

0081 Karl H. Mueller, "1 Kor 1,18-25: Die Eschatologisch-Kritische Funktion der Verkuendigung des Kreuzes," *BZ* 10/2 (1966): 246-72.

0082 A. Penna, "La δύναμις θεου: reflessioni in margine a 1 Cor. 1:18-25," *RBib* 15 (1967): 281-94.

0083 Gordon H. Clark, "Wisdom in First Corinthians," *JETS* 15/4 (1972): 197-205.

0084 Bishoi Kamel, "The Cross: Stumbling Block, Folly and Power," *CCR* 6/3 (1985): 64-67.

1:20

0085 L. Hartman, "Universal Reconciliation (Col 1.20)," *SNTU-A* 10 (1985): 109-21.

0086 Daniel Hoffman, "The Authority of Scripture and Apostolic Doctrine in Ignatius of Antioch," *JETS* 28 (1985): 71-79.

0087 M. Lautenschlager, "Abschied vom Disputierer. Zur Bedeutung von συζητητὴς in 1 Kor 1,20," *ZNW* 83/3-4 (1992): 276-85.

1:21

0088 L. Ligier, "Le peche du monde: 1 Cor.. 1:21," in *Péché d'Adam et péché du monde*. 2 vols. Paris: Aubier, 1960-1961. 2:163-69.

1:22-2:13

0089 John R. Levison, "Did the Spirit Inspire Rhetoric? An Exploration of George Kennedy's Definition of Early Christian Rhetoric," in Duane F. Watson, ed., *Persuasive Artistry* (festschrift for George A. Kennedy). Sheffield: JSOT Press, 1991. Pp. 25-40.

1:22-24

0090 Settimio Ciproani, "Sapientia crucis e sapienza "umana" in Paolo," *RBib* 36 (1988): 343-61.

1:22-23

0091 Gregory M. Corigan, "Paul's Shame for the Gospel," *BTB* 16/1 (1986): 23-27.

1:22

0092 Jos Janssens, "Il cristiano di fronte al martirio imminente: testimonianze e dottrina nella chiesa antica," *Greg* 66/3 (1985): 405-27.

0093 R. Garland Young, "Greek Wisdom," *BI* 14/2 (1989): 20-22.

1:23

0094 K. Romaniuk, "Nos autem praedicamus Christum et hunc crucifixum," *VD* 47 (1969): 232-36.

0095 Wolfgang Schrage, "Den Juden ein Skandalon: Der Anstoss des Kreuzes nach 1 Kor 1,23," in Edna Brocke and Jürgen Seim, eds., *Gottes Augapfel: Beiträge zur Erbeuerung des Verhältnisses von Christen und Juden*. Neukirchener-Vluyn: Neukirchener Verlag, 1986. Pp. 59-76.

1:24

0096 Andrew Chester, "Jewish Messianic Expectations and Mediatorial Figures and Pauline Christology," in Martin Hengel and Ulrich Heckel, eds., *Paulus und das antike Judentum*. Tübingen: Mohr, 1991. Pp. 17-89.

1:25

0097 L. D. Hurst, "Re-enter the Pre-existent Christ in Philippians 2:5-11," *NTS* 32 (1986): 449-57.

1:26-31

0098 G. R. O'Day, "Jeremiah 9:22-23 and 1 Corinthians 1:26-31: A Study in Intertextuality," *JBL* 109/2 (1990): 259-67.

1:26-29

0099 Klaus Schreiner, "Zur Biblischen Legitimation des Adels: Auslegungsgeschichtliche Studien zu 1 Kor. 1,26-29," *ZKG* 85/3 (1974): 317-57.

0100 Terrell R. Blair, "Little-known Laborers," *FundJ* 5/1 (1986): 32-33.

1:26

0101 D. Sänger, "Die δυνατοι in 1 Kor 1:26," *ZNW* 76 (1985): 285-91.

0102 F. Montagnini, " 'Videte vocationem vestram' (1 Cor 1,26)," *RBib* 39/2 (1991): 217-21.

1:27

0103 Robert T. Osborn, "The Christian Blasphemy," *JAAR* 53 (1985): 339-63.

1:29-31

0104 Sigfred Pedersen, "Theologische Uberlegungen zur Isagogik des Römerbriefs," *ZNW* 76/1-2 (1985): 47-67.

1:30

0105 Wilhelm Bender, "Bemerkungen Zur Übersetzung von 1 Korinther 1:30," *ZNW* 71/3-4 (1980): 263-68.

0106 Andrew Chester, "Jewish Messianic Expectations and Mediatorial Figures and Pauline Christology," in Martin Hengel and Ulrich Heckel, eds., *Paulus und das antike Judentum.* Tübingen: Mohr, 1991. Pp. 17-89.

2-3

0107 K. Maly, *Mündige Gemeinde. Untersuchungen Zaire pastoral en Führung des Apostels Paulus im 1. Korintherbrief.* Stuttgart: Katholisches Bibelwerk, 1967.

2

0108 D. W. Martin, "Spirit in 1 Cor. 2," *CBQ* 5 (1943): 381-95.

0109 Norman M. Pritchard, "Profession of Faith and Admission to Communion in the Light of 1 Corinthians 2 and Other Passages," *SJT* 33/1 (1980): 55-70.

0110 Allen R. Hunt, *The Inspired Body: Paul, the Corinthians, and Divine Inspiration.* Macon GA: Mercer University Press, 1995.

2:1-13

0111 Charles B. Cousar, "1 Corinthians 2:1-13," *Int* 44 (1990): 169-73.

2:1-11

0112 Ronald Byars, "Sectarian Division and the Wisdom of the Cross: Preaching from First Corinthians," *QR* 9/4 (1989): 65-97.

2:1-5

0113 Timothy H. Lim, "Not in Persuasive Words of Wisdom but in the Demonstration of the Spirit and Power," *NovT* 29/2 (1987): 137-49.

0114 George J. Zemek, "First Corinthians 2:1-5: Paul's Personal Paradigm for Preaching," in Gary Meadows, ed., *New Testament Essays* (festschrift for Homer A Kent). Winona Lake IN: BMH Books, 1991. Pp. 265-88.

0115 M. A. Bullmore, "St. Paul's Theology of Rhetorical Style: An Examination of 1 Corinthians 2.1-5 in the Light of First Century Graeco-Roman Rhetorical Culture," doctoral dissertation, Northwestern University, Evanston Il, 1993.

2:1

0116 James L. Blevins, " 'Wisdom' in Paul's Writings," *BI* 8/2 (1982): 15-17.

0117 Gordon D. Fee, "Textual-Exegetical Observations on 1 Corinthians 1:2, 2:1, and 2:10," in David A. Black, ed., *Scribes and Scripture* (festschrift for J. Harold Greenlee). Winona Lake INL Eisenbrauns, 1993. Pp. 1-15

2:2-16

0118 A. Rose, "L'épouse dans l'assemblée liturgique," *BVC* 34 (1960): 13-19.

2:4-7

0119 James L. Blevins, " 'Wisdom' in Paul's Writings," *BI* 8/2 (1982): 15-17.

2:4-5

0120 P. Rossano, "La Parola e lo Spirito. Riflffsioni su 1 Tess 1,5 e 1 Cor 2,4-5," in *Mélanges bibliques en homage au R. P. Beda Rigaux*. Gembloux: Dululot, 1970. Pp. 437-44.

2:6-3:4

0121 Benjamin Fiore, " 'Covert Allusion' in 1 Corinthians 1-4," *CBQ* 47/1 (1985): 85-102.

2:6-16

0122 Martin Widmann, "1 Kor 2:6-16: Ein Einspruch Gegen Paulus," *ZNW* 70/1-2 (1979): 44-53.

0123   W. C. Kaiser, "A Neglected Text in Bibliography Discussions:
       1 Corinthians 2:6-16," *WTJ* 43/2 (1981): 301-319.

0124   Jerome Murphy-O'Connor, "Interpolations in 1 Corinthians," *CBQ*
       48 (1986): 81-94.

0125   A. B. Spencer and W. D. Spencer, "The Truly Spiritual in Paul:
       Biblical Background Paper on 1 Corinthians 2:6-16," in Mark L.
       Branson and C. René Padilla, eds., *Conflict and Context:
       Hermeneutics in the Aemricas.* Grand Rapids: Eerdmans, 1986. Pp.
       242-48.

0126   W. Robert Cook, "The Word as a Revelation of God: Its Divine
       Focus," in Earl D. Radmacher, et al., eds., *Celebrating the Word.*
       Portland OR: Multnomah Press, 1987. Pp. 55-63.

0127   Peter Stuhlmacher, "The Hermeneutical Significance of 1 Cor
       2:6-16," in Gerald F. Hawthorne and Otto Betz, eds., *Tradition
       and Interpretation in the New Testament* (festschrift for E. Earle
       Ellis). Grand Rapids: Eerdmans, 1987. Pp. 328-47.

0128   J. Reiling, "Wisdom and the Spirit: An Exegesis of 1 Corinthians
       2,6-16," in Tjitze Baarda, ed., *Text and Testimony: Essays on New
       Testament and Apocryphal Literature* (festschrift for A. F. J. Klijn).
       Kampen: Kok, 1988. Pp. 200-11

0129   Judith L. Kovacs, "The Archons, the Spirit, and the Death of
       Christ: Do We Need the Hypothesis of Gnostic Opponents to
       Explain 1 Corinthians 2:6-16?" in Joel Marcus and Marion L.
       Soards, eds., *Apocalyptic and the New Testament* (festschrift J.
       Louis Martyn). Sheffield: JSOT Press, 1989. Pp. 217-36.

0130   Thomas W. Gillespie, "Interpreting the Kerygma: Early Christian
       Prophecy according to 1 Corinthians 2:6-16," in James E.
       Goehring, et al., eds., *Gospel Origins and Christian Beginnings.*
       Sonoma CA: Polebridge Press, 1990, Pp. 151-66.

0131   William O. Walker, "1 Corinthians 2:6-16: A Non-Pauline
       Interpolation?" *JSNT* 47 (1992): 75-94.

0132   R. B. Gaffin, "Some Epistemological Reflections on 1 Corinthians
       2:6-16," *WTJ* 57 (1995): 103-24.

0133 Allen R. Hunt, *The Inspired Body: Paul, the Corinthians, and Divine Inspiration.* Macon GA: Mercer University Press, 1995.

2:6-15

0134 Paul W. Gooch, "Margaret, Bottom, Paul, and the Inexpressible," *WW* 6/3 (1986): 313-25.

2:6-8

0135 E. Driessen, "Promissio Redemptoris apud S. Paulum," *VD* 21 (1941): 233-38, 264-71, 280-305.

0136 P. Bormann, "Bemerkungen zu zwei lesenswerten Aufsatzen," *TGl* 50 (1960): 112-14.

0137 A. Feuillet, "Les 'chefs de ce siecle,' et la Sagesse divine: d'après 1 Cor 2,6-8," in *Studiorum Paulinorum Congressus, 1961.* 2 vols. Rome: Pontifical Biblical Institute, 1963. 1:383-93.

0138 Henry I. Lederle, "Better the Devil You Know: Seeking a Biblical Basis for the Societal Dimension of Evil and/or the Demonic in the Pauline Concept of the 'Powers'," in Pieter G. R. Villiers, ed., *Like a roaring lion: Essays on the Bible, the Church and Demonic Powers.* Pretoria: University of South Africa, 1987. Pp. 102-20.

2:6

0139 William Baird, "Among the Mature: The Idea of Wisdom in 1 Corinthians 2:6," *Int* 13 (1959): 425-32.

0140 Vincent P. Branick, "Apocalyptic Paul?" *CBQ* 47 (1985): 664-75.

2:7-8

0141 Bishoi Kamel, "The Cross: Stumbling Block, Folly and Power," *CCR* 6/3 (1985): 64-67.

2:7

0142 Leslie C. Allen, "The Old Testament Background of (Pro)Orizein in the New Testament," *NTS* 17/1 (1970): 104-08.

0143 Galen W. Wiley, "A Study of 'Mystery' in the New Testament," *GTJ* 6/2 (1985): 349-60.

0144 J. K. Grider, "Predestination as Temporal Only," *WTJ* 22 (1987): 56-64.

2:9

0145 A. Feuillet, "The Enigma of 1 Cor 2:9," *TD* 14 (1966): 143-48.

0146 Eckhard Nordheim, "Das Zitat des Paulus in 1 Kor 2:9 und seine Beziehung zum Koptischen Testament Jakobs," *ZNW* 65/1-2 (1974): 112-120.

0147 Herve Ponsot, "D'Isaie 64:3 à 1 Corinthiens 2:9," *RB* 90/2 (1983): 229-42.

0148 Bo Frid, "The Enigmatic ἀλλά in 1 Corinthians 2:9," *NTS* 31 (1985): 603-11.

0149 Luis F. Ladaria, "Presente y futuro en la escatología cristiana," *EE* 60 (1985): 351-59.

0150 Oda Wischmeyer, "Theon agapan bei Paulus: eine traditionsgeschichtliche Miszelle," *ZNW* 78/1-2 (1987): 141-44.

0151 Takashi Onuki, "Traditionsgeschichte von Thomas 17 und ihre christologische Relevanz," in Cilliers Breytenbach and Henning Paulsen, eds., *Anfänge der Christologie* (festschrift for Ferdinand Hahn). Göttingen: Vandenhoeck & Ruprecht, 1991. Pp. 399-415.

2:10-12

0152 M. A. G. Haykin, "The Spirit of God: The Exegesis of 1 Cor 2:10-12 by Origen and Athanasius," *SJT* 35/6 (1982): 513-28.

2:10

0153 Gordon D. Fee, "Textual-Exegetical Observations on 1 Corinthians 1:2, 2:1, and 2:10," in David A. Black, ed., *Scribes and Scripture* (festschrift for J. Harold Greenlee). Winona Lake INL Eisenbrauns, 1993. Pp. 1-15

2:12-15

0154 David R. Nichols, "The Problem of Two-Level Christianity at Corinth," *Pneuma* 11 (1989): 99-112.

2:13

0155 James L. Blevins, " 'Wisdom' in Paul's Writings," *BI* 8/2 (1982): 15-17.

2:14-3:4

0156 Stanley D. Toussaint, "The Spiritual Man," *BSac* 125/498 (1968): 139-146.

2:15-16

0157 John D. Lawrence, "The Eucharist as the Imitation of Christ," *TS* 47 (1986): 286-96.

0158 Roger L. Omanson,"Acknowledging Paul's Quotations," *BT* 43/2 (1992): 201-13.

2:16

0159 W. L. Willis, "The 'Mind of Christ' in 1 Corinthians 2:16," *Bib* 70/1 (1989): 110-122.

2:19

0160 R. Trevijano Etcheverría, "La valoración de los dichos no canónicos: el caso de 1 Cor 2.9 y Ev Tom log 17," in Elizabeth A. Livingstone, ed., *Studia Patristica, 24: Historica, Theologica et Philosophica*. Louvain: Peeters, 1993. Pp. 406-14.

3-6

0161 Michael D. Goulder, "Did Luke Know Any of the Pauline Letters," *PRS* 13 (1986): 97-112.

3

0162 Brendan Byrne, "Ministry and Maturity in 1 Corinthians 3," *ABR* 35 (1987): 83-87.

0163 J. P. M. Sweet, "A House Not Made with Hands," in William Horbury, ed., *Templum Amicitiae: Essays on the Second Temple* (festschrift for Ernst Bammel). Sheffield: JSOT Press, 1991. Pp. 368-90.

0164 John Proctor, "Fire in God's House: Influence of Malachi 3 in the NT," *JETS* 36 (1993): 9-14.

0165 Allen R. Hunt, *The Inspired Body: Paul, the Corinthians, and Divine Inspiration*. Macon GA: Mercer University Press, 1995.

3:1-9

0166 C. Thomas Rhyne, "1 Corinthians 3:1-9," *Int* 44 (1990): 174-79.

3:1-3

0167 J. Francis, " 'As Babes in Christ': Some Proposals regarding 1 Corinthians 3:1-3," *JSNT* 7 (1980): 41-60.

0168 David R. Nichols, "The Problem of Two-Level Christianity at Corinth," *Pneuma* 11 (1989): 99-112.

3:1-2

0169 W. Thüsing, " 'Milch' und 'feste Speise'," *TTZ* 76 (1967): 233-46, 261-80.

3:5-4:5

0170 Benjamin Fiore, " 'Covert Allusion' in 1 Corinthians 1-4," *CBQ* 47/1 (1985): 85-102.

0171 D. Kuck, "Paul and Pastoral Ambition: A Reflection on 1 Corinthians 3-4," *CThM* 19/3 (1992): 174-83.

3:5-17

0172 Max A. Chevallier, "L'unité plurielle de l'église d'après le Nouveau Testament," *RHPR* 66 (1986): 3-20.

3:5-11

0173 Sigfred Pedersen, "Theologische Uberlegungen zur Isagogik des Römerbriefs," *ZNW* 76/1-2 (1985): 47-67.

3:5

0174 Gerhard L. Miller, "Purgatory," *TD* 33/4 (1986): 31-36.

3:6-9

0175 Richard Bauckham, "The Parable of the Vine: Rediscovering a Lost Parable of Jesus," *NTS* 33/1 (1987): 84-101.

3:8-15

0176 W. Pesch, "Der Sonderlohn für die Verkündiger des Evangeliums," in J. Blinzler, et al., eds., *Neutestamentliche Aufsätze* (festschrift for Josef Schmid). Regensburg: Pustet, 1963. Pp. 199-206.

3:9-17

0177 Jay Shanor, "Paul as Master Builder: Construction Terms in First Corinthians," *NTS* 34/3 (1988): 461-71.

0178 K. Romaniuk, "... wie ein guter Baumeister ...." in J. J. Degenhardt, ed., *Die Freude an Gott - unsere Kraft* (festschrift for Otto B. Knoch). Stuttgart: Verlag Katholisches Bibelwerk, 1991. Pp. 164-69.

3:9

0179 E. Peterson "Ἔργον in der Bedeutung 'Bau' bei Paulus," *Bib* 22 (1941): 439-41.

0180 Victor P. Furnish, " 'Fellow Workers in God's Service'," *JBL* 80 (1961): 364-70.

3:10-3:23
0181 A. Miranda, "L' 'uomo spirituale' nella Prima ai Corinzi," *RBib* 43 (1995): 485-519.

3:10-15
0182 S. Cipriani, "Insegna 1 Cor. 3,10-15 la dottrina del Purgatorio?" *RBib* 7 (1959): 25-43.

'   **0183** Charles W. Fishburne, "1 Cor. 3:10-15 and the Testament of Abraham," *NTS* 17/1 (1970): 109-15.

0184 Craig A. Evans, "How Are the Apostles Judged? A Note On 1 Corinthians 3:10-15," *JETS* 27/2 (1984): 149-50.

0185 G. L. Müller, "Fegfeuer: zur Hermeneutik eines umstrittenen Lehrstücks in der Eschatologie," *TQ* 166 (1986): 25-39.

0186 H. W. Hollsnder, "The Testing by Fire of the Builder's Works: 1 Corinthians 3.10-15," *NTS* 40 (1994): 89-104.

3:10
0187 H. von Lips, "Der Apostolat des Paulus - en Charisma: semantische Aspekte zu charis-charisma und anderen Wortpaaren im Sprachgebrauch des Paulus," *Bib* 66/3 (1985): 305-43.

3:12-15
0188 J. Michl, "Gerichtsfeuer und Purgatorium zu 1 Kor 3,12-15," in *Studiorum Paulinorum Congressus, 1961*. 2 vols. Rome: Pontifical Biblical Institute, 1963. 1:395-401.

3:12

0189 James E. Rosscup, "A New Look at 1 Corinthians 3:12—'Gold, Silver, Precious Stones'," *MSJ* 1 (1990): 33-51.

3:13

0190 Harm W. Hollander, "Revelation by Fire: 1 Corinthians 3:13," *BT* 44 (1993): 242-44.

3:15

0191 J. R. Busto Saiz, "Se salvará como atravesando fuego? 1 Cor 3:15b reconsiderado," *EE* 68 (1993): 333-38.

3:16-23

0192 M. Trimaille, "La communauté, sanctuaire de Dieu, et son unité dans le Christ," *AsSeign* N.S. 38 (1970): 34-41.

3:16-17

0193 A.-M. Denis, "La fonction apostolique et la liturgie nouvelle en esprit: l'Apôtre, constructeur du temple spirituel," *RSPT* 42 (1958): 408-26.

0194 Jonathan A. Draper, "The Tip of an Ice-berg: The Temple of the Holy Spirit," *JTSA* 59 (1987): 57-65.

0195 Brian S. Rosner, "Temple and Holiness in 1 Corinthians 5," *TynB* 42/1 (1991): 137-45.

3:16

0196 Peter T. O'Brien, "The Church as a Heavenly and Eschatological Entity," in Don A Carson, ed., *The Church in the Bible and the World*. Exeter: Paternoster Press, 1987. Pp. 88-119.

0197 Douglas R. de Lacey, "ohitines este Hymeis: The Function of a Metaphor in St. Paul," in William Horbury, ed., *Templum Amicitiae: Essays on the Second Temple* (festschrift for Ernst Bammel). Sheffield: JSOT Press, 1991. Pp. 391-409

0198 F. W. Horn, "Wandel im Geist: zur pneumatologischen Begründung der Ethik bei Paulus," *KD* 38 (1992): 149-70.

3:18

0199 Dennis Ormseth, "Showing the Body: Reflections on 1 Corinthians 12-13 for Epiphany," *WW* 6 (1986): 97-103.

3:20

0200 Roy A. Harrisville, "Paul and the Psalms: A Formal Study," *WW* 5 (1985): 168-79.

3:21

0201 Sigfred Pedersen, "Theologische Überlegungen zur Isagogik des Römerbriefs," *ZNW* 76/1-2 (1985): 47-67.

3:23

0202 W. Thüsing, "Ihr seid Christi-Christus ist Gottes," in *Per Christum in Deum: Studien zum Verhältnis von Christozentrik und Theozentrik in den paulinischen Hauptbriefen.* Münster: Aschendorff, 1965. P. 1020.

3:28-29

0203 W. C. Linss, "St. Paul and Women," *Dia* 24 (1985): 36-40.

3:28

0204 Daniel P. Fuller, "Paul and Galatians 3:28," *TSFB* 9/2 (1985): 9-13.

4:1-13

0205 Jonathan J. Bonk, "Doing Mission out of Affluence: Reflections on Recruiting 'End of the Procession' Missionaries from 'Front of the Procession' Churches," *Miss* 17/4 (1989): 427-52.

4:1-5

0206 J. L. Lilly, "Missal Epistles from 1 Corinthians," *CBQ* 13 (1951): 308-13, 432-38.

0207 M. Coune, "L'apôtre sera jugé," *AsSeign* 7 (1967): 16-31.

0208 Jouette M. Bassler, "1 Corinthians 4:1-5," *Int* 44 (1990): 179-83.

4:2

0209 W. Hulitt Gloer, "Stewards in the First Century," *BI* 11/1 (1985): 31-33.

4:4

0210 Charles H. Cosgrove, "Justification in Paul: A Linguistic and Theological Reflection," *JBL* 106/4 (1987): 653-70.

4:6-13

0211 Benjamin Fiore, " 'Covert Allusion' in 1 Corinthians 1-4," *CBQ* 47/1 (1985): 85-102.

4:6

0212 Morna D. Hooker, "Beyond the Things Which Are Written: An Examination of 1 Corinthians 4:6," *NTS* 10 (1963): 127-32.

0213 John Strugnell, "A Plea Conjectural Emendation in the New Testament with a Coda on 1 Cor. 4:6," *CBQ* 36/4 (1974): 543-58.

0214 Jerome Murphy-O'Connor, "Interpolations in 1 Corinthians," *CBQ* 48 (1986): 81-94.

0215 L. L. Wellborn, "A Conciliatory Principle in 1 Cor. 4:6," *NovT* 29/4 (1987): 300-46.

0216 Roger L. Omanson, "Acknowledging Paul's Quotations," *BT* 43/2 (1992): 201-13.

0217 David R. Hall, "A Disguise for the Wise: μετεσχηματισμος in 1 Corinthians 4.6," *NTS* 40 (1994): 143-49.

0218 B. J. Dodd, "Pauls's Paradigmatic 'I' and 1 Corinthians 6:12," *JSNT* 59 (1995): 39-58.

4:7

0219 Sigfred Pedersen, "Theologische Uberlegungen zur Isagogik des Römerbriefs," *ZNW* 76/1-2 (1985): 47-67.

4:8-9

0220 William Klassen, "The King as 'Living Law' with Particular Reference to Musonius Rufus," *SR* 14/1 (1985): 63-71.

4:8

0221 A. C. Wire, "Theological and Biblical Perspective: Liberation for Women Calls for a Liberated World," *ChS* 76 (1986): 7-17.

0222 David R. Nichols, "The Problem of Two-Level Christianity at Corinth," *Pneuma* 11 (1989): 99-112.

0223 Mark A. Plunkett, "Eschatology at Corinth," in *EGLMBS* 9 (1989): 195-211.

4:9-20

    0224 W. D. Spencer, "The Power in Paul's Teaching (1 Cor 4:9-20),"
            JETS 32/1 (1989): 51-61.

4:12

    0225 Jürgen Sauer, "Traditionsgeschichtliche Erwägungen zu den
            synoptischen und paulinischen Aussagen über Feindesliebe und
            Wiedervergeltungsverzicht," *ZNW* 76/1-2 (1985): 1-28.

4:14-21

    0226 Benjamin Fiore, " 'Covert Allusion' in 1 Corinthians 1-4," *CBQ*
            47/1 (1985): 85-102.

    0227 E. M. Lassen, "The Use of the Father Image in Imperial
            Propaganda and 1 Corinthians 4:14-21," *TynB* 42/1 (1991): 127-36.

4:14-17

    0228 Wolfgang Schrage, "Das Apostolische Amt des Paulus nach 1 Kor
            4,14-17," in Albert Vanhoye, ed., *L'Apôtre Paul: personnalité,*
            style et conception du ministre. Louvain: Peeters, 1986. Pp. 103-19.

4:14-15

    0229 Dennis Ormseth, "Showing the Body: Reflections on 1 Corinthians
            12-13 for Epiphany," *WW* 6 (1986): 97-103.

4:15

    0230 M. Saillard, "C'est moi qui, par l'Évangile, vous ai enfantés dans
            le Christ," *RechSR* 56 (1968): 5-42.

    0231 Norman H. Young, "Paidagogos: The Social Setting of a Pauline
            Metaphor," *NovT* 29 (1987): 150-76.

4:16

    0232 Otto Merk, "Nachahmung Christi: zu ethischen Perspektiven in der
            paulinischen Theologie," in Helmut Merklein, ed., *Neues*
            Testament und Ethik (festschrift for Rudolf Schnackenburg).
            Freiburg: Herder, 1989. Pp. 172-206.

4:17

    0233 Kenneth E. Bailey, "The Structure of 1 Corinthians and Paul's
            Theological Method with Special Reference to 4:17," *NovT* 25/2
            (1983): 152-81.

    0234 M. C. Griffths, "Today's Missionary, Yesterday's Apostle," *EMQ*
            21/2 (1985): 154-65.

4:18

0235 Luis F. Ladaria, "Presente y futuro en la escatología cristiana," *EE* 60 (1985): 351-59.

4:20

0236 Günter Haufe, "Reich Gottes bei Paulus und in der Jesustradition," *NTS* 31 (1985): 467-72.

0237 Karl P. Donfried, "The Kingdom of God in Paul," in Wendell Willis, ed., *The Kingdom of God in 20th-Century Interpretation.* Peabody MA: Hendrickson, 1987. Pp. 175-90.

5-7

0238 Horst Balz, "Biblische Aussagen zur Homosexualität," *ZEE* 31/1 (1987): 60-72.

0239 Jürgen Becker, "Zum Problem der Homosexualität in der Bibel," *ZEE* 31/1 (1987): 36-59.

5-6

0240 Paul S. Pinear, "Christ and the Congregation: 1 Corinthians 5-6," *RevExp* 80/3 (1983): 341-50.

0241 Arthur J. Dewey, "Paulos pornographos: the mapping of sacred space," *EGLMBS* 6 (1986): 104-13.

0242 Gerhard Sellin, "1 Korinther 5-6 und der 'Vorbrief' nach Korinth. Indizien für eine Mehrschichtigkeit von Kommunikationsakten im ersten Korintherbrief," *NTS* 37/4 (1991): 535-58.

0243 R. Trevijano Etchevrria, "A propósito del incestuoso (1 Cor 5-6)," *Salm* 38/2 (1991): 129-53.

0244 Will Deming, "The Unity of 1 Corinthians 5-6," *JBL* 115 (1996): 289-312.

5:1-6:20

0245 A. C. Wire, "Theological and Biblical Perspective: Liberation for Women Calls for a Liberated World," *ChS* 76 (1986): 7-17.

<u>5</u>

0246   B. N. Wambacq, "Matthieu 5, 31-32: Possibilite de Divorce ou Obligation de Rompre une Union Illigitime," *NRT* 104/1 (1982): 34-49.

0247   Andreas Lindemann, "Die biblischen Toragebote und die paulinische Ethik," in Wolfgand Schrage *Studien zum Text und zur Ethik des Neuen Testaments* (festschrift for Heinrich Greeven). Berlin: de Gruyter, 1986. Pp. 242-65.

0248   Colin G. Kruse, "The Offender and the Offence in 2 Corinthians 2:5 and 7:12," *EQ* 60 (1988): 129-39.

0249   Peter Zaas, "Catalogues and Context: 1 Corinthians 5 and 6," *NTS* 34/4 (1988): 622-629.

0250   J. J. Engelbrecht, "Kerklike Tug Volgens 1 Korintiers 5 en 6 (Ecclesiastical Discipline According to 1 Cor 5 & 6)," *HTS* 45/2 (1989): 387-400.

0251   G. Harris, "The Beginnings of Church Discipline: 1 Corinthians 5," *NTS* 37/1 (1991): 1-21.

0252   Brian S. Rosner, "Temple and Holiness in 1 Corinthians 5," *TynB* 42/1 (1991): 137-45.

0253   M. Lattke, "Verfluchter Inzest: War der 'Pornos' von 1 Kor 5 ein persischer 'Magos'?" in A. Kessler, et al., eds., *Peregrina Curiositas* (festschrift for Dirk Van Damme). Göttingen: Vandenhoeck & Ruprecht, 1994. Pp. 29-55.

<u>5:1</u>

0254   G. Al Wright, "First-Century AD Greek Morals," *BI* 14/2 (1989): 35-38.

<u>5:1-13</u>

0255   David W. Miller, "The Uniqueness of New Testament Church Eldership," *GTJ* 6/2 (1985): 315-27.

0256   J. W. MacGorman, "The Discipline of the Church," in Paul Basden and David Dockery, eds., *The People of God*. Nashville: Broadman Press, 1991. Pp. 74-84.

0257 Kathleen Callow, "Patterns of Thematic Development in 1 Corinthians 5:1-13," in David A. Black, et al., eds., *Linguistics and New Testament Interpretation: Essays on Discourse Analysis.* Nashville: Broadman Press, 1992. Pp. 194-206.

5:1-8

0258 James Benedict, "The Corinthian Problem of 1 Corinthians 5:1-8," *BLT* 32 (1987): 70-73.

0259 James T. South, "A Critique of the 'Curse/Death' Interpretation of 1 Corinthians 5:1-8," *NTS* 39 (1993): 539-61.

5:1-5

0260 V. C. Pfitzner, "Purified Community-Purified Sinner: Explusion from the Communion According to Matthew 18:15-18 and 1 Corinthians 5:1-5," *ABR* 30 (1982): 34-55.

0261 A. C. Perriman, "Paul and the Parousia: 1 Corinthians 15:50-57 and 2 Corinthians 5:1-5," *NTS* 35/4 (1989): 512-21.

5:2

0262 J. McHugh, "Num solus panis triticeus sit materia valida SS. Eucharistiae?" in *Studiorum Paulinorum Congressus, 1961.* 2 vols. Rome: Pontifical Biblical Institute, 1963. 2:289-98.

0263 Brian S. Rosner, " Οὐσχὶ μᾶλλον ἐπενθήσατε': Corporate Responsibility in 1 Corinthians 5," *NTS* 38/3 (1992): 470-73.

5:3-5

0264 Jerome Murphy-O'Connor, "1 Corinthians 5:3-5," *RB* 84/2 (1977): 239-45.

0265 B. McDonald, "Spirit, Penance and Perfection: The Exegesis of 1 Corinthians 5:3-5 from A.D. 200-241," doctoral dissertation, University of Edinburgh, 1993.

5:4

0266 G. A. Cole, "1 Cor 5:4: 'With my Spirit'," *ET* 8 (1987): 205.

5:5-11

0267 Joseph Plevnik, "Paul's Appeals to His Damascus Experience and 1 Cor 15:5-7: Are They Legitimations?" *TJT* 4 (1988): 101-11.

5:5

0268 J. Cambier, "La Chair et l'esprit en 1 Cor. 5:5," *NTS* 15/2 (1969): 221-32.

0269 N. George Joy, "Is the Body Really to be Destroyed?" *BT* 39/4 (1988): 429-36.

0270 Simon J. Kistemaker, " 'Deliver This Man to Satan': A Case Study in Church Discipline," *McMJT* 3 (1992): 33-46.

0271 Barth Campbell, "Flesh and Spirit in 1 Cor 5:5: An Exercise in Rhetorical Criticism of the New Testament," *JETS* 36 (1993): 331-42.

5:6

0272 A. Schon, "Eine weitere metrische Stelle bei St. Paulus," *Bib* 30 (1949): 510-13.

0273 Luis F. Ladaria, "Presente y futuro en la escatología cristiana," *EE* 60 (1985): 351-59.

5:6-8

0274 J. Keir Howard, " 'Christ Our Passover': A Study of the Passover-Exodus Theme in 1 Corinthians," *EQ* 41/2 (1969): 97-108.

5:7-8

0275 F. Ogara, "Dominica Resurrectionis," *VD* 13 (1933): 97-103.

0276 L. D. Hurst, "Apollos, Hebrews, and Corinth: Bishop Montefiore's Theory Examined," *SJT* 38/4 (1985): 505-13.

5:7

0277 Christian Grappe, "Essai sur l'arrière-plan Pascal des récits de la dernière nuit de Jésus," *RHPR* 65/2 (1985): 105-25.

0278 Antonio Orbe, "Cristo, sacrificio y manjar," *Greg* 66/2 (1985): 185-239.

0279 Pasquale Colella, "Cristo nostra pasqua? 1 Cor 5:7," *BibO* 28 (1986): 197-217.

5:12

0280 B. J. Dodd, "Pauls's Paradigmatic 'I' and 1 Corinthians 6:12," *JSNT* 59 (1995): 39-58.

5:16-21

0281 Paul D. Hanson, "The Identity and Purpose of the Church," *TT* 42 (1985): 342-52.

6-7

0282 David R. Catchpole, "The Synoptic Divorce Material as a Traditio-Historical Problem," *BJRL* 57/1 (1974): 92-127.

0283 Jens Christensen, "Paulus livsfornaegteren? For og imod Vilhelm Gronbechs Paulustolkning," *DTT* 53/1 (1990): 1-18.

6

0284 William Klassen, "The King as 'Living Law' with Particular Reference to Musonius Rufus," *SR* 14/1 (1985): 63-71.

0285 Peter Zaas, "Catalogues and Context: 1 Corinthians 5 and 6," *NTS* 34/4 (1988): 622-629.

0286 J. J. Engelbrecht, "Kerklike Tug Volgens 1 Korintiers 5 en 6 (Ecclesiastical Discipline According to 1 Cor 5 & 6)," *HTS* 45/2 (1989): 387-400.

6:1-11

0287 Erich Dinkler, "Zum Problem der Ethik bei Paulus: Rechtsnahme und Rechtsverzicht," *ZTK* 49 (1952): 167-200.

0288 Peter Richardson, "Judgment in Sexual Matters in 1 Corinthians 6:1-11," *NovT* 25/1 (1983): 37-58.

0289 Reginald H. Fuller, "An exegetical paper: 1 Corinthians 6:1-11," *ExA* 2 (1986): 96-104.

0290 Mauro Pesce, "Marginalità e sottomissione: la concezione escatologica del potere politico in Paolo," in Paolo Prodi and Luigi Sartori, eds., *Cristianesimo e potere*. Bologna: Centro Editoriale Dehoniano, 1986. Pp. 43-82.

0291 V. George Shillington, "People of God in the Courts of the World: A Study of 1 Corinthians 6:1-11," *Dir* 15 (1986): 40-50.

0292 Robert D. Taylor, "Toward a Biblical Theology of Litigation: A Law Professor Looks at 1 Cor 6:1-11," *ExA* 2 (1986): 105-16.

0293 Lloyd A. Lewis, "The Law Courts in Corinth: An Experiment in the Power of Baptism," *ATR* suppl. 11 (1990): 88-98.

0294 J. D. M. Derrett, "Judgement and 1 Corinthians 6," *NTS* 37/1 (1991): 22-36.

0295 Alan C. Mitchell, "Rich and Poor in the Courts of Corinth: Litigiousness and Status in 1 Corinthians 6:1-11," *NTS* 39 (1993): 562-86.

6:1-8

0296 B. W. Winter, "Civil Litigation in Secular Corinth and the Church. The Forensic Background to 1 Corinthians 6.1-8," *NTS* 37/4 (1991): 559-72.

6:1-6

0297 Brian S. Rosner, "Moses Appointing Judges. An Antecedent to 1 Cor 6,1-6?" *ZNW* 82 (1991): 275-78.

6:5-11

0298 L. Nieder, *Die Motive der religios-sittlichen Paränese in den paulinischen Gemeindebriefen.* Münich, Zink, 1953. Pp. 19-23.

6:9-20

0299 Kenneth E. Bailey, "Paul's Theological Foundation for Human Sexuality: 1 Cor 6:9-20—in the Light of Rhetorical Criticism," *TRev* 3/1 (1980): 27-41.

6:9-11

0300 Paul D. Feinberg, "Homosexuality and the Bible," *FundJ* 4/3 (1985): 17-19.

6:9-10

0301 Randolph A. Nelson, "Homosexuality and Social Ethics," *WW* 5 (1985): 380-94.

0302 John R. W. Stott, "Homosexual Marriage: Why Same Sex Partnerships Are Not a Christian Option," *CT* 29/17 (1985): 21-28.

0303   Karl P. Donfried, "The Kingdom of God in Paul," in Wendell
       Willis, ed., *The Kingdom of God in 20th-Century Interpretation.*
       Peabody MA: Hendrickson, 1987. Pp. 175-90.

0304   David L. Tiede, "Will Idolaters, Sodomizers, or the Greedy Inherit
       the Kingdom of God? A Pastoral Exposition of 1 Cor 6:9-10," *WW*
       10 (1990): 147-55.

0305   Abraham Smith, "The New Testament and Homosexuality," *QR*
       11 (1991): 18-32.

0306   Charles D. Myers, "What the Bible Really Says about
       Homosexuality," *Anima* 19 (1992): 47-56.

6:9

0307   Richard B. Hays, "Relations Natural and Unnatural," *JREth* 14
       (1986): 184-215.

0308   William L. Petersen, "Can ἀρσενοκοῖται Be Translated by
       'Homosexuals'?" *VC* 40 (1986): 187-91.

0309   David F. Wright, "Translating arsenokoitai," *VC* 41/4 (1987):
       396-98.

0310   James B. de Young, "The Source and NT Meaning of
       ἀρσενοκοῖται, with Implications for Christian Ethics and
       Ministry," *MSJ* 3/2 (1992): 191-215.

0311   David E. Malick, "The Condemnation of Homosexuality in
       1 Corinthians 6:9," *BSac* 150 (1993): 479-92.

6:11

0312   R. Schnackenburg, "Die Taufe als Bad der Reinigung," in *Das
       Heilsgeschehen bei der Taufe nach dem Apostel Paulus.* Münich:
       Zink, 1950. Pp. 1-8.

0313   Günter Haufe, "Reich Gottes bei Paulus und in der Jesustradition,"
       NTS 31 (1985): 467-72.

6:12-7:40

0314   G. Claudel, "1 Kor 6:12-7:40 neu gelesen," *TTZ* 94 (1985): 20-36.

0315 G. Claudel, "Une lecture de 1 Co 6,12-7,40," *SémBib* 41 (1986): 3-19.

0316 J.-J. Fauconnet, "La morale sexuelle chez Saint Paul: Analyse et commentaire de 1 Cor 6,12 à 7,40," *BullLittEccl* 93/4 (1992): 359-78.

6:12-7:39

0317 Angela West, "Sex and Salvation: A Christian Feminist Study of 1 Corinthians 6:12-7:39," *MC* 29/3 (1987): 17-24.

6:12-7:16

0318 Walter J. Bartling, "Sexuality, Marriage, and Divorce in 1 Corinthians 6:12-7:16," *CTM* 39/6 (1968): 355-66.

6:12-30

0319 Janice R. Huie, "A Call to Christian Integrity: preaching from 1 Corinthians," *QR* 7 (1987): 83-104.

0320 Robert Jewett, "Paul's Dialogue with the Corinthians . . . and Us," *QR* 13 (1993): 89-112.

6:12-20

0321 Emanuel Miguens, "Christ's 'Members' and Sex (1 Cor 6, 12-20)," *Thomist* 39/1 (1975): 24-48.

0322 Jerome Murphy-O'Connor, "Corinthian Slogans in 1 Cor. 6:12-20," *CBQ* 40/3 (1978): 391-96.

0323 Brendan Byrne, "Eschatologies of Resurrection and Destruction: The Ethical Significance of Paul's Dispute with the Corinthians," *DR* 104/357 (1986): 280-98.

0324 Terrance Callan, "Toward a Psychological Interpretation of Paul's Sexual Ethic," *EGLMBS* 6 (1986): 57-71.

0325 Timothy Radcliffe, " 'Glorify God in Your Bodies': 1 Corinthians 6:12-20 as a Sexual Ethic," *NBlack* 67 (1986): 306-14.

0326 Roy B. Ward, "Porneia and Paul," *EGLMBS* 6 (1986): 219-28.

0327 R. Kirchhof, *Die Sünde gegen den eigenen Leib: Studien zu πορνῃ und πορνείαν in 1 Kor 6,12-20 und dem sozio-kulturellen Kontext* *der paulinischen Adressaten.* SUNT #18. Göttingen: Vandenhoeck & Ruprecht, 1994.

6:12

0328   Roger L. Omanson,"Acknowledging Paul's Quotations," *BT* 43/2 (1992): 201-13.

0329   B. J. Dodd, "Pauls's Paradigmatic 'I' and 1 Corinthians 6:12," *JSNT* 59 (1995): 39-58.

6:13-20

0330   W. J. McGarry, "St. Paul's Magnificent Appeal for Purity," *AmER* 92 (1935): 47-56.

0331   M. Coune, "La dignité chrétienne du corps," *AsSeign* N.S. 33 (1970): 46-52.

6:14

0332   Udo Schnelle, "1 Kor. 6:14: Eine Nachpaulinische Glosse," *NovT* 25/3 (1983): 217-19.

0333   Jerome Murphy-O'Connor, "Interpolations in 1 Corinthians," *CBQ* 48 (1986): 81-94.

6:16-17

0334   S. E. Porter, "How Should ὁ κολλώμενος in 1 Cor 6,16.17 Be Translated?" *ETL* 67/1 (1991): 105-106.

6:16

0335   Bruce N. Kaye, "One Flesh and Marriage," *CANZTR* 22 (1990): 46-57.

6:17-20

0336   L. D. Hurst, "Apollos, Hebrews, and Corinth: Bishop Montefiore's Theory Examined," *SJT* 38/4 (1985): 505-13.

6:17

0337   O. Wieslaw J. Roslon, " 'A Ten, Kto Przylgnie do Pana, Stanowi z nim Jednego Ducha' (1 Kor 6, 17)," *RoczTK* 12 (1965): 58-73.

6:18

0338   Brendan Byrne, "Sinning Against One's Own Body: Paul's Understanding of the Sexual Relationship in 1 Corinthians 6:18," *CBQ* 45/4 (1983): 608-16.

0339 Gerhard Dautzenburg, "Pheugete ten porneian (1 Kor 6,18): eine Fallstudie zur paulinischen Sexualethik in ihrem Verhältnis zur Sexualethik des Frühjudentums," in Helmut Merklein, ed., *Neues Testament und Ethik* (festschrift for Rudolf Schnackenburg). Freiburg: Herder, 1989. Pp. 271-98.

0340 Brian S. Rosner, "A Possible Quotation of Test. Reuben 5:5 in 1 Corinthians 6:18a," *JTS* 43/1 (1992): 123-27.

6:19-20

0341 Vigen Guroian, "Seeing Worship as Ethics: An Orthodox Perspective," *JRE* 13 (1985): 332-59.

0342 Jonathan A. Draper, "The Tip of an Ice-berg: The Temple of the Holy Spirit," *JTSA* 59 (1987): 57-65.

0343 George L. Klein, "Hosea 3:1-3—Background to 1 Cor 6:19b-20?" *CTR* 3 (1989): 373-75.

6:19

0344 John Chryssavgis, "Soma - Sarx: The Body and the Flesh - An Insight into Patristic Anthropology," *Coll* 18/1 (1985): 61-66.

0345 Harold S. Songer, "The Temple in Roman Thought," *BI* 11/1 (1985): 14-18.

0346 F. W. Horn, "Wandel im Geist: zur pneumatologischen Begründung der Ethik bei Paulus," *KD* 38 (1992): 149-70.

7-11

0347 Andreas Lindemann, "Die biblischen Toragebote und die paulinische Ethik," in Wolfgand Schrage *Studien zum Text und zur Ethik des Neuen Testaments* (festschrift for Heinrich Greeven). Berlin: de Gruyter, 1986. Pp. 242-65.

7

0348 P. Schoonenberg, "Le sens de la virginité," *Chr* 5 (1958): 32-44.

0349 E. Neuhäusler, "Ruf Gottes und Stand des Christen: Bemerkungen zu 1 Kor 7," *BZ* 3 (1959): 43-60.

0350 C. de Villapadierna, "¿Ley del levirato en 1 Corintios 7?" *EstFr* 67 (1966): 77-87.

0351 Terri Williams, ''The Forgotten Alternative in First Corinthians 7,''
CT 17/17 (1973): 870-72.

0352 Elaine H. Pagels, ''Paul and Women: A Response to Recent
Discussion,'' *JAAR* 42/3 (1974): 538-49.

0353 David R. Cartlidge, ''1 Corinthians 7 as a Foundation for a
Christian Sex Ethic,'' *JR* 55/2 (1975): 220-34.

0354 Darrell Doughty, ''The Presence and Future of Salvation in
Corinth,'' *ZNW* 66/1-2 (1975): 61-90.

0355 Marco Adinolfi, ''Il Matrimonio Nella Liberta Dell' Etica
Escatologica di 1 Cor. 7,''*Ant* 51/2-3 (1976): 133-69.

0356 J. Cambier, ''Doctrine Paulinienne du Mariage Chrétien. Etude
Critique de 1 Co 7 et d'Ep 5, 21-33 et Essai de Leur Traduction
Actuelle,'' *EgT* 10/1 (1979): 13-59.

0357 C. Benton Kline, ''Marriage Today: A Theological Carpet Bag,''
JPC 33/1 (1979): 24-37.

0358 J. Carl Laney, ''Paul and the Permanence of Marriage in
1 Corinthians 7,'' *JETS* 25/3 (1982): 283-94.

0359 David E. Garland, ''The Christian's Posture Toward Marriage and
Celibacy: 1 Corinthians 7,'' *RevExp* 80/3 (1983): 351-62.

0360 Paul W. Gooch, ''Authority and Justification in Theological Ethics:
A Study in 1 Corinthians 7,'' *JREth* 11/1 (1983): 62-74.

0361 Jeremy Moiser, ''A Reassessment of Paul's View of Marriage With
Reference to 1 Cor. 7,'' *JSNT* 18 (1983): 103-22.

0362 Terrance Callan, ''Toward a Psychological Interpretation of Paul's
Sexual Ethic,'' *EGLMBS* 6 (1986): 57-71.

0363 William A. Heth, ''Matthew's 'Eunuch Saying' (19:12) and Its
Relationship to Paul's Teaching on Singleness in 1 Corinthians 7,''
doctoral dissertation, Dallas Theological Seminary, Dallas TX,
1986.

0364   Wolfgang Trilling, "Zum Thema: Ehe und Ehescheidung im Neuen Testament," in Joachim Rogge and Gottfried Schille, eds., *Theologische Versuche, 16*. Berlin: Evangelische Verlagsanstalt, 1986. Pp. 73-84.

0365   Piet Farla, "The Two Shall Become One Flesh: Gen 1.27 and 2.24 in the New Testament Marriage Texts," trans. Richard Rosser in Sipke Draisma, ed., *Intertextuality in Biblical Writings* (festschrift for Bas van Iersel). Kampen: Kok, 1989. Pp. 67-82.

0366   Margaret Y. MacDonald, "Women Holy in Body and Spirit: The Social Setting of 1 Corinthians 7," *NTS* 36/2 (1990): 161-81.

0367   Vincent L. Wimbush, "The Ascetic Impulse in Early Christianity: Methodological Challenges and Opportunities," in Elizabeth A. Livingstone, ed., *Studia Patristica, 25: Biblica et Arocrypha*. Louvain: Peeters, 1993. Pp. 462-78. See *TT* 50 (1993): 417-28.

0368   J. M. Gundry-Volf, "Male and Female in Creation and New Creation: Interpretations of Galatians 3.28c in 1 Corinthians 7," in T. E. Schmidt and M. Silva, eds., *To Tell the Mystery: Essays on New Testament Eschatology* (festschrift for R. H. Gundry). Sheffield: JSOT Press, 1994. Pp. 95-121.

7:1-16

0369   John J. Bandy, "Paul's Teaching Concerning Marriage in 1 Corinthians 7:1-16," master's thesis, Southern Baptist Theological Seminary, Louisville KY, 1952.

7:1-11

0370   H. Richards, "Christ on Divorce," *Scr* 11 (1959): 22-32.

7:1-9

0371   William A. Heth, "Unmarried 'for the Sake of the Kingdom' in the Early Church," *GTJ* 8 (1987): 55-88.

7:1-7

0372   Wolfgang Schrage, "Zur Frontstellung der Paulinischen Ehebewertung in 1 Kor 7:1-7," *ZNW* 67/3-4 (1976): 214-34.

0373   R. F. Collins, "The Unity of Paul's Paraenesis in 1 Thess. 4:3-8. 1 Cor. 7:1-7, A Significant Parallel," *NTS* 29/3 (1983): 420-29.

7:1-5

0374 Alan Padgett, "Feminism in First Corinthians: A Dialogue with Elisabeth Schüssler Fiorenza," *EQ* 58/2 (1986): 121-32.

0375 R. E. Oster, "Use, Misuse and Neglect of Archaeological Evidence in Some Modern Works on 1 Corinthians)," *ZNW* 83/1-2 (1992): 52-73.

7:1

0376 Gordon D. Fee, "1 Corinthians 7:1 in The NIV," *JETS* 23/4 (1980): 307-14.

0377 W. E. Phipps, "Is Paul's Attitude Towards Sexual Relations Contained in 1 Cor. 7.1?" *NTS* 28/1 (1982): 125-31.

0378 B. H. Throckmorton, "Language and the Bible," *REd* 80 (1985): 523-38.

0379 William J. Ireland, "Letter-Writing in the First Century AD," *BI* 14/2 (1989): 56-58.

0380 Roger L. Omanson,"Acknowledging Paul's Quotations," *BT* 43/2 (1992): 201-13.

7:2-40

0381 A. C. Wire, "Theological and Biblical Perspective: Liberation for Women Calls for a Liberated World," *ChS* 76 (1986): 7-17.

7:2

0382 Roy B. Ward, "Porneia and Paul," *EGLMBS* 6 (1986): 219-28.

7:7-8

0383 Christian Wolff, "Niedrigkeit und Verzicht in Wort und Weg Jesu und in der apostolischen Existenz des Paulus," *NTS* 34/2 (1988): 183-96.

7:7

0384 H. von Lips, "Der Apostolat des Paulus - en Charisma: semantische Aspekte zu charis-charisma und anderen Wortpaaren im Sprachgebrauch des Paulus," *Bib* 66/3 (1985): 305-43.

0385 Norbert Baumert, "Charisma und Amt bei Paulus," in Albert Vanhoye, ed., *L'Apôtre Paul: personnalité, style et conception du ministre*. Louvain: Peeters, 1986. Pp. 203-28.

0386 John J. Kilgallen, "Reflections on Charisma(ta) in the New Testament," *SM* 41 (1992): 289-323.

0387 B. J. Dodd, "Pauls's Paradigmatic 'I' and 1 Corinthians 6:12," *JSNT* 59 (1995): 39-58.

7:8-9

0388 Robert Macina, "Pour éclairer le terme: digamoi," *RevSR* 61 (1987): 54-73.

7:9

0389 M. L. Barré, "To Marry or to Burn: Purousthai in 1 Cor. 7:9," *CBQ* 36/2 (1974): 193-202.

7:10-16

0390 H. G. Coiner, "Those 'Divorce and Remarriage' Passages," *CTM* 39/6 (1968): 367-84.

0391 Richard N. Soulen, "Marriage and Divorce: A Problem in New Testament Interpretation," *Int* 23/4 (1969): 439-50.

7:10-15

0392 B. Byron, "1 Cor. 7:10-15: A Basis for Future Catholic Discipline on Marriage and Divorce?" *TS* 34/3 (1973): 429-45.

7:10-11

0393 E. Vogt, "Zu 1 Kor 7,10-11," *TGl* 31 (1939): 68-76.

0394 M. Zerwick, "De matrimonio et divortio in Evangelio," *VD* 38 (1960): 193-212.

0395 W. Harrington, "Jesus' Attitude towards Divorce," *ITQ* 37 (1970): 199-209.

0396 Augustine Stock, "Matthean Divorce Texts," *BTB* 8/1 (1978): 24-33.

0397 Jerome Murphy-O'Connor, "The Divorced Woman in 1 Cor 7:10-11," *JBL* 100/4 (1981): 601-606.

0398 Edward Dobson, "Divorce and the Teaching of Paul; pt 7," *FundJ* 5 (1986): 26-27.

0399 Frans Neirynck, "Paul and the Sayings of Jesus," in Albert Vanhoye, ed., *L'Apôtre Paul: personnalité, style et conception du ministre*. Louvain: Peeters, 1986. Pp. 265-321.

7:10

0400 Roger L. Omanson, "Some Comments about Style and Meaning: 1 Corinthians 9:15 and 7:10," *BT* 34/1 (1983): 135-39.

0401 Nikolaus Walter, "Paulus und die urchristliche Jesustradition," *NTS* 31 (1985): 498-522.

0402 Traugott Holtz, "Paul and the Oral Gospel Tradition," in Henry Wansbrough, ed., *Jesus and the Oral Gospel Tradition*. Sheffield: JSOT Press, 1991. Pp. 380-93.

7:12-15

0403 J. Bauer, "Das sogenannte Privilegium Paulinum," *BL* 20 (1952-1953): 82-83.

7:12

0404 John J. O'Rourke, "A Note on an Exception: Mt 5:32 (19:9) and 1 Cor 7:12 Compared," *HeyJ* 5 (1964): 299-302.

7:14-8:30

0405 J.-J. Suurmond, "The Ethical Influence of the Spirit of God: An Exegetical and Theological Study with Special Reference to 1 Corinthians, Romans 7:14-8:30, and the Johannine Literature," doctoral dissertation, Fuller Theological Seminary, Pasadena CA, 1983.

7:14

0406 J. Blinzler, "Zur Auslegung von 1 Kor 7,14," in *Neutestamentliche Aufsätze* (festschrift for Josef Schmid). Regensburg: Pustet, 1963. Pp. 23-41.

0407 Lester J. Kuyper, "Exegetical Study on 1 Corinthians 7:14," *RR* 31/1 (1977): 62-64.

0408 Jerome Murphy-O'Connor, "Works Without Faith in 1 Cor. 7:14," *RB* 84/3 (1977): 349-61.

0409 John C. O'Neill, "1 Corinthians 7,14 and Infant Baptism," in Albert Vanhoye, ed., *L'Apôtre Paul: personnalité, style et conception du ministre.* Louvain: Peeters, 1986. Pp. 357-61.

7:15-24

0410 D. Wiederkehr, *Die Theologie der Berufung in den Paulusbriefen.* Freiburg: Universitätsverlag, 1963. Pp. 125-46.

7:15

0411 H. U. Willi, "Das Privilegium Paulinum (1 Kor 7,15f) Pauli eigene Lebenserinnerung?" *BZ* 22/1 (1978): 100-108.

7:16

0412 C. Burchard, "Ei nach einem Ausdruck des Wissens oder Nichtwissens Joh 9:25, Act 19:2, 1 Cor 1:16, 7:16," *ZNW* 52/1-2 (1961): 73-82.

0413 Sakae Kubo, "1 Corinthians 7:16: Optimistic or Pessimistic?" *NTS* 24/4 (1978): 539-544.

7:17-24

0414 Gregory W. Dawes, "But If You Can Gain Your Freedom (1 Corinthians 7:17-24)," *CBQ* 52 (1990): 681-97.

7:17

0415 Sigfred Pedersen, "Theologische Uberlegungen zur Isagogik des Römerbriefs," *ZNW* 76/1-2 (1985): 47-67.

7:19

0416 F. Thielman, "The Coherence of Paul's View of the Law: The Evidence of First Corinthians," *NTS* 38/2 (1992): 235-53.

7:20-24

0417 Daniel Marguerat, "Paul: un génie théologique et ses limites," *FV* 84/5 (1985): 65-76.

7:21-22

0418 W. Deming, "A Diatribe Pattern in 1 Corinthians 7:21-22: A New Perspective on Paul's Directions to Slaves," *NovT* 37 (1995): 130-37.

0419 L. Boston, "A Womanist Reflection on 1 Corinthians 7:21-24 and 1 Corinthians 14:33-35," *JWR* 9-10 (1990-1991): 81-89.

7:21

0420   A. Callahan, "A Note on 1 Corinthians 7:21," *JITC* 17/1-2 (1989-1990): 110-14.

0421   J. A. Harrill, "Paul and Slavery: The Problem of 1 Cor 7:21," *BR* 39 (1994): 5-28.

7:22

0422   L. Cerfaux, "Service du Christ et liberte," *BVC* 8 (1954-1955): 7-15.

7:25-40

0423   Diane Payette-Bucci, "Voluntary Childlessness," *Dir* 17 (1988): 26-41.

0424   P. Genton, "1 Corinthiens 7,25-40. Notes exégétiques," *ÉTR* 67/2 (1992): 249-53.

7:25-38

0425   M. Navarro Puerto, "La παρθενος: Un futuro significativo en el aquí y ahora de la comunidad (1 Cor 7,25-38)," *EB* 49/3 (1991): 353-87.

7:25-35

0426   X. Leon-Dufour, "L'appel au célibat consacré," *AsSeign* 95 (1966): 17-32.

0427   James F. Bound, "Who Are The "Virgins" Discussed in 1 Corinthians 7:25-35?" *EvJ* 2/1 (1984): 3-15.

7:25-28

0428   William A. Heth, "Unmarried 'for the Sake of the Kingdom' in the Early Church," *GTJ* 8 (1987): 55-88.

7:25

0429   K. G. E. Dolfe, "1 Cor 7,25 Reconsidered (Paul a Supposed Adviser)," *ZNW* 83/1-2 (1992): 115-18.

7:26

0430   L. Legrand, " 'À cause de la détresse présente' saint Paul," in *La virginité dans la Bible*. Paris: Cerf, 1964. Pp. 25-31.

0431 B. B. Blue, "The House Church at Corinth and the Lord's Supper: Famine, Food Supply, and the *Present Distress*," *CTR* 5/2 (1991): 221-39.

0432 Roger L. Omanson,"Acknowledging Paul's Quotations," *BT* 43/2 (1992): 201-13.

7:27

0433 Bruce W. Winter, "Secular and Christian Responses to Corinthian Famines," *TynB* 40 (1989): 86-106.

7:29-35

0434 F. Puzo, "Maria y Maria (Nota exegetica a Lc. 10,38-42 y 1 Cor 7,29-35)," *EE* 34 (1960): 851-57.

0435 Janice R. Huie, "A Call to Christian Integrity: Preaching from 1 Corinthians," *QR* 7 (1987): 83-104.

7:29-31

0436 Y. Congar, "In the World and not of the World," *Scr* 9 (1957): 53-64.

0437 Romano Penna, "San Paolo (1 Cor 7, 29b-31a) e Diogene il Cinico," *Bib* 58/2 (1977): 237-45.

0438 H. Russell Botman, et al., "Exegesis and Proclamation—1 Corinthians 7:29-31: 'To Live . . . as if It Were not'," *JTSA* 65 (1988): 73-79.

0439 W. E. Glenny, "1 Corinthians 7:29-31 and the Teaching of Continence in *The Acts of Paul and Thecla*," *GTJ* 11/1 (1990): 53-70.

0440 Robert Jewett, "Paul's Dialogue with the Corinthians . . . and Us," *QR* 13 (1993): 89-112.

7:29

0441 Vincent P. Branick, "Apocalyptic Paul?" *CBQ* 47 (1985): 664-75.

7:30

0442 F.-J. Steinmetz, " 'Wejnen mit den Weinenden': Auslegung und Meditation von Lk 6,25; 1 Kor 7,30; Rom 12,15," *GeistL* 42 (1969): 391-94.

7:31

0443 A. V. Cernuda, "Engañan la oscuridad y el mundo; la luz era y manifiesta lo verdadero," *EB* 27 (1968): 153-75, 215-32.

0444 I. L. Grohar, "El 'mundo' en los escritos juanicos: un ensayo de interpretación," *RevB* 47 (1985): 221-27.

0445 Luis F. Ladaria, "Presente y futuro en la escatología cristiana," *EE* 60 (1985): 351-59.

7:32-35

0446 David L. Balch, "1 Cor 7:32-35 and Stoic Debates About Marriage, Anxiety and Distraction," *JBL* 102/3 (1983): 429-39.

7:34-40

0447 William A. Heth, "Unmarried 'for the Sake of the Kingdom' in the Early Church," *GTJ* 8 (1987): 55-88.

7:34

0448 Roger L. Omanson, "Acknowledging Paul's Quotations," *BT* 43/2 (1992): 201-13.

7:36-38

0449 R. Kugelmann, "1 Cor. 7,36-38," *CBQ* 10 (1948): 63-71, 458-59.

0450 L.-A. Richard, "Sur 1 Cor. vii, 36-38. Cas de conscience d'un père chrétien ou 'mariage ascétiqu?' Un essai d'interprétation," in *Mémorial J. Chaine* (festschrift for J. Chaine). Lyon: Facultés catholiques, 1950. Pp. 309-20.

0451 John J. O'Rourke, "Hypotheses regarding 1 Corinthians 7,36-38," *CBQ* 20 (1958): 292-98.

0452 Roger L. Omanson, "Translations: Text and Interpretation," *EQ* 57 (1985): 195-210.

7:37

0453 J. Leal, "Super virgine sua (1 Cor. 7,37)," *VD* 35 (1957): 97-102.

7:39-40

0454 Robert Macina, "Pour éclairer le terme: digamoi," *RevSR* 61 (1987): 54-73.

7:39

0455 Richard H. Hiers, "Binding and 'Loosing': The Matthean Authorizations," *JBL* 104 (1985): 233-50.

0456 J. B. Bauer, "Was las Tertullian 1 Kor 7,39?" *ZNW* 77 (1986): 284-87.

0457 Edward Dobson, "Divorce and the Teaching of Paul; pt 7," *FundJ* 5 (1986): 26-27.

8-11

0458 Michael D. Goulder, "Did Luke Know Any of the Pauline Letters," *PRS* 13 (1986): 97-112.

0459 E. de la Serna, "¿'Ver-juzgar-actuar' in San Pablo?" *RevB* 52/2 (1990): 85-98.

8:1-11:1

0460 Harold S. Songer, "Problems Arising From Worship of Idols: 1 Corinthians 8:1-11:1," *RevExp* 80/3 (1983): 363-75.

0461 John C. Brunt, "Rejected, Ignored, or Misunderstood? The Fate of Paul's Approach to the Problem of Food Offered to Idols in Early Christianity," *NTS* 31 (1985): 113-24.

8-10

0462 M. Coune, "Le problème des idolothytes et l'éducation de la syneitêsis," *RechSR* 51 (1963): 497-534.

0463 K. Maly, *Mündige Gemeinde. Untersuchungen zur pastoral en Führung des Apostels Paulus im 1. Korintherbrief.* Stuttgart: Katholisches Bibelwerk, 1967.

0464 Eugene J. Cooper, "Man's Basic Freedom and Freedom of Conscience in the Bible: Reflections on 1 Corinthians 8-10," *ITQ* 42/4 (1975): 272-83.

0465 R. A. Horsley, "Consciousness and Freedom Among the Corinthians: 1 Corinthians 8-10," *CBQ* 40/4 (1978): 574-89.

0466 Gordon D. Fee, "Eidolothuta Once Again: An Interpretation of 1 Corinthians 8-10," *Bib* 61/2 (1980): 172-97.

0467 Charles A. Kennedy, "The Cult of the Dead in Corinth," in *Love and Death in the Ancient Near East* (festschrift for Marvin H. Pope). Guillford CN: Four Quarters Publishinh Company, 1987. Pp. 227-36.

0468 Bruce Fisk, "Eating Meat Offered to Idols: Corinthian Behavior and Pauline Response in 1 Corinthians 8-10," *TriJ* 10/1 (1989): 49-70.

0469 O. Lamar Cope, "First Corinthians 8-10: Continuity or Contradiction?" *ATR* suppl. 11 (1990): 114-23.

0470 T. Söding, "Starke und Schwache: Der Götzenopferstreit in 1 Kor 8-10 als Paradigma paulinischer Ethik," *ZNW* 85 (1994): 69-92.

8-9

0471 Andreas Lindemann, "Die biblischen Toragebote und die paulinische Ethik," in Wolfgand Schrage *Studien zum Text und zur Ethik des Neuen Testaments* (festschrift for Heinrich Greeven). Berlin: de Gruyter, 1986. Pp. 242-65.

0472 Abraham J. Malherbe, "Determinism and Free Will in Paul: The Argument of 1 Corinthians 8 and 9," in T. Engberg-Pedersen, ed., *Paul in His Hellenistic Context*. Edinburgh: T. & T. Clark, 1994. Pp. 231-55.

8

0473 J. M. Ford, "Levirate Marriage in St. Paul," *NTS* 10 (1964): 361-65.

0474 J. M. Ford, "St. Paul, the Philogamist: 1 Cor. 8 in Early Patristic Exegesis," *NTS* 11/4 (1965): 326-48.

0475 Jean Marc Laporte, "Kenosis and Koinonia: The Path Ahead for Anglican-Roman Catholic Dialogue," *OC* 21/2 (1985): 102-20.

0476 Paul W. Gooch, "Conscience in 1 Corinthians 8 and 10," *NTS* 33/2 (1987): 244-54.

0477 Charles A. Kennedy, "1 Corinthians 8 as a Mishnaic List," in Jacon Neusner, ed., *Religious Writings and Religious Systems: Systemic Analysis of Holy Books*. Vol. 2. Atlanta: Scholars Press, 1989. Pp. 17-24.

0478 Peter D. Gooch, *Dangerous Food: 1 Corinthians 8-10 in Its Context.* Studies in Christianity and Judaism #5. New York: Edwin Mellen Press, 1993.

0479 K.-K. Yeo, "The Rhetorical Hermeneutic of 1 Corinthians 8 and Chinese Ancester Worship," *BibInt* 3 (1994): 294-311.

8:1-13

0480 L. D. Hurst, "Apollos, Hebrews, and Corinth: Bishop Montefiore's Theory Examined," *SJT* 38/4 (1985): 505-13.

0481 Janice R. Huie, "A Call to Christian Integrity: Preaching from 1 Corinthians," *QR* 7 (1987): 83-104.

0482 Robert Jewett, "Paul's Dialogue with the Corinthians . . . and Us," *QR* 13 (1993): 89-112.

8:1-11

0483 Michael D. Goulder, "Did Luke Know any of the Pauline Letters?" *PRS* 13/2 (1986): 97-112.

8:1-10

0484 Eduardo de la Serna, "Ver-juzgar-actuar en San Pablo?" *RevB* 52/2 (1990): 85-98.

8:1-6

0485 R. A. Horsley, "Gnosis in Corinth: 1 Corinthians 8: 1-6," *NTS* 27/1 (1980): 32-51.

8:1

0486 James E. Taulman, "The Greek Gods," *BI* 14/2 (1989): 66-69.

0487 D. W. Odell-Scott, "Paul's Skeptical Critique of a Primitive Christian Metaphysical Theology," *Encounter* 56 (1995): 127-46.

8:3

0488 Oda Wischmeyer, "Theon agapan bei Paulus: eine traditionsgeschichtliche Miszelle," *ZNW* 78/1-2 (1987): 141-44.

8:4-6

0489 A. Feuillet, "La profession de foi monothéiste de 1 Co viii, 4-6," in *Le Christ, sagesse de Dieu.* Paris: Gabalda, 1966. Pp. 59-85.

8:6

0490 M. M. Sagnard, "À propos de 1 Cor. 8,6," *ETL* 26 (1950): 54-58.

0491 W. Thüsing, "Allwirksamkeit Gottes durch Christus und Hinordnung auf Gott durch Christus," in *Per Christum in Deum: Studien zum Verhältnis von Christozentrik und Theozentrik in den paulinischen Hauptbriefen.* Münster: Aschendorff, 1965. Pp. 225-32.

0492 Hugolin Langkammer, "Jednostki Literackie i Teologiczne w i Kor 8, 6," *RoczTK* 15/1 (1968): 97-109.

0493 E. Earle Ellis, "Traditions in 1 Corinthians," *NTS* 32/4 (1986): 481-502.

8:8-11

0494 W. J. McGarry, "St. Paul and the Weaker Brother," *AmER* 94 (1936): 609-17.

8:8

0495 Jerome Murphy-O'Connor, "Food and Spiritual Gifts in 1 Cor. 8:8," *CBQ* 41/2 (1979): 292-98.

8:10

0496 B. N. Wambacq, "Quid S. Paulus de usu carnium decuerit," *VD* 19 (1939): 18-21, 60-69.

0497 James Custer, "When is Communion Communion," *GTJ* 6 (1985): 403-10.

0498 R. E. Oster, "Use, Misuse and Neglect of Archaeological Evidence in Some Modern Works on 1 Corinthians)," *ZNW* 83/1-2 (1992): 52-73.

8:13-9:27

0499 B. J. Dodd, "Pauls's Paradigmatic 'I' and 1 Corinthians 6:12," *JSNT* 59 (1995): 39-58.

9

0500 Gerhard Dautzenberg, "Der Verzicht auf das apostolische Unterhaltsrecht. Eine exegetische Untersuchung zu 1 Kor 9," *Bib* 50 (1969): 212-32.

0501 W. L. Willis, "An Apostolic Apologia? The Form and Function of 1 Corinthians 9," *JSNT* 24 (1985): 33-48.

0502 Wilhelm Wuellner, "Where Is Rhetorical Criticism Taking Us?" *CBQ* 49 (1987): 448-63.

0503 Harry P. Nasuti, "The Woes of the Prophets and the Rights of the Apostle: The Internal Dynamics of 1 Corinthians 9," *CBQ* 50/2 (1988): 246-64.

0504 Peter D. Gooch, *Dangerous Food: 1 Corinthians 8-10 in Its Context.* Studies in Christianity and Judaism #5. New York: Edwin Mellen Press, 1993.

9:1-2

0505 Joseph Plevik, " 'The Eleven and Those with Them' According to Luke," *CBQ* 40/2 (1978): 205-11.

9:1

0506 Ulrich Luck, "Die Bekehrung des Paulus und das paulinische Evangelium: zur Frage der Evidenz in Botschaft und Theologie des Apostels," *ZNW* 76/3-4 (1985): 187-208.

0507 Frans Neirynck, "Paul and the Sayings of Jesus," in Albert Vanhoye, ed., *L'Apôtre Paul: personnalité, style et conception du ministre.* Louvain: Peeters, 1986. Pp. 265-321.

0508 Joseph Plevnik, "Paul's Appeals to His Damascus Experience and 1 Cor 15:5-7: Are They Legitimations?" *TJT* 4 (1988): 101-11.

9:2

0509 Jean-Noël Aletti, "L'autorité apostolique de Paul: théorie et pratique," in Albert Vanhoye, ed., *L'Apôtre Paul: personnalité, style et conception du ministre.* Louvain: Peeters, 1986. Pp. 229-46.

9:4-10:5

0510 A. Sisti, "Guardare fissi alla meta," *BibO* 5 (1963): 14-21.

9:5

0511 J. B. Bauer, "Uxores circumducere (1 Kor 9,5)," *BZ* 3 (1959): 94-102.

9:6-13
> **0512** H. Rosman, "Tolle' lege," *VD* 20 (1940): 120-21.

9:8-10
> **0513** W. C. Kaiser, "The Current Crisis in Exegesis and the Apostolic Use of Deuteronomy 25:4 in 1 Corinthians 9:8-10," *JETS* 21/1 (1978): 3-18.

9:8-9
> **0514** F. Thielman, "The Coherence of Paul's View of the Law: The Evidence of First Corinthians," *NTS* 38/2 (1992): 235-53.

9:9-18
> **0515** A. Miranda, "L' 'uomo spirituale' nella Prima ai Corinzi," *RBib* 43 (1995): 485-519.

9:9-11
> **0516** David I. Brewer, "1 Corinthians 9:9-11: A Literal Interpretation of 'Do not Muzzle the Ox'," *NTS* 38 (1992): 554-65.

9:12-18
> **0517** Peter Richardson, "Temples, Altars and Living from the Gospel," in L. A. Jervis and P. Richardson, eds., *Gospel in Paul: Studies on Corinthians, Galatians, and Romans* (festschrift for R. N. Longenecker). Sheffield: Academic Press, 1994. Pp. 89-110.

9:13-14
> **0518** Armando J. Levoratti, "Tú no has querido sacrificio ni oblación: Salmo 40:7; Hebreos 10:5; pt 1," *RevB* 48 (1986): 1-30.

9:14-27
> **0519** G. Didier, "Le salaire du désintéressement (1 Cor. 9,14-27)," *RechSR* 43 (1955): 228-52.

9:14-18
> **0520** Ernst Käsemann, "Eine Paulinische Variation des 'Amor Fati'," *ZTK* 56 (1959): 138-154.

9:14
> **0521** Nikolaus Walter, "Paulus und die urchristliche Jesustradition," *NTS* 31 (1985): 498-522.

9:15-16
> **0522** Sigfred Pedersen, "Theologische Uberlegungen zur Isagogik des Römerbriefs," *ZNW* 76/1-2 (1985): 47-67.

9:15

0523   Roger L. Omanson, "Some Comments about Style and Meaning: 1 Corinthians 9:15 and 7:10," *BT* 34/1 (1983): 135-39.

9:16-23

0524   Janice R. Huie, "A Call to Christian Integrity: Preaching from 1 Corinthians," *QR* 7 (1987): 83-104.

0525   Robert Jewett, "Paul's Dialogue with the Corinthians . . . and Us," *QR* 13 (1993): 89-112.

9:16

0526   Siegfried Kreuzer, "Der Zwang des Botenbeobachtungen zu Lk 14,23 und 1 Kor 9,16," *ZNW* 76(1/2) (1985); 123-28.

9:19-23

0527   Peter Richardson, "Pauline Inconsistency," *NTS* 26/3 (1980): 347-62.

0528   Jerome Hall, "Paul, the Lawyer, on Law," *JLR* 3/2 (1985): 331-79.

0529   Jean Marc Laporte, "Kenosis and Koinonia: The Path Ahead for Anglican-Roman Catholic Dialogue," *OC* 21/2 (1985): 102-20.

0530   Heikki Räisänen, "Galatians 2:16 and Paul's Break with Judaism," *NTS* 31 (1985): 543-53.

0531   Donald A. Carson, "Pauline Inconsistency: Reflections on 1 Corinthians 9:19-23 and Galatians 2:11-14," *Ch* 100 (1986): 6-45.

0532   Bruce Wilson, "Notes toward a Theology of Everyday Life," *SMR* 126 (1986): 16-25.

0533   Kenneth V. Neller, "1 Corinthians 9:19-23," *RQ* 29/3 (1987): 129-42.

0534   Barbara Hall, "All Things to All People: A Study of 1 Corinthians 9:19-23," in Robert T. Fortna and Beverly R. Gaventa, eds., *The Conversation Continues: Studies in John and Paul* (festschrift for J. Louis Martyn). Nashville: Abingdon Press, 1990. Pp. 137-57.

0535 F. Thielman, "The Coherence of Paul's View of the Law: The Evidence of First Corinthians," *NTS* 38/2 (1992): 235-53.

0536 P. V. Reid, "Paul as a Model for Evangelization," *Listening* 30 (1995): 83-93.

9:19

0537 Ronald F. Hock, "Paul's Tentmaking and the Problem of His Social Class," *JBL* 97/4 (1978): 555-64.

9:20

0538 E. G. Edwards, "On Using the Textual Apparatus of the UBS Greek New Testament," *BT* 28/1 (1977): 121-42.

9:22

0539 David Alan Black, "A Note on 'The Weak' in 1 Corinthians 9:22," *Bib* 64/2 (1983): 240-42.

0540 David Stanley, "The Apostle Paul as Saint," *SM* 35 (1986): 71-97.

9:24-10:5

0541 G. Martelet, "But et sens d'une double comparison," *AsSeign* 22 (1965): 19-27.

0542 F. Ogara, "Bibebant... de spiritali consequente eos petra, petra autem erat Christus," *VD* 16 (1936): 33-40.

9:24-27

0543 Robert J. Karris, "Pauline Literature," in John J. Collins and John Dominic Crossan, eds., *The Biblical Heritage in Modern Catholic Scholarship*. Wilmington: Glazier, 1986. Pp. 156-83.

0544 Robert Jewett, "Paul's Dialogue with the Corinthians . . . and Us," *QR* 13 (1993): 89-112.

9:24-26

0545 Roman Garrison, "Paul's Use of the Athlete Metaphor in 1 Corinthians 9," *SR* 22/2 (1993): 209-17.

9:24

0546 François Refoulé, "Note sur Romains 9:30-33," *RB* 92 (1985): 161-86.

0547 Timothy N. Boyd, "Paul's Use of Analogy," *BI* 14/2 (1989): 24-28.

9:27

0548 Daniel Hoffman, "The Authority of Scripture and Apostolic Doctrine in Ignatius of Antioch," *JETS* 28 (1985): 71-79.

10-13

0549 Colin G. Kruse, "The Relationship Between the Opposition to Paul Reflected in 2 Corinthians 1-7 and 10-13," *EQ* 61/3 (1989): 195-202.

10-11

0550 P. S. Minear, "Paul's Teaching on the Eucharist in First Corinthians," *Worship* 44 (1970): 83-92.

0551 C. Burchard, "The Importance of Joseph and Aseneth for the Study of the New Testament: A General Survey and a Fresh Look at the Lord's Supper," *NTS* 33/1 (1987): 102-34.

10

0552 John D. Serkland, "The Dissension at Corinth: An Exploration," *LTQ* 8/1 (1973): 27-36.

0553 Paul W. Gooch, "Conscience in 1 Corinthians 8 and 10," *NTS* 33/2 (1987): 244-54.

10:1-13

0554 T. Baarda, "1 Corinthe 10:1-13: Een Schets (1 Corinthians 10:1-13: A Sketch)," *GTT* 76/1 (1976): 1-14.

0555 E. Earle Ellis, "Traditions in 1 Corinthians," *NTS* 32/4 (1986): 481-502.

0556 Ingo Broer, "Darum: Wer da meint zu stehen, der sehe zu, dass er nicht falle: 1 Kor 10,12f im Kontext von 1 Kor 10,1-13," in Helmut Merklein, ed., *Neues Testament und Ethik* (festschrift for Rudolf Schnackenburg). Freiburg: Herder, 1989. Pp. 299-325.

0557 William Baird, "1 Corinthians 10:1-13," *Int* 44 (1990): 286-90.

0558 G. D. Collier, " 'That We Might Not Crave Evil': The Structure and Argument of 1 Corinthians 10:1-13," *JSNT* 55 (1994): 55-75.

10:1-11
> **0559**   G. Martelet, "Sacraments, Figures et Exhortation en 1 Cor. 10,1-11," *RSR* 44 (1956): 323-59, 515-59.
>
> **0560**   A. Rose, "L'Église au desert," *BVC* 13 (1956): 49-59.
>
> **0561**   Andrew J. Bandstra, "Interpretation in 1 Corinthians 10:1-11," *GTJ* 6/1 (1971): 5-21.
>
> **0562**   M. Collin and P. Lenhardt, *Évangile et tradition d'Israël.* Paris: Cerf, 1990.

10:1-22
> **0563**   Wayne A. Meeks, "And Rose Up To Play: Midrash and Paraenesis in 1 Corinthians 10:1-22," *JSNT* 16 (1982): 64-78.
>
> **0564**   Terrance Callan, "Paul and the Golden Calf," *EGLMBS* 10 (1990): 1-17.

10:1-6
> **0565**   A. Miranda, "L' 'uomo spirituale' nella Prima ai Corinzi," *RBib* 43 (1995): 485-519.

10:1-4
> **0566**   A. Feuillet, "L'explication 'typologique,' des événements du désert en 1 Co 10,1-4," *SMR* 8 (1965): 115-35.

10:1-2
> **0567**   R. Schnackenburg, "Ein alt. Vorbild der Taufe (1 Kor 10,1f)," in *Das Heilsgeschehen bei der Taufe nach dem Apostel Paulus.* Münich: Zink, 1950. Pp. 86-89.
>
> **0568**   J. Bonduelle, "Les trois temps de notre exode: Tous, en Moïse, furent baptisés dans la nuée et dans la mer (1 Cor. 10,2)," *VS* 84 (1951): 276-302.

10:2
> **0569**   M. A. G. Haykin, " 'In the Cloud and in the Sea': Basil of Caesarea and the Exegesis of 1 Cor 10:2," *VC* 40 (1986): 135-44.
>
> **0570**   William B. Badke, "Baptised into Moses-Baptised into Christ: A Study in Doctrinal Development," *EQ* 60/1 (1988): 23-29.

0571 Giuseppe Barbaglio, "E tutti in Mosè sono stati battezzati nella nube e nel mare," in Pius Tragan, ed., *Alle origini del battesimo cristiano*. Rome: Pontificio Ateneo St. Anselmo, 1991. Pp. 167-91.

10:3-7

0572 James Custer, "When is Communion Communion," *GTJ* 6 (1985): 403-10.

10:4

0573 J. Schmitt, "Petra autem erat Christus," *MD* 29 (1952): 18-31.

0574 E. Earle Ellis, "Christos in 1 Corinthians 10:4,9," in Martinus de Boer, ed., *From Jesus to John: Essays on New Testament Christology* (festschrift of Marinus de Jonge). Sheffield: JSOT Press, 1993. Pp: 168-73.

10:6-16

0575 Charles Perrot, "Les Exemples du Desert," *NTS* 29/4 (1983): 437-52.

10:6-13

0576 F. Ogara, "Haec... in Figaro contingebant illis," *VD* 15 (1935): 227-32.

10:9

0577 E. Earle Ellis, "Christos in 1 Corinthians 10:4,9," in Martinus de Boer, ed., *From Jesus to John: Essays on New Testament Christology* (festschrift of Marinus de Jonge). Sheffield: JSOT Press, 1993. Pp: 168-73.

10:11

0578 I. Peri, "Gelangen zur Vollkommenheit: Zur Lateinischen Interpretation von Katantao in Eph 4:13," *BZ* 23/2 (1979): 269-78.

10:13

0579 R. J. Foster, "The Meaning of 1 Cor X,13," *Scr* 2 (1947): 45.

0580 D. M. Ciocchi, "Understanding Our Ability to Endure Temptation: A Theological Watershed," *JETS* 35/4 (1992): 463-79.

10:14-22

0581 Donald Farner, "The Lord's Supper until He Comes," *GTJ* 6/2 (1985): 391-401.

0582   David T. Adamo, "The Lord's Supper in 1 Cor. 10:14-22; 11:17-34," *AfTJ* 18/1 (1989): 36-48.

0583   Calvin Porter, "An Interpretation of Paul's Lord's Supper Texts: 1 Corinthians 10:14-22 and 11:17-34," *Enc* 50/1 (1989): 29-45.

10:14-21
0584   M.-É. Boismard, "L'Eucharistie selon saint Paul," *LV* 31 (1957): 93-106.

10:15-16
0585   Sigfred Pedersen, "Theologische Uberlegungen zur Isagogik des Römerbriefs," *ZNW* 76/1-2 (1985): 47-67.

10:15
0586   James Custer, "When is Communion Communion," *GTJ* 6 (1985): 403-10.

10:16-22
0587   P. C. Potgieter, "The Influence of Zwingli on Calvin concerning the Lord's Supper," in B. J. van der Walt, et al., eds., *John Calvin's Institutes*. Potcherstroom: Institute for Reformational Studies, 1986. Pp. 148-62.

10:16-17
0588   Peter E. Fink, "The Challenge of God's Koinonia," *Worship* 59 (1985): 386-403.

0589   L. M. Russell, "Inclusive Language and Power," *REd* 80 (1985): 582-602.

0590   Richard L. Thulin, "Retelling Biblical Narratives as the Foundation for Preaching," in Wayne R. Robinson, ed., *Journeys toward Narrative Preaching*. New York: Pilgrim Press, 1990. Pp. 7-22.

10:16
0591   Phillip Sigal, "Another Note to 1 Corinthians 10:16," *NTS* 29/1 (1983): 134-39.

0592   Guillermo J. Garlatti, "La eucaristia como memoria y proclamacion de la muerte del Señor: aspectos de la cena del Señor según San Pablo [2 pts]," *RevB* 46/4 (1984): 321-41; (1984) 47/1-2 (1985): 1-25.

0593 Walter Kasper, "The Unity and Multiplicity of Aspects in the Eucharist," *Communio (US)* 12 (1985): 115-38.

0594 Inge Mager, "Die theologische Lehrfreiheit in Göttingen und ihre Grenzen: Der Abendmahlskonflikt um Christoph August Heumann," in Bernd Moeller, ed., *Theologie in Göttingen: eine Vorlesungsreihe*. Göttingen: Vandenhoeck & Ruprecht, 1987. Pp. 41-57.

0595 A. McGowan, " 'First Regarding the Cup . . .': Papias and the Diversity of Early Eucharistic Practice," *JTS* 46 (1995): 551-55.

10:17

0596 Michel Albaric, "Une catéchèse eucharistique: le sermon 227," in A.-M. La Bonnardière, ed., *Saint Augustin et la Bible*. Paris: Editions Beauchesne, 1986. Pp. 87-98.

10:18-22

0597 James Custer, "When is Communion Communion," *GTJ* 6 (1985): 403-10.

10:18

0598 Jean-Noël Aletti, "L'autorité apostolique de Paul: théorie et pratique," in Albert Vanhoye, ed., *L'Apôtre Paul: personnalité, style et conception du ministre*. Louvain: Peeters, 1986. Pp. 229-46.

10:20-21

0599 Roy B. Ward, "Porneia and Paul," *EGLMBS* 6 (1986): 219-28.

10:22

0600 Brian S. Rosner, " 'Stronger Than He?' The Strength of 1 Corinthians 10:22b," *TynB* 43/1 (1992): 171-79.

10:23-11:1

0601 Duane F. Watson, "1 Corinthians 10:23-11:1 in the Light of Greco-Roman Rhetoric," *JBL* 108/2 (1989): 301-18.

10:23-24

0602 Morna D. Hooker, "Interchange in Christ and Ethics," *JSNT* 25 (1985): 3-17.

10:23

0603 Dennis Ormseth, "Showing the Body: Reflections on 1 Corinthians 12-13 for Epiphany," *WW* 6 (1986): 97-103.

0604 B. J. Dodd, "Pauls's Paradigmatic 'I' and 1 Corinthians 6:12," *JSNT* 59 (1995): 39-58.

10:25

0605 David W. J. Gill, "The Meat-Market at Corinth," *TynBll* 43/2 (1992): 389-93.

10:26

0606 Roy A. Harrisville, "Paul and the Psalms: A Formal Study," *WW* 5 (1985): 168-79.

10:27

0607 Paul W. Gooch, "St. Paul on the Strong and the Weak: A Study in the Resolution of Conflict," *Crux* 13/2 (1976): 10-20.

10:28

0608 B. Witherington, "Why Not Idol Meat?" *BibRev* 10 (1994): 38-43, 54-55.

10:29

0609 Jean Delumeau, "La difficile émergence de la tolérance," in Roger Zuber and Laurent Theis, eds., *La Révocation de l'Edit de Nantes et le protestantisme français en 1685*. Paris: Société de l'Historie du Protestantisme Français, 1986. Pp. 359-74

11-14

0610 R. F. White, "Richard Gaffin and Wayne Grudem on 1 Cor 13:10: A Comparison of Cessationist and Noncessationist Argumentation," *JETS* 35/2 (1992): 173-81.

11

0611 G. G. Blum, "Das Amt der Frau im Neuen Testament," *NovT* 7 (1964): 142-61.

0612 Elaine H. Pagels, "Paul and Women: A Response to Recent Discussion," *JAAR* 42/3 (1974): 538-49.

0613 Bruce W. Winter, "The Lord's Supper at Corinth: An Alternative Reconstruction," *RTR* 37/3 (1978): 73-82.

11:1-16

0614 E. Haulotte, *Symbolique du vêtement selon la Bible* "Le 'voile' des femmes dans l'assemblée liturgique (1 Co 11,1-16)," *VD* 22 (1942): 237-71.

0615 Cindy Weber-Han, "Sexual Equality according to Paul: An Exegetical Study of 1 Corinthians 11:1-16 and Ephesians 5:21-33," *BLT* 22/3 (1977): 167-70.

0616 Leonidas Kalugila, "Women in the Ministry of Priesthood in the Early Church: An Inquiry," *AfTJ* 14/1 (1985): 35-45.

11:1-12

0617 Paul S. Fiddes, "Woman's Head Is Man: A Doctrinal Reflection upon a Pauline Text," *BQ* 31 (1986): 370-83.

11:1

0618 Otto Merk, "Nachahmung Christi: zu ethischen Perspektiven in der paulinischen Theologie," in Helmut Merklein, ed., *Neues Testament und Ethik* (festschrift for Rudolf Schnackenburg). Freiburg: Herder, 1989. Pp. 172-206.

11:2-34

0619 David K. Lowery, "The Head Covering and the Lord's Supper in 1 Corinthians 11:2-34," *BSac* 143 (1986): 155-63.

11:2-16

0620 C. V. Beyler, "Meaning and Relevance of the Devotional Covering: A Study in the Interpretation of 1 Corinthians 11:2-16," master's thesis, Southern Baptist Theological Seminary, Louisville KY, 1954.

0621 J. W. Roberts, "The Veils in 1 Corinthians 11:2-16," *RQ* 3 (1959): 183-98.

0622 Graydon F. Snyder, "Jesus Power: A Confrontation with Women's Lib at Corinth," *BLT* 16/3 (1971): 161-67.

0623 James B. Hurley, "Did Paul Require Veils or the Silence of Women? A Consideration of 1 Corinthians 11:2-16 and 1 Corinthians 14:33b-36," *WTJ* 35/2 (1973): 190-202.

0624   William O. Walker, "1 Corinthians 11:2-16 and Paul's Views Regarding Women," *JBL* 94/1 (1975): 94-110.

0625   Jerome Murphy-O'Connor, "The Non-Pauline Character of 1 Corinthians 11:2-16," *JBL* 95/4 (1976): 615-21.

0626   Bruce K. Waltke, "1 Corinthians 11:2-16: An Interpretation," *BSac* 135 (1978): 46-57.

0627   Linda Mercandante, "The Male-Female Debate: Can We Read the Bible Objectively?" *Crux* 15/2 (1979): 20-25.

0628   Jerome Murphy-O'Connor, "Sex and Logic in 1 Corinthians 11:2-16," *CBQ* 42/4 (1980): 482-500.

0629   Alan Padgett, "Paul on Women in the Church: The Contradictions of Coiffure in 1 Corinthians 11:2-16," *JSNT* 20 (1984): 69-86.

0630   Lyle Vander Broek, "Women and the Church: Approaching Difficult Passages," *RR* 38 (1985): 225-31.

0631   Terrance Callan, "Toward a Psychological Interpretation of Paul's Sexual Ethic," *EGLMBS* 6 (1986): 57-71.

0632   Joël Delobel, "1 Cor 11,2-16: Towards a Coherent Interpretation," in Albert Vanhoye, ed., *L'Apôtre Paul: personnalité, style et conception du ministre.* Louvain: Peeters, 1986. Pp. 369-89.

0633   Alan Padgett, "Feminism in First Corinthians: A Dialogue with Elisabeth Schüssler Fiorenza," *EQ* 58/2 (1986): 121-32.

0634   David Peterson, "The Ordination of Women: Balancing the Scriptural Evidence," *SMR* 125 (1986): 13-21.

0635   Ronald Y. K. Fung, "Ministry in the New Testament," in Don A Carson, ed., *The Church in the Bible and the World.* Exeter: Paternoster Press, 1987. Pp. 154-212.

0636   David M. Scholer, "Feminist Hermeneutics and Evangelical Biblical Interpretation," *JETS* 30 (1987): 407-20.

0637   Thomas P. Shoemaker, "Unveiling of Equality: 1 Corinthians 11:2-16," *BTB* 17/2 (1987): 60-63.

0638   Ron Johnson, "The Theology of Gender," *JPsyC* 7 (1988): 39-49.

0639   Dennis R. MacDonald, "Corinthian Veils and Gnostic Androgynes," in Karen L. King, ed., *Images of the Feminine in Gnosticism*. Philadelphia: Fortress Press, 1988. Pp. 276-92.

0640   Jerome Murphy-O'Connor, "1 Corinthians 11:2-16 Once Again," *CBQ* 50/2 (1988): 265-74.

0641   Cynthia L. Thompson, "Hairstyles, Head-Coverings, and St. Paul. Portraits from Roman Corinth," *BA* 51/2 (1988): 99-115.

0642   Huub van de Sandt, "1 Kor. 11:2-16 als een retorische eenheid," *Bij* 49/4 (1988): 410-25.

0643   Danielle Ellul, "Sois belle et tais -toi!" Est-ce vraiment ce que Paul a dit? A propos de 1 Co 11:2-16," *FV* 88/5 (1989): 49-58.

0644   David W. J. Gill, "The Importance of Roman Portraiture for Head-Coverings in 1 Corinthians 11:2-16," *TynB* 41 (1990): 245-60.

0645   Timothy Radcliffe, "Paul and Sexual Identity: 1 Corinthians 11:2-16," in J. M. Soskice, ed., *After Eve*. Basingstoke: Marshal Pickering, 1990. Pp. 62-72.

0646   Christine Amjad-Ali, "The Equality of Women: Form or Substance," in R. S. Sugirtharajah, ed., *Voices from the Margin: Interpreting the Bible in the Third World*. Maryknoll NY: Orbis, 1991. Pp. 205-13.

0647   Gail P. Corrington, "The 'Headless Woman': Paul and the Language of the Body in 1 Cor 11:2-16," *PRS* 18/3 (1991): 223-31.

0648   A. Rowe, "Hermeneutics and 'Hard Passages' in the NT on the Role of Women in the Church: Issues from Recent Literature," *EpRev* 18 (1991): 82-88.

0649   Thomas R. Schreiner, "Head Coverings, Prophecies and the Trinity: 1 Corinthians 11:2-16," in John Piper and Wayne Grudem, eds., *Recovering Biblical Manhood and Womanhood*. Wheaton IL: Crossway Books, 1991. Pp. 124-39, 485-87.

0650   K. T. Wilson, "Should Women Wear Headcoverings?" *BSac* 148/592 (1991): 442-62.

0651   Edward B. Anderson, "Power on Her Head," *LO* 14 (1992): 19-22.

0652   R. E. Oster, "Use, Misuse and Neglect of Archaeological Evidence in Some Modern Works on 1 Corinthians)," *ZNW* 83/1-2 (1992): 52-73.

0653   L. Ann Jervis, " 'But I Want You to Know . . .': Paul's Midrashic Intertextual Response to the Corinthian Worshipers," *JBL* 112 (1993): 231-46.

0654   I. R. Reimer, "Da Memória à Novidade de Vida," *EstT* 33/3 (1993): 201-12.

0655   T. Schlirrmacher, *Paulus im Kampf gegen den Schleier: Eine alternative Auslegung von I. Korinther 11,2-16.* Biblia et Symbiotica #4. Bonn: Verlag für Kultur und Wissenschaft, 1993.

11:2-6
0656   Walter L. Liefeld, "Women, Submission and Ministry in 1 Corinthians," in Alvera Mickelsen, ed., *Women, Authority and the Bible.* Downers Grove IL: InterVarsity Press, 1986. Pp. 134-54.

11:3-35
0657   A. C. Wire, "Theological and Biblical Perspective: Liberation for Women Calls for a Liberated World," *ChS* 76 (1986): 7-17.

11:3-17
0658   J. Keir Howard, "Niether Male nor Female: An Examination of the Status of Womem in the New Testament," *EQ* 55/1 (1983): 31-42.

11:3-16
0659   A. Isaksson, *Mariage and Ministry in the New Temple. A Study with Special Reference to Mt. 19.13-12 and 1. Cor. 11.3-16* . Lund: Gleerup, 1965.

0660   G. W. Trompf, "On Attitudes Toward Women in Paul and Paulinist Literature: 1 Corinthians 11:3-16 and Its Context," *CBQ* 42/2 (1980): 196-215.

0661 Jerome Murphy-O'Connor, "Interpolations in 1 Corinthians," *CBQ* 48 (1986): 81-94.

0662 William O. Walker, "The Vocabulary of 1 Corinthians 11:3-16: Pauline or Non-Pauline?" *JSNT* 35 (1989): 75-88.

11:3-9

0663 Lone Fatum, "Image of God and Glory of Man: Women in the Pauline Congregations," in Karl E. Borresen, ed., *Image of God and Gender Models*. Oslo: Solum Forlag, 1991. Pp. 56-137.

11:3

0664 W. Thüsing, "Christi Haupt ist Gott," in *Per Christum in Deum: Studien zum Verhältnis von Christozentrik und Theozentrik in den paulinischen Hauptbriefen*. Münster: Aschendorff, 1965. Pp. 20-29.

0665 Joseph A. Fitzmyer, "Another Look at Kephalē in 1 Corinthians 11:3," *NTS* 35/4 (1989): 503-11.

0666 Wayne Grudem, "The Meaning of Kephale ('head'): A Response to Recent Studies," *TriJ* 11 (1990): 3-72.

0667 A. C. Perriman, "The Head of a Woman: The Meaning of κεφαλὴ in 1 Cor. 11:3," *JTS* 45 (1994): 602-22.

11:4-21

0668 F. Thielman, "The Coherence of Paul's View of the Law: The Evidence of First Corinthians," *NTS* 38/2 (1992): 235-53.

11:4

0669 Richard Oster, "When Men Wore Veils to Worship: The Historical Context of 1 Corinthians 11:4," *NTS* 34/4 (1988): 481-505.

11:6-8

0670 Wesley Carr, "The Rulers of this Age—1 Corinthians 11:6-8," *NTS* 23/1 (1976): 20-35.

11:6

0671 Halvor Moxnes, "Paulus og den norske vaerematen: 'skam' og 'aere' i Romerbrevet," *NTT* 86/3 (1985): 129-40.

11:7-12

0672 Mary Rose D'Angelo, "The Garden: Once and not Again: Traditional Interpretations of Genesis 1:26-27 in 1 Corinthians

11:7-12," in G. A. Robbins, ed., *Genesis 1-3 in the History of Exegesis*. Lewiston NY: Mellen, 1988. Pp. 1-41.

0673   G. E. Sterling, " 'Wisdom among the Perfect': Creation Traditions in Alexanderian Judaism and Corinthian Christianity," *NovT* 37/4 (1995): 355-84.

11:7

0674   T. J. van Bavel, "Women as the Image of God in Augustine's De trinitate XII," in *Signum Pietatis* (festschrift for Cornelius P. Mayer). Würzburg: Augustinus-Verlag, 1989. Pp. 267-88.

0675   Kari E. Borresen, "God's Image, Is Woman Excluded? Medieval Interpretation of Gen 1:27 and 1 Cor 11:7," in Karl E. Borresen, ed., *Image of God and Gender Models*. Oslo: Solum Forlag, 1991. Pp. 208-27.

11:9

0676   T. Gallus, "Non est creatus vir propter mulierem, sed mulier propter virum (1 Cor 11,9)," *VD* 22 (1942): 141-51.

11:10

0677   I. Mezzacasa, "Propter angels," *VD* 11 (1931): 39-42.

0678   C. Rösch, "Um tar Engel willen (1 Kor. 11,10)," *TGl* 24 (1932): 363-65.

0679   Morna D. Hooker, "Authority on Her Head: An Examination of 1 Corinthians 11:10," *NTS* 10 (1964): 410-17.

0680   A. Feuillet, "Le Signe de Puissance sur la Tête de la Femme: 1 Co 11, 10," *NRT* 95/9 (1973): 945-54.

0681   Günther Schwarz, "Exousian echein eip tes kephales? (1. Korinther 11:10)," *ZNW* 70/3-4 (1979): 249.

0682   Robert C. Newman, "The Ancient Exegesis of Genesis 6:2,4," *GTJ* 5/1 (1984): 13-36.

0683   David R. Hall, "A Problem of Authority," *ET* 102 (1990): 39-42.

0684   J. Winandy, "Un curieux *casus pendens:* 1 Corinthiens 11.10 et son interprétation," *NTS* 38/4 (1992): 621-29.

11:11-13

0685 Nikolaus Walter, "Paulus und die urchristliche Jesustradition," *NTS* 31 (1985): 498-522.

11:11-12

0686 Madeleine Boucher, "Some Unexplored Parallels to 1 Corinthians 11,11-12 and Gal 3,28: The NT on the Role of Women," *CBQ* 31 (1969): 50-58.

11:11

0687 K. Wennemer, "Jedoch is weder die Frau ohne den Mann, noch der Mann ohne die Frau im Herrn (1 Kor 11,11)," *GeistL* 26 (1953): 288-97.

11:12

0688 Karl H. Schelkle, "1 Cor 11:12: 'Woman from Man, Man from Woman'," *TD* 32/2 (1985): 145-47.

11:13

0689 Joseph A. Fitzmyer, "Kephalē in 1 Corinthians 11:3," *Int* 47/1 (1993): 52-59.

11:14-15

0690 Halvor Moxnes, "Paulus og den norske vaerematen: 'skam' og 'aere' i Romerbrevet," *NTT* 86/3 (1985): 129-40.

11:15

0691 Alan Padgett, "The Significance of ἀντί in 1 Corinthians 11:15," *TynB* 45 (1994): 181-87.

11:16

0692 T. Engberg-Pedersen, "1 Corinthians 11:16 and the Character of Pauline Exhortation," *JBL* 110/4 (1991): 679-89.

11:17-34

0693 L. Dequeker and W. Zuidema, "L'Eucharistie selon saint Paul," *Conci* 40 (1968): 45-53.

0694 John C. Middlekauff, "The Lord's Supper: 1 Corinthians 11:17-34," *BLT* 24 (1979): 225-29.

0695 J. Timothy Coyle, "The Agape/Eucharist Relationship in 1 Corinthians 11," *GTJ* 6/2 (1985): 411-24.

0696   Donald Farner, "The Lord's Supper until He Comes," *GTJ* 6/2 (1985): 391-401.

0697   Daniel Marguerat, "Paul: un génie théologique et ses limites," *FV* 84/5 (1985): 65-76.

0698   Stephen C. Barton, "Paul's Sense of Place: An Anthropological Approach to Community Formation in Corinth," *NTS* 32/2 (1986): 225-46.

0699   H.-J. Klauck, "Eucharistie und Kirchengemeinschaft bei Paulus," *WuW* 49 (1986): 1-14.

0700   G. C. Nicholson, "Houses for Hospitality: 1 Cor 11:17-34," *CANZTR* 19 (1986): 1-6.

0701   Peter Stuhlmacher, "Das neutestamentliche Zeugnis vom Herrenmahl," *ZTK* 84/1 (1987): 1-35.

0702   Otfried Hofius, "Herrenmahl und Herrenmahlsparadosis," *ZTK* 85/4 (1988): 371-408.

0703   David T. Adamo, "The Lord's Supper in 1 Cor. 10:14-22; 11:17-34," *AfTJ* 18/1 (1989): 36-48.

0704   Calvin Porter, "An Interpretation of Paul's Lord's Supper Texts: 1 Corinthians 10:14-22 and 11:17-34," *Enc* 50/1 (1989): 29-45.

0705   Eduardo de la Serna, "Ver-juzgar-actuar en San Pablo?" *RevB* 52/2 (1990): 85-98.

0706   Victor P. Furnish, "Belonging to Christ: A Paradigm for Ethics in First Corinthians," *Int* 44/2 (1990): 145-57.

0707   B. B. Blue, "The House Church at Corinth and the Lord's Supper: Famine, Food Supply, and the *Present Distress*," *CTR* 5/2 (1991): 221-39.

0708   T. Engberg-Pedersen "Proclaiming the Lord's Death: 1 Corinthians 11:7-34 and the Forms of Paul's Theological Argument," *SBLSP* (1991): 592-617.

0709 Peter Lampe, "Das korinthische Herrenmahl im Schnittpunkt hellenistisch-römischer Mahlpraxis und paulinischer Theologia Crucis (1Kor 11,17-34)," *ZNW* 82/3-4 (1991): 183-213.

0710 Hans Weder, "Le souvenir évangélique: réflexions néotestamentaires sur la présence du passé," in Daniel Marguerat and Jean Zumstein, eds., *La mémoire et le temps*. Geneva: Labor et Fides, 1991. Pp. 31-46.

11:17-22

0711 Willem S. Vorster, "On Early Christian Communities and Theological Perspectives," *JTSA* 59 (1987): 26-34.

11:19

0712 R. A. Campbell, "Does Paul Acquiesce in Divisions at the Lord's Supper?" *NovT* 33/1 (1991): 61-70.

11:20-25

0713 John D. Lawrence, "The Eucharist as the Imitation of Christ," *TS* 47 (1986): 286-96.

11:20

0714 Gerard S. Sloyan, "Jewish Ritual of the 1st Century CE and Christian Sacramental Behavior," *BTB* 15 (1985): 98-103.

0715 Joe O. Lewis, "Paul and the Lord's Supper," *BI* 14/2 (1989): 73-75.

11:21-34

0716 James Custer, "When is Communion Communion," *GTJ* 6 (1985): 403-10.

11:21-23

0717 Paul D. Fueter, "The Therapeutic Language of the Bible," *IRM* 75 (1986): 211-21.

0718 William R. Herzog, "The New Testament and the Question of Racial Injustice," *ABQ* 5 (1986): 12-32.

11:21

0719 J. D. M. Derrett, "Intoxication, Joy, and Wrath: 1 Cor 11:21 and Jn 2:10," *FilN* 2/1 (1989): 41-56.

11:23-34
> **0720** Reinhard Schwarz, "Das Abendmahl - die Testamentshandlung Jesu," *Luther* 59/1 (1988): 13-25.

11:23-32
> **0721** M.-É. Boismard, "L'Eucharistie selon saint Paul," *LV* 31 (1957): 93-106.

11:23-30
> **0722** H. Maccoby, "Paul and the Eucharist," *NTS* 37/2 (1991): 247-67.

11:23-29
> **0723** E. J. Kilmartin, "The Eucharistic Cup in the Primitive Liturgy," *CBQ* 24 (1962): 32-43.

> **0724** C. Spicq, "L'authentique participation au repas du Seigneur (1 Co 11,23-29)," *AsSeign* 54 (1966): 27-40.

11:23-26
> **0725** William L. Craig, "The Historicity of the Empty Tomb of Jesus," *NTS* 31 (1985): 39-67.

> **0726** William R. Farmer, "Peter and Paul, and the Tradition concerning 'the Lord's Supper' in 1 Corinthians 11:23-26," *CTR* 2 (1987): 119-40.

> **0727** H.-J. Klauck and Barry D. Smith, "Presence in the Lord's Supper: 1 Corinthians 11:23-26 in the Context of Hellenistic Religious History," in Ben F. Meyer, ed., *One Loaf, One Cup: Ecumenical Studies of 1 Cor 11 and Other Eucharistic Texts: The Cambridge Conference on the Eucharist, August 1988.* Macon GA: Mercer University Press, 1993. Pp. 57-74.

11:23-25
> **0728** A. Grail, "Sacrement de la Croix," *LV* 7 (1952): 11-27.

> **0729** P. Benoit, "Les récits de l'institution et leur portée," *LV* 31 (1957): 49-76.

> **0730** J. Betz, "Die Eucharistie als sakramentale Gegenwart des Heilsereignisses 'Jesus,' nach dem ältesten Abendmahlsbericht," *GeistL* 33 (1960): 166-75.

0731 Walter Kasper, "The Unity and Multiplicity of Aspects in the Eucharist," *Communio (US)* 12 (1985): 115-38.

0732 Inge Mager, "Die theologische Lehrfreiheit in Göttingen und ihre Grenzen: Der Abendmahlskonflikt um Christoph August Heumann," in Bernd Moeller, ed., *Theologie in Göttingen: eine Vorlesungsreihe*. Göttingen: Vandenhoeck & Ruprecht, 1987. Pp. 41-57.

0733 Charles H. Talbert, "Paul on the Covenant," *RevExp* 84 (1987): 299-313.

0734 Bonnie B. Thurston, "Do This: A Study on the Institution of the Lord's Supper," *RQ* 30/4 (1988): 207-17.

0735 Martin Karrer, "Der Kelch des neuen Bundes: Erwägungen zum Verständnis des Herrenmahls nach 1 Kor 11:23b-25," *BZ* 34/2 (1990): 198-221.

0736 Peter Lampe, "The Eucharist: Identifying with Christ on the Cross," *Int* 48 (1994): 36-49.

0737 Nikolaus Walter, "Paulus und die urchristliche Jesustradition," *NTS* 31 (1985): 498-522.

0738 Guillermo J. Garlatti, "La eucaristia como memoria y proclamacion de la muerte del Señor: aspectos de la cena del Señor según San Pablo [2 pts]," *RevB* 46/4 (1984): 321-41; (1984) 47/1-2 (1985): 1-25.

11:23-24
0739 Peder Borgen, "Nattverdtradisjonen i 1.Kor. 10 og 11 som evangelietradisjon," *SEÅ* 51-52 (1985-1986): 32-39.

11:23
0740 George O. Evenson, "The Force of "Apo" in 1 Cor. 11:23," *LQ* 11 (1959): 244-46.

0741 Robert Paul Roth, "Paradosis and Apokalupsis in 1 Corinthians 11:23," *Lutheran Quarterly* 12 (1960): 64-67.

0742 Christian Grappe, "Essai sur l'arrière-plan Pascal des récits de la dernière nuit de Jésus," *RHPR* 65/2 (1985): 105-25.

11:24-25

0743 F. Porporato, "Hoc facite in meam commemorationem," *VD* 13 (1933): 264-70.

0744 F. P. Chenderlin, "The Semantic and Conceptual Background and Value of 'ANAMNHSIS in 1 Corinthians 11:24-25," doctoral dissertation, Claremont Graduate School, Claremont CA, 1982.

0745 Peter Henrici, "Do This in Remembrance of Me: The Sacrifice of Christ and the Sacrifice of the Faithful," *Communio* 12 (1985): 146-57.

0746 John N. Suggit, "The Perils of Bible translation: An Examination of the Latin Versions of the Words of Institution of the Eucharist," in K. J. H. Petzer and Patrick Hartin, eds., *A South African Perspective on New Testament* (festschrift for Bruce Metgzer). Leiden: Brill, 1986. Pp. 54-61.

0747 R. A. D. Clancy, "The Old Testament Roots of Remembrance in the Lord's Supper," *CJ* 19/1 (1993): 35-50.

11:24

0748 Jakob J. Petuchowski, "Do This In Remembrance of Me (1 Cor. 11:24)," *JBL* 76 (1957): 293-98.

0749 Michel Albaric, "Une catéchèse eucharistique: le sermon 227," in A.-M. La Bonnardière, ed., *Saint Augustin et la Bible*. Paris: Editions Beauchesne, 1986. Pp. 87-98.

0750 Otfried Hofius, "Tὸ σῶμα τὸ ὑπὲρ ὑμῶν 1 Cor 11:24," *ZNW* 80/1-2 (1989): 80-88.

11:25

0751 R. Kugelmann, "This Is My Blood of the New Covenant," *Worship* 35 (1961): 421-24.

0752 Homer A. Kent, "The New Covenant and the Church," *GTJ* 6/2 (1985): 289-98.

0753 Niels Hyldahl, "Μετὰ τὸ δειπνῆσαι, 1 Kor 11,25 (og Luk 22, 20)," *SEÅ* 51/52 (1986-1987): 100-107.

0754 N. Kobayashi, "The Meaning of Jesus' Death in the 'Last Supper' Traditions," *TJT* 8/1 (1992): 95-105.

11:26

0755 Otfried Hofius, " 'Bis dass kommt': 1 Kor. xi. 26," *NTS* 14/3 (1968): 439-41.

0756 F. G. Schafer, "Der 'Heilstod,' Jesu im paulinischen Verständnis von Taufe und Eucharistie," *BZ* 14 (1970): 227-39.

0757 Beverly R. Gaventa, " 'You Proclaim the Lord's Death': 1 Corinthians 11:26 and Paul's Understanding of Worship," *RevExp* 80/3 (1983): 377-87.

0758 Ray C. Jones, "The Lord's Supper and the Concept of Anamnesis," *WW* 6 (1986): 434-45.

11:27-34
0759 H. U. von Balthasar, "The Holy Church and the Eucharistic Sacrifice," *CICR* 12 (1985): 139-45.

11:27-33
0760 Peter E. Fink, "The Challenge of God's Koinonia," *Worship* 59 (1985): 386-403.

11:27-29
0761 J. M. R. Tillard, "L'Eucharistie, Purification de l'Eglise Peregrinante," *NRT* 84 (1962): 449-74; 579-97.

0762 Jesús Sancho Bielsa, "El comentario de Santo Tomás a 1 Cor 11,27-29," in Antonio Piolanti, ed., *Atti del IX Congresso tomistico internazionale*, 6. Vatican City: Libreria Editrice Vaticana, 1991. Pp. 66-77.

11:27
0763 George A. F. Knight, "The Cup of Wrath," *Int* 12 (1958): 412-17.

11:28
0764 J. E. Sanchez Caro, " 'Probet autem seipsum homo' (1 Cor 11:28). Influjo de la praxis penitential Eclesiástica en la interpretacion de un texto biblico," *Salm* 32 (1985): 293-334.

11:29-30

0765 Mauro Pesce, "Manigiare e bere il proprio giudizio. Una concezione culturale comune a 1 Cor e a So[dot under]ta?" *RBib* 38/4 (1990): 495-513.

<u>12-16</u>

0766 Stephen S. Smalley, "Spiritual Gifts and 1 Corinthians 12-16," *JBL* 87/4 (1968): 417-33.

<u>12-14</u>

0767 K. Maly, *Mündige Gemeinde. Untersuchungen zur pastoralen Führung des Apostels Paulus im 1. Korintherbrief.* Stuttgart: Katholisches Bibelwerk, 1967. Pp. 186-228.

0768 Daniel Fraikin, "Charismes et Ministeres" a la Lumiere de 1 Cor 12-14," *ÉgTie* 9/3 (1978): 455-63.

0769 Mauro Pesce, "L'Apostolo di Fronte Alla Crescita Pneumatica dei Corinti," *CrNSt* 3/1 (1982): 1-39.

0770 David L. Baker, "The Interpretation of 1 Corinthians 12-14," *EQ* 46/4 (1974): 224-34.

0771 Bert Dominy, "Paul and Spiritual Gifts: Reflections on 1 Corinthians 12-14," *SouJT* 26/1 (1983): 49-68.

0772 Charles H. Talbert, "Paul's Understanding of the Holy Spirit: The Evidence of 1 Corinthians 12-14," *PRS* 11/4 (1984): 95-108.

0773 Benoît Standaert, "La rhétorique ancienne dans saint Paul," in Albert Vanhoye, ed., *L'Apôtre Paul: personnalité, style et conception du ministre.* Louvain: Peeters, 1986. Pp. 78-92.

0774 D. B. Martin, "Tongues of Angels and Other Status Indicators," *JAAR* 59/3 (1991): 547-89.

0775 U. Heckel, "Paulus und die Charismatiker. Zur theologischen Einordnung der Geistesgaben in 1 Kor 12-14," *TBe* 23/3 (1992): 117-38.

0776 J. Smit, "Argument and Genre of 1 Corinthians 12-14," in Stanley E. Porter and Thomas H. Olbricht, eds., *Rhetoric and the New Testament: Essays from the 1992 Heidelberg Conference.* Sheffield: JSOT Press, 1993. Pp. 211-30.

12-13

0777 Gail P. Corrington, "The Beloved Community: A Roycean Interpretation of Paul," *EGLMBS* 7 (1987): 27-38.

12

0778 A. Alvarez de Linera, "El glosolalo y su intérpret," *EB* 9 (1950): 193-208.

0779 J. M. Bover, "Los carismas espirituales en San Pablo," *EB* 9 (1950): 295-328.

0780 I. Hermann, "Die Auferbauung der Gemeinde nach 1 Kor 12," in *Kyrios und Pneuma. Studien zur Christologie der paulinischen Hauptbriefe.* Münich: Kösel, 1961. Pp. 69-85.

0781 Walter J. Bartling, "The Congregation of Christ: A Charismatic Body: An Exegetical Study of 1 Corinthians 12," *CTM* 40/2 (1969): 68-80.

0782 Robert L. Thomas, " 'Tongues. . . Will Cease'," *JETS* 17/2 (1974): 81-89.

0783 Terrance Callan, "Prophecy and Ecstasy in Greco-Roman Religion and in 1 Corinthians," *NovT* 27/2 (1985): 125-40.

0784 Dennis Ormseth, "Showing the Body: Reflections on 1 Corinthians 12-13 for Epiphany," *WW* 6 (1986): 97-103.

0785 Walter Kirchschläger, "Das Geistwirken in der Sicht des Neuen Testaments: dargestellt an seinen Hauptzeugen," in Walter Kirchschläger, et al., eds. *Pneumatologie und Spiritualität.* Zürich: Benziger Verlag, 1987. Pp. 15-52.

0786 Thomas A. Jackson, "Concerning Spiritual Gifts: A Study of 1 Corinthians 12," *FM* 7/1 (1989): 61-69.

0787 Albert Vanhoye, "Nécessité de la diversité dans l'unité selon 1 Co 12 et Rom 12," in J. E. Martins Terra, et al., eds., *Unité et diversité dans l'église.* Vatican City: Libreria Editrice Vaticana, 1989. Pp. 143-56.

0788 E. J. Vledder and A. G. van Aarde, "A Holistic View of the Holy Spirit as Agent of Ethical Responsibility," *HTS* 47 (1991): 503-25.

0789 Enrique Nardoni, "Charism in the Early Church since Rudolph Sohm: An Ecumenical Challenge," *TS* 53 (1992): 646-62.

0790 Ola Tjorhom, "Enhet og mangfold innenfor Kristi legeme i 1 Kor 12—og i dag," *NTT* 94/4 (1993): 247-63.

0791 Allen R. Hunt, *The Inspired Body: Paul, the Corinthians, and Divine Inspiration.* Macon GA: Mercer University Press, 1995.

12:1-31

0792 B. Hennen, "Ordines sacri. Ein Deutungsversuch zu 1 Cor 12,1-31 und Rom 12,3-8," *TQ* 119 (1938): 427-69.

12:1-13

0793 Gary W. Charles, "1 Corinthians 12:1-13," *Int* 44/1 (1990): 65-68.

12:1-11

0794 A. Sisti, "Unita nella varieta," *BibO* 7 (1965): 187-95.

0795 Norbert Baumert, "Charisma und Amt bei Paulus," in Albert Vanhoye, ed., *L'Apôtre Paul: personnalité, style et conception du ministre.* Louvain: Peeters, 1986. Pp. 203-28.

0796 A. Miranda, "L' 'uomo spirituale' nella Prima ai Corinzi," *RBib* 43 (1995): 485-519.

12:1-3

0797 K. Maly, "1 Kor 12:1-3: Eine Regel zur Unterscheidung der Geister? *BZ* 10 (1967): 57-95.

0798 Traugott Holtz, "Das Kennzeichen Des Geistes," *NTS* 18/3 (1972): 365-76.

0799 Michel Bouttier, "Complexio Oppositorum: Sur les Formules de 1 Cor. 12:13; GAL. 3:26-28; Col. 3:10-11," *NTS* 23/1 (1976): 1-19.

0800 Andre Mehat, "L'Enseignement sur 'Les Choses de L'Esprit'," *RHPR* 63/4 (1983): 395-415.

0801 J. S. Vos, "Das Rätsel von 1 Kor 12:1-3," *NovT* 35 (1993): 251-69.

12:1

    0802   David R. Nichols, "The Problem of Two-Level Christianity at Corinth," *Pneuma* 11 (1989): 99-112.

12:2

    0803   T. Paige, "1 Corinthians 12.2: A Pagan *Pompe?*" *JSNT* 44 (1991): 57-65.

12:3-13

    0804   H. Schürmann, "Unité dans l'Esprit et diversité spirituelle (1 Co 12,3b-7.12-13)," *AsSeign* N.S. 30 (1970): 35-41.

12:3

    0805   N. Brox, "Ἀνάθεμα Ἰησοῦς," *BZ* 12 (1968): 103-11.

    0806   W. F. Albright, "Two Texts in 1 Corinthians," *NTS* 16/3 (1970): 271-76.

    0807   J. D. M. Derrett, "Cursing Jesus (1 Cor. 12:3): The Jews as Religious 'Persecutors'," *NTS* 21/4 (1975): 544-54.

12:10-14

    0808   Justin S. Upkong, "Pluralism and the Problem of the Discernment of Spirits," *EcumRev* 41 (1989): 416-25.

12:10

    0809   Gerhard Dautzenberg, "Zum Religionsgeschichten Hin-Tergrund der Diakrisis (1 Kor 12:10)," *Biblische Zeitschrift* 15/1 (1971): 93-104.

    0810   Wayne Grudem, "A Response to Gerhard Dautzenberg on 1 Cor. 12:10," *BZ* 22/2 (1978): 253-70.

    0811   G. L. Lasebikan, "Glossolalia: Its Relationship with Speech Disabilities and Personality Disorders," *AfTJ* 14/2 (1985): 111-20.

12:12-13

    0812   Luther L. Grubb, "The Church Reaching Tomorrow's World," *GTJ* 12/3 (1971): 13-22.

    0813   W. Stephen Sabom, "The Gnostic World of Anorexia Nervosa," *JPT* 13 (1985): 243-54.

12:12

0814 L. Cerfaux, "Le Christ (le corps du Christ) dans 1 Cor. 12,12," in *Le Christ dans la théologie de saint Paul.* 2nd ed. Paris: Cerf, 1945. Pp. 253-55.

0815 J. Havet, " 'Christ collectif,' ou 'Christ individual,' en 1 Cor. 12,12," *ETL* 23 (1947): 499-520.

0816 Arno Schilson, "Sein in Christus: dogmatische Uberlegungen zur Grundstruktur christlicher Identität," in J. G. Ziegler, ed., *In Christus: Beiträge zum ökumenischen Gespräch.* Sankt Ottilien: EOS Verlag, 1987. Pp. 45-98.

12:13

0817 R. Schnackenburg, "Eingliederung in den Leib Christi (1 Kor 12,13)," in *Das Heilsgeschehen bei der Taufe nach dem Apostel Paulus.*München: Zink, 1950. Pp. 23-26.

0818 Joseph Hanimann, "Nous Avons ete Abreuves D'un Seul Esprit: Note Sur 1 Co 12, 13b," *NRT* 94/4 (1972): 400-405.

0819 Daniel Marguerat, "Paul: un génie théologique et ses limites," *FV* 84/5 (1985): 65-76.

0820 Warren McWilliams, "Paul's View of Freedom," *BI* 12/3 (1986): 50-53.

0821 B. Macías, "1 Cor 12.13: Una conjetura renacentista: . . .καὶ πάντες ἕν πνεῦμα ἐποτίσθημεν," *FilN* (1994): 209-13.

12:14-26

0822 R. E. Oster, "Use, Misuse and Neglect of Archaeological Evidence in Some Modern Works on 1 Corinthians)," *ZNW* 83/1-2 (1992): 52-73.

12:14

0823 Timothy N. Boyd, "Paul's Use of Analogy," *BI* 14/2 (1989): 24-28.

12:20

0824 G. L. Lasebikan, "Glossolalia: Its Relationship with Speech Disabilities and Personality Disorders," *AfTJ* 14/2 (1985): 111-20.

12:22-27

0825 L. D. Hurst, "Apollos, Hebrews, and Corinth: Bishop Montefiore's Theory Examined," *SJT* 38/4 (1985): 505-13.

12:26

0826 T. Söding, " 'Ihr aber seid der Leib Christi' (1 Kor 12,26). Exegetische Beobachtungen an einem zentralen Motiv paulinischer Ekklesiologie," *Cath* 45/2 (1991): 135-62.

12:27

0827 T. Zapelena, "Vos estis corpus Christi 1 Cor. 12,27," *VD* 37 (1959): 78-95, 162-70.

0828 Fika van Rensburg, "The Church as the Body of Christ," in Paul G. Schrotenboer, ed., *Catholicity and Secession: A Dilemma.* Kampen: Kok, 1992. Pp. 28-44.

12:28-31

0829 H. von Lips, "Der Apostolat des Paulus - en Charisma: semantische Aspekte zu charis-charisma und anderen Wortpaaren im Sprachgebrauch des Paulus," *Bib* 66/3 (1985): 305-43.

0830 Norbert Baumert, "Charisma und Amt bei Paulus," in Albert Vanhoye, ed., *L'Apôtre Paul: personnalité, style et conception du ministre.* Louvain: Peeters, 1986. Pp. 203-28.

0831 John J. Kilgallen, "Reflections on Charisma(ta) in the New Testament," *SM* 41 (1992): 289-323.

12:28

0832 Agustín del Agua Perez, "El papel de la 'escuela midrásica' en la configuración del Nuevo Testamento," *EB* 60 (1985): 333-49.

0833 M. C. Griffths, "Today's Missionary, Yesterday's Apostle," *EMQ* 21/2 (1985): 154-65.

0834 George W. Knight, "Two Offices and Two Orders of Elders: A New Testament Study," *Pres* 11/1 (1985): 1-12.

0835 Jerry R. Young, "Shepherds, Lead," *GTJ* 6/2 (1985): 329-35.

0836 James E. Carter, "Paul's View of Church Administration," *BI* 12/3 (1986): 77-79.

12:31

0837 Gerhard Iber, "Zum Verstandnis von 1 Cor. 12:31," *ZNW* 54 (1963): 43-52.

0838 Johannes Louw, "The Function of Discourse in a Sociosemiotic Theory of Translation: Illustrated by the Translation of *Zeloute* in 1 Corinthians 12:31," *BT* 39/3 (1988): 329-35.

0839 J. Smit, "Two Puzzles: 1 Corinthians 12:31 and 13:3: A Rhetorical Solution," *NTS* 39 (1993): 246-64.

0840 W. C. van Unnik, "The Meaning of 1 Corinthians 12:31," *NovT* 35 (1993): 142-59.

12:4-9

0841 H. von Lips, "Der Apostolat des Paulus - en Charisma: semantische Aspekte zu charis-charisma und anderen Wortpaaren im Sprachgebrauch des Paulus," *Bib* 66/3 (1985): 305-43.

12:4-6

0842 Fred B. Craddock, "From Exegesis To Sermon: 1 Corinthians 12:4-6," *RevExp* 80/3 (1983): 417-25.

12:4-5

0843 James E. Carter, "Paul's View of Church Administration," *BI* 12/3 (1986): 77-79.

12:4

0844 Watson E. Mills, "Charismatic Gifts in the New Testament Church," *BI* 1/2 (1975): 28-33.

0845 Luis F. Ladaria, "Presente y futuro en la escatología cristiana," *EE* 60 (1985): 351-59.

0846 John J. Kilgallen, "Reflections on Charisma(ta) in the New Testament," *SM* 41 (1992): 289-323.

12:7-11

0847 John F. Walvoord, "The Holy Spirit and Spiritual Gifts," *BSac* 143 (1986): 109-22.

12:8-11

0848 Donald Gee, "The Gifts and Fruit of the Spirit," *Para* 21 (1987): 21-26.

12:8-10

0849 Andrew G. Hadden, "Gifts of the Spirit in Assemblies of God Writings," *Para* 24 (1990): 20-32.

0850 David S. Lim, "Many Gifts, One Spirit," *Para* 26 (1992): 3-7.

12:9-10

0851 John J. Kilgallen, "Reflections on Charisma(ta) in the New Testament," *SM* 41 (1992): 289-323.

13

0852 H.-C. Desroches, "Le 'portrait,' de la charite," *VS* 74 (1946): 518-36.

0853 J. Brennan, "The Exegesis of 1 Cor. 13," *ITQ* 21 (1954): 270-78.

0854 C. Spicq, "L'Agapè de 1 Cor. 13. Un example de contribution de la sémantique à l'exégèse neo-testamentaire," *ETL* 31 (1955): 357-70.

0855 H. Schlier, "Über die Liebe. 1 Kor 13," in *Die Zeit der Kirche.* Freiburg: Herder, 1956. Pp. 186-93.

0856 John Wick Bowman, "The Three Imperishables," *Int* 13 (1959): 433-43.

0857 Eric L. Titus, "Did Paul Write 1 Cor. 13?" *JBR* 27 (1959): 299-302.

0858 Stanley D. Toussaint, "First Corinthians Thirteen and the Tongues Question," *BSac* 120 (1963): 311-16.

0859 Nils Johansson, "1 Cor. 13 and 1 Cor. 14," *NTS* 10 (1964): 383-92.

0860 Jack T. Sanders, "First Corinthians 13," *Int* 20/2 (1966): 159-87.

0861 Arthus G. Vella, " 'Agape' in 1 Corinthians 13," (part 1) *MeliT* 18/1 (1966): 22-31; 18/2 (1966): 56-66; 19/1-2 (1967): 44-54.

0862 A. Sisti, "L'inno della carità," *BibO* 10 (1968): 39-51.

0863 Terrance Callan, "Prophecy and Ecstasy in Greco-Roman Religion and in 1 Corinthians," *NovT* 27/2 (1985): 125-40.

0864 Dennis Ormseth, "Showing the Body: Reflections on 1 Corinthians 12-13 for Epiphany," *WW* 6 (1986): 97-103.

0865 Andries H. Andries, "Remarks on the Stylistic Parallelisms in 1 Cor 13," in K. J. H. Petzer and Patrick Hartin, eds., *A South African Perspective on New Testament* (festschrift for Bruce Metzger). Leiden: Brill, 1986. Pp. 202-13.

0866 Carl R. Holladay, "1 Corinthians 13: Paul as Apostolic Paradigm," in David L. Balch, et al., eds., *Greeks, Romans, and Christians* (festschrift for Abraham J. Malherbe). Minneapolis: Fortress Press, 1990. Pp. 80-98.

0867 J. Smit, "The Genre of 1 Corinthians 13 in the Light of Classical Rhetoric," *NovT* 33/3 (1991): 193-216.

0868 E. Stuart, "Love is . . . Paul," *ET* 102/9 (1991): 264-66.

0869 C. J. Waters, " 'Love is . . . Paul'—A Response," *ET* 103/3 (1991): 75.

0870 J. Lambrecht, "The Most Eminent Way: A Study of 1 Connthians 13," in *Pauline Studies: Collected Essays.* Louvain: Peeters, 1994. Pp. 79-107.

13:1

0871 Ivor H. Jones, "Musical Instruments in the Bible," *BT* 37 (1986): 101-16.

0872 William W. Klein, "Noisy Gong or Acoustic Vase? A Note 1 Corinthians 13:1," *NTS* 32/2 (1986): 286-89.

0873 Todd K. Sanders, "A New Approach to 1 Corinthians 13:1," *NTS* 36 (1990): 614-18.

13:3

0874 Ken Smith, "The Stewardship of Money," *FundJ* 4/4 (1985): 31-33.

0875 J. H. Petzer, "Contextual Evidence in Favor of Kauchesomai in 1 Corinthians 13:3," *NTS* 35/2 (1989): 229-53.

0876 J. Smit, "Two Puzzles: 1 Corinthians 12:31 and 13:3: A Rhetorical Solution," *NTS* 39 (1993): 246-64.

13:4-7

0877 J. J. McGovern, "The Gamut of Charity," *Worship* 35 (1961): 155-59.

13:7

0878 Jean Marc Laporte, "Kenosis and Koinonia: The Path Ahead for Anglican-Roman Catholic Dialogue," *OC* 21/2 (1985): 102-20.

0879 E. Wong, "1 Corinthians 13:7 and Christian Hope," *LouvS* 17/2-3 (1992): 232-42.

13:8-13

0880 Emanuel Miguens, "1 Cor 13:8-13 Reconsidered," *CBQ* 37/1 (1975): 76-97.

13:8

0881 Walter Kasper, "Die Hoffnung auf die endgültige Ankunft Jesu Christi in Herrlichkeit," *IKaZ* 14/1 (1985): 1-14.

13:10

0882 R. L. Roberts, " 'That which Is Perfect': 1 Cor. 13:10," *RQ* 3 (1959): 199-204.

0883 John R. McRay, "Tò τέλειον in 1 Corinthians 13:10," *RQ* 14 (1971): 168-83.

0884 Jean-Noël Aletti, "L'autorité apostolique de Paul: théorie et pratique," in Albert Vanho ye, ed., *L'Apôtre Paul: personnalité, style et conception du ministre*. Louvain: Peeters, 1986. Pp. 229-46.

0885 Randy Tate, "Christian Childishness and 'That Which is Perfect'," *Para* 24/1 (1990): 11-15.

0886 R. F. White, "Richard Gaffin and Wayne Grudem on 1 Cor 13:10: A Comparison of Cessationist and Noncessationist Argumentation," *JETS* 35/2 (1992): 173-81.

13:11

0887 Robert L. Thomas, "1 Cor 13:11 Revisited: An Exegetical Update," *MSJ* 4 (1993): 187-201.

13:12

0888 J. Beumer, "Tunc... cognoscam, sicut et cognitus sum (1 Cor 13,12)," *VD* 22 (1942): 166-73.

0889 J. Dupont, "Dans un miroir, en enigme (1 Co 13,12)," in *Gnosis: La connaissance religieuse dans les épîtres de saint Paul*. Louvain: Nauwlaerts, 1949. Pp. 106-48.

0890 D. H. Gill, "Through a Glass Darkly: A Note on 1 Corinthians 13,12," *CBQ* 25 (1963): 427-29.

0891 Raoul Mortley, "The Mirror and 1 Cor. 13:12 in the Epistemology of Clement of Alexandria,"*VC* 30/2 (1976): 109-20.

0892 Ronald W. Graham, "Now . . . and Then," *LTQ* 17/4 (1982): 79-81.

0893 Richard Seaford, "1 Corinthians 13:12," *JTS* 35/1 (1984): 117-20.

0894 Gerald Downing, "Revelation, Disagreement and Obscurity," *RStud* 21 (1985): 219-30.

0895 Luis F. Ladaria, "Presente y futuro en la escatología cristiana," *EE* 60 (1985): 351-59.

0896 Norman W. Porteous, "Through a Glass Darkly," in Jacon Neusner, ed., *Approaches to Ancient Judaism*. New series, vol. 1. Atlanta: Scholars Press, 1990. Pp. 59-65.

0897 Michael Johnson, "Face to Face," *EGLMBS* 11 (1991): 222-37.

13:13

0898 M.-F. Lacan, "Les trois qui demeurent. 1 Cor 13,13," *RechSR* 46 (1958): 321-43.

0899 F. Dreyfus, "Maintenant la foi, l'espérance et la charité demeurent toutes les trois (1 Cor 13,13)," in *Studiorum Paulinorum Congressus, 1961*. 2 vols. Rome: Pontifical Biblical Institute, 1963. 1:403-12.

0900 Frans Neirynck, "De grote drie bij een Nieuve Vertalling van 1 Cor., xiii, 13," *ETL* 39 (1963): 595-615.

0901 Richard Morgan, "Faith, Hope and Love Abide," *Ch* 101/2 (1987): 128-39.

0902 Wolfgang Weiss, "Glaube—Liebe—Hoffnung: Zu der Trias bei Paulus," *ZNW* 84/3-4 (1993): 196-217.

13:23-25

0903 H. Schlier, "Die Verkündigung im Gottesdienst der Kirche: Das Mahl des Herrn, Die Liturgie, Die Predigt," in *Die Zeit der Kirche.* Freiburg: Herder, 1956. Pp. 244-64.

14

0904 Eduard Schweizer, "The Service of Worship," *Int* 13 (1959): 400-407.

0905 G. G. Blum, "Das Amt der Frau im Neuen Testament," *NovT* 7 (1964): 142-61.

0906 Nils Johansson, "1 Cor. 13 and 1 Cor. 14," *NTS* 10 (1964): 383-92.

0907 Robert L. Thomas, " 'Tongues. . . Will Cease'," *JETS* 17/2 (1974): 81-89.

0908 Watson E. Mills, "Glossolalia in Asia Minor," *BI* 8/2 (1982): 81-85.

0909 Terrance Callan, "Poropecy and Ecstasy in Greco-Roman Religion and in 1 Corinthians," *NovT* 27/2 (1985): 125-40.

0910 Pui Lan Kwok, "The Feminist Hermeneutics of Elisabeth Schüssler Fiorenza: An Asian Feminist Response," *EAJT* 3/2 (1985): 147-53.

0911 Eileen Kearney, "Scientia and Sapientia: Reading Sacred Scriptures at the Paraclete," in E. R. Elder, ed., *From Cloister to Classroom: Monastic and Scholastic Approaches to Truth.* Kalamazoo MI: Cistercian Publicatians, 1986. Pp. 111-29.

0912 Alan Padgett, "Feminism in First Corinthians: A Dialogue with Elisabeth Schüssler Fiorenza," *EQ* 58/2 (1986): 121-32.

0913 Robert A. Kelly, "Luther's Use of 1 Corinthians 14," in James E. Bradley and Richard A. Muller, eds., *Church, Word and Spirit: Historical and Theological Essays* (festschrift for Geoffrey W. Bromiley). Grand Rapids: Eerdmans, 1987. Pp. 123-34.

0914 R. K. Levang, "The Content of an Utterance in Tongues," *Para* 23/1 (1989): 14-20.

0915 Ingo Broer, "Fundamentalistische Exegese oder kritische Bibelwissenschaft? Anmerkungen zum Fundamentalismusproblem anhand des paulinischen Offenbarungsverständnisses," in Jürgen Werbick, ed., *Offenbarungsanspruch und fundamentalistische Versuchung*. Freiburg: Herder, 1991. Pp. 59-88.

0916 D. Littin, *St. Paul's Theology of Proclarnation: 1 Corinthians 14 and Greco-Roman Rhetoric*. SNTSMS #79. Cambridge: University Press, 1994.

0917 Allen R. Hunt, *The Inspired Body: Paul, the Corinthians, and Divine Inspiration*. Macon GA: Mercer University Press, 1995.

14:1-40
0918 A. C. Wire, "Theological and Biblical Perspective: Liberation for Women Calls for a Liberated World," *ChS* 76 (1986): 7-17.

14:1-12
0919 A. Miranda, "L' 'uomo spirituale' nella Prima ai Corinzi," *RBib* 43 (1995): 485-519.

14:1-9
0920 J. Cantinat, "Charismes et bien commun de L'Église," *BVC* 63 (1956): 16-25.

14:2-25
0921 Vigen Guroian, "Seeing Worship as Ethics: An Orthodox Perspective," *JRE* 13 (1985): 332-59.

14:2
0922 G. L. Lasebikan, "Glossolalia: Its Relationship with Speech Disabilities and Personality Disorders," *AfTJ* 14/2 (1985): 111-20.

14:7-8

0923 David W. Music, "Musical Instruments of the First Century," *BI* 8/2 (1982): 77-80.

14:13-27

0924 G. L. Lasebikan, "Glossolalia: Its Relationship with Speech Disabilities and Personality Disorders," *AfTJ* 14/2 (1985): 111-20.

14:20-25

0925 Wayne Grudem, "1 Corinthians 14:20-25: Prophecy and Tongues as Signs of God's Attitude," *WTJ* 41/2 (1979): 381-96.

0926 Bruce C. Johanson, "Tongues: A Sign for Unbelievers?" *NTS* 25/2 (1979): 180-203.

14:20-22

0927 D. E. Lanier, "With Stammering Lips and Another Tongue: 1 Cor 14:20-22 and Isa 28:11-12," *CTR* 5/2 (1991): 259-85.

14:20

0928 H. U. von Balthasar, "Jesus als Kind und sein Lob des Kindes," *IKaZ* 14/2 (1985): 101-108.

14:22-25

0929 Walter Rebell, "Gemeinde als Missionsfaktor im Urchristentum: 1 Kor 14:24f, als Schlüsselsituation," *TZ* 44/2 (1988): 117-34.

14:22

0930 J. Smit, "Tongues and Prophecy: Deciphering 1 Cor 14,22," *Bib* 75 (1994): 175-90.

14:23-26

0931 Marlis Gielen, "Zur Interpretation der paulinischen Formel He kat' oikon ekklesia," *ZNW* 77 (1986): 109-25.

14:26-33

0932 W. Stephen Sabom, "The Gnostic World of Anorexia Nervosa," *JPT* 13 (1985): 243-54.

0933 W. E. Richardson, "Liturgical Order and Glossolalia in 1 Corinthians 14.26c-33a," *NTS* 32 (1986): 144-53. See *AUSS* 24 (1986): 47-48.

14:27-32
> **0934** William R. Herzog, "The New Testament and the Question of Racial Injustice," *ABQ* 5 (1986): 12-32.

14:33-40
> **0935** Walter L. Liefeld, "Women, Submission and Ministry in 1 Corinthians," in Alvera Mickelsen, ed., *Women, Authority and the Bible*. Downers Grove IL: InterVarsity Press, 1986. Pp. 134-54.

14:33-38
> **0936** W. A. Maier, "An Exegetical Study of 1 Corinthians 14:33b-38," *CTQ* 55/2-3 (1991): 81-104.

14:33-36
> **0937** James B. Hurley, "Did Paul Require Veils or the Silence of Women? A Consideration of 1 Corinthians 11:2-16 and 1 Corinthians 14:33b-36," *WTJ* 35/2 (1973): 190-202.

> **0938** Stephen C. Barton, "Paul's Sense of Place: An Anthropological Approach to Community Formation in Corinth," *NTS* 32/2 (1986): 225-46.

> **0939** Robert J. Karris, "Pauline Literature," in John J. Collins and John Dominic Crossan, eds., *The Biblical Heritage in Modern Catholic Scholarship*. Wilmington: Glazier, 1986. Pp. 156-83.

> **0940** Ronald Y. K. Fung, "Ministry in the New Testament," in Don A Carson, ed., *The Church in the Bible and the World*. Exeter: Paternoster Press, 1987. Pp. 154-212.

> **0941** David W. Odell-Scott, "In Defense of an Egalitarian Interpretation of 1 Cor 14:34-36: A Reply to Murphy-O'Connor's Critique," *BTB* 17/3 (1987): 100-103.

> **0942** Charles H. Talbert, "Biblical Criticism's Role: The Pauline View of Women as a Case in Point," in Robison B. James, ed., *The Unfettered Word*. Waco TX: Word Books, 1987. Pp. 62-71.

> **0943** Robert W. Allison, "Let Women be Silent in the Churches: What Did Paul Really Say, and What Did It Mean?" *JSNT* 32 (1988): 27-60.

0944 A. Rowe, "Silence and the Christian Women of Corinth. An Examination of 1 Corinthians 14:33b-36," *CVia* 33/1-2 (1990): 41-84.

0945 Donald A. Donald, "Silent in the Churches: On the Role of Women in 1 Corinthians 14:33b-36," in John Piper and Wayne Grudem, eds., *Recovering Biblical Manhood and Womanhood.* Wheaton IL: Crossway Books, 1991. Pp. 140-53, 487-90.

0946 I. R. Reimer, "Da Memória à Novidade de Vida," *EstT* 33/3 (1993): 201-12.

14:33-35

0947 L. Boston, "A Womanist Reflection on 1 Corinthians 7:21-24 and 1 Corinthians 14:33-35," *JWR* 9-10 (1990-1991): 81-89.

0948 D. J. Nadeau, "Le problème des femmes en 1 Cor 14:33-35," *ÉTR* 69 (1994): 63-65.

14:34-36

0949 David W. Odell-Scott, "In Defense of an Egalitarian Interpretation of 1 Cor 14:34-36," *BTB* 17 (1987): 100-103.

0950 Linda M. Bridges, "Silencing the Corinthian Men, not the Women," in Anne Neil and Virginia Neely, eds., *The New Has Come.* Washington: Southern Baptist Alliance, 1989. Pp. 40-50.

14:34-35

0951 Jerome Murphy-O'Connor, "Interpolations in 1 Corinthians," *CBQ* 48 (1986): 81-94.

0952 A. Rowe, "Hermeneutics and 'Hard Passages' in the NT on the Role of Women in the Church: Issues from Recent Literature," *EpRev* 18 (1991): 82-88.

0953 J. Keir Howard, "Niether Male nor Female: An Examination of the Status of Womem in the New Testament," *EQ* 55/1 (1983): 31-42.

0954 J. H. Petzer, "Reconsidering the Silent Women of Corinth—A Note on 1 Corinthians 14:34-35," *ThEv* 26 (1993): 132-38.

14:34
    0955 B. M. F. van Iersel, "Keep Quiet about Women in the Church (with Apologies to 1 Corinthians 14.34)," *Conci* 5 (1994): 137-39.

14:35
    0956 Winsome Munro, "Women, Text and the Canon: The Strange Case of 1 Corinthians 14:35," *BTB* 18/1 (1988): 26-31.

14:36
    0957 I. Peri, "Gelangen zur Vollkommenheit: Zur Lateinischen Interpretation von Katantao in Eph 4:13," *BZ* 23/2 (1979): 269-78.

14:37-40
    0958 A. Miranda, "L' 'uomo spirituale' nella Prima ai Corinzi," *RBib* 43 (1995): 485-519.

15
    0959 William A. Lawson, "Historical and Exegetical Commentary on the Fifteenth Chapter of the First Epistle of Paul to the Corinthians," master's thesis, Midwestern Baptist Theological Seminary, Kansas City KN, 1955.

    0960 Ernest Lussier, "The Biblical Theology on Purgatory," *AmER* 142 (1960): 225-33.

    0961 S. Lyonnet, "Redemption through Death and Resurrection," *Worship* 35 (1961): 281-87.

    0962 Y.-B. Trémel, "À l'image du dernier Adam. Lecture de 1 Cor. 15," *VS* 108 (1963): 395-406.

    0963 F. Mussner, " 'Schichten' in der paulinischen Theologie dargetan an 1 Kor 15," *BZ* 9 (1965): 59-70.

    0964 C. F. Sleeper, "Pentecost and Resurrection," *JBL* 84 (1965): 389-99.

    0965 John H. Schütz, "Apostolic Authority and the Control of Tradition: 1 Cor. 15," *NTS* 15/4 (1969): 439-57.

    0966 J. Kremer, "La résurrection de Jésus, principe et modèle de notre résurrection, d'après saint Paul," *Conci* 60 (1970): 71-80.

0967 Elaine H. Pagels, " 'The Mystery of the Resurrection': A Gnostic Reading of 1 Corinthians 15," *JBL* 93/2 (1974): 276-88.

0968 Kathryn W. Trim, "Paul: Life after Death: An Analysis of 1 Corinthians 15," *Crux* 14/4 (1978): 129-50.

0969 Gerald Borchert, "The Resurrection: 1 Corinthians 15," *RevExp* 80/3 (1983): 401-15.

0970 Robert Sloan, "Resurrection in 1 Corinthians," *SouJT* 26/1 (1983): 69-91.

0971 Stephen T. Davis, "Was Jesus Raised Bodily," *CSR* 14/2 (1985): 140-52.

0972 Gary R. Habermas, "Knowing that Jesus' Resurrection Occurred," *FP* 2/3 (1985): 295-302.

0973 Werner Georg Kümmel, "Das Urchristentum II. Arbeiten zu Spelialproblemen," *TR* 50/2 (1985): 132-64.

0974 M. Pamment, "Raised a Spiritual Body. Bodily Resurrection according to Paul," *NBlack* 66 (1985): 372-88.

0975 Günter Haufe, "Individuelle Eschatologie des Neuen Testaments," *ZTK* 83/4 (1986): 436-63.

0976 Ben F. Meyer, "Did Paul's View of the Resurrection of the Dead Undergo Development?" *TS* 47 (1986): 363-87.

0977 G. W. E. Nickelsburg, "An ἐκτρώμη, Though Appointed from the Womb: Paul's Apostolic Self-Description in 1 Corinthians 15 and Galatians 1," *HTR* 79/1-3 (1986): 198-205.

0978 A. G. Pérez Gordo, "¿Es 1 Co 15 una homilia?" *Bur* 27 (1986): 9-98.

0979 Benoît Standaert, "La rhétorique ancienne dans saint Paul," in Albert Vanhoye, ed., *L'Apôtre Paul: personnalité, style et conception du ministre.* Louvain: Peeters, 1986. Pp. 78-92.

0980 Larry Kreitzer, "Adam as Analogy: Help or Hindrance?" *KingsTR* 11 (1988): 59-62.

0981   Larry Kreitzer, "Christ and Second Adam in Paul," *CVia* 32 (1989): 55-101.

0982   J. N. Vorster, "Resurrection Faith in 1 Corinthians 15," *Neo* 23/2 (1989): 287-307.

0983   Edgar M. Krentz, "Images of the Resurrection in the New Testament," *CTM* 18 (1991): 98-108.

0984   Andreas Lindemann, "Paulus und die korinthische Eschatologie. zur These von einer 'Entwicklung' im paulinischen Denken," *NTS* 37/3 (1991): 373-99.

0985   Gerhard Barth, "Zur Frage nach der in 1 Korinther 15 bekämpften Auferstehungsleugnung," *ZNW* 83/3-4 (1992): 187-201.

0986   Jeremy Moiser, "1 Corinthians 15," *IBS* 14/1 (1992): 10-30.

0987   I. Saw, "Paul's Rhetoric in 1 Corinthians 15: An Analysis," doctoral dissertation, Lutheran School of Theology, Chicago, 1993.

0988   Duane F. Watson, "Paul's Rhetorical Strategy in 1 Corinthians 15," in Stanley E. Porter and Thomas H. Olbricht, eds., *Rhetoric and the New Testament: Essays from the 1992 Heidelberg Conference*. Sheffield: JSOT Press, 1993. Pp. 231-49.

15:1-58

0989   Ernst Haag, "Seele und Unsterblichkeit in biblischer Sicht," in Wilhelm Breuning, ed., *Seele: Problembegriff christlicher Eschatologie*. Freiburg: Herder, 1986. Pp. 31-93.

15:1-20

0990   Ted Peters, "What Is the Gospel?" *PRS* 13 (1986): 21-43.

15:1-19

0991   Ronald J. Sider, "St. Paul's Understanding of the Nature and Significance of the Resurrection in 1 Corinthians 15:1-19," *NovT* 19/2 (1977): 124-41.

15:1-11

0992   J. Kremer, *Das älteste Zeugnis von der Auferstehung Christi. Eine bibeltheologische Studie zur Aussage und Bedeutung von 1 Kor 15,1-11*. Stuttgart: Katholisches Bibelwerk, 1966.

0993 K. Kertelge, "Das Apostelamt des Paulus, sein Ursprung und seine Bedeutung," *BZ* 14 (1970): 161-81.

0994 P. von der Osten-Sacken, "Die Apologie des Paulinischen Apostolats in 1 Kor 15:1-11," *ZNW* 64/3-4 (1973): 245-62.

0995 Josef Blank, "Secundum Scripturas: Ursprung und Struktur der theologischen Hermeneutik im Neuen Testament," in Hans Küng and David Tracy, eds., *Das neue Paradigma von Theologie*. Zürich: Benzinger Verlag, 1986. Pp. 35-52.

0996 J. Lambrecht, "Line of Thought in 1 Cor 15,1-11," in *Pauline Studies: Collected Essays*. Louvain: Peeters, 1994. Pp. 109-24.

15:1-10

0997 J. Cambier, "L'affirmation de la résurrection du Christ (1 Co 15,1-10)," *AsSeign* 65 (1963): 12-30.

15:1-3

0998 Knox Chamblin, "Revelation and Tradition in the Pauline Euangelion," *WTJ* 48 (1986): 1-16.

15:1

0999 Dieter Lührmann, "Confesser sa foi à l'époque apostolique," *RTP* 117 (1985): 93-110.

1000 J. Terry Young, "The Gospel of Jesus Christ," *BI* 15/1 (1988): 16-17.

15:2

1001 Willard M. Aldrich, "Perseverence," *BSac* 115 (1958): 9-19.

15:3-12

1002 William L. Craig, "The Historicity of the Empty Tomb of Jesus," *NTS* 31 (1985): 39-67.

15:3-8

1003 William Baird, "What Is the Kerygma? A Study of 1 Cor 15:3-8 and Gal 1:11-17," *JBL* 76 (1957): 181-91.

1004 P. Seidemsticker, "Das Antiochenische Glaubensbekenntnis 1 Kor 15,3-7 im Lichte seiner Traditionsgeschichte," *TGl* 57 (1967): 286-323.

1005 P. Seidemsticker, "The Resurrection Seen from Antioch," *TD* 17 (1969): 104-109.

1006 Byung-Mu Ahn, "The Body of Jesus-Event Tradition," *EAJT* 3/2 (1985): 293-309.

1007 Ronald Y. K. Fung, "Revelation and Tradition: The Origins of Paul's Gospel," *EQ* 57 (1985): 23-41.

1008 Christian Grappe, "Essai sur l'arrière-plan Pascal des récits de la dernière nuit de Jésus," *RHPR* 65/2 (1985): 105-25.

15:3-7

1009 Barnabas Lindars, "Jesus Risen: Bodily Resurrection but no Empty Tomb," *Theology* 89 (1986): 90-96.

1010 Jacob Kremer, "Vor allem habe ich euch überliefert ...: bibeltheologische Erwägungen zum unverkürzten Verkünden von Gottes Wort," in J. J. Degenhardt, ed., *Die Freude an Gott - unsere Kraft* (festschrift for Otto B. Knoch). Stuttgart: Verlag Katholisches Bibelwerk, 1991. Pp. 176-82.

15:3-5

1011 J. Schmitt, "La tradition apostolic dans 1 Cor. xv, 3b-5," in *Jesus ressuscité dans la prédication apostolique*. Paris: Galbalda, 1949. Pp. 37-61

1012 Hans Conzelmann, "On the Analysis of the Confessional Formula in 1 Corinthians 15:3-5," *Int* 20/1 (1966): 13-25.

1013 K. Lehman, *Auferweckt am dritten Tag nach der Schrift*. Freiburg: Herder, 1968.

1014 John Kloppenborg, "An Analysis of the Pre-Pauline Formula 1 Cor. 15:3b-5 in Light of Some Recent Literature," *CBQ* 40:3 (1978): 351-67.

1015 Randall C. Webber, "A Note on 1 Corinthians 15:3-5," *JETS* 26/3 (1983): 265-69.

1016 Rinaldo Fabris, "San Pietro apostolo nella prima chiesa," *SM* 35 (1986): 41-70.

1017 Beimund Bieringer, "Traditionsgeschichtlicher Ursprung und theologische Bedeutung der Hyper Aussagen im Neuen Testament," in Frans van Segbroeck, et al., eds.. *The Four Gospels 1992* (festschrift for Frans Neirynck). 2 vols. Louvain: Peeters, 1992. 1:219-48.

1018 Helmut Koester, "Jesu Leiden und Tod als Erzählung," in Rüdiger Bartelmus, et al., eds., *Konsequente Traditionsgeschichte* (festschrift for Klaus Baltzer). Fribourg: Universitätsverlag, 1993. Pp. 199-204.

15:3-4

1019 J. Dupont, "Ressuscité le troisième jour," *Bib* 40 (1959): 742-61.

1020 Kenneth O. Gangel, "According to the Scriptures," *BSac* 128 (1968): 123-28.

15:3

1021 C. de Beus, "Paulus en de traditie over de opstanding in 1 Cor. 15:3," *NTT* 22/3 (1968): 185-99.

1022 Erhardt Güttgemanns, "Christos in 1 Kor. 15.3b: Titel oder Eigenname?" *EvT* 28/10 (1968): 533-54.

1023 J. M. van Cangh, "Mort pour nos péchés selon les Écritures," *RTL* 1 (1970): 191-99.

1024 Christophe Senft, "Paul et Jésus," *FV* 84/5 (1985): 49-56.

1025 F. Pastor-Ramos, " 'Murió por nuestros pecados' (1 Cor 15,3; Gal 1,4). Observaciones sobre el origen de esta fórmula en Is 53," *EE* 61 (1986): 385-93.

1026 Franz Zeilinger, "Das 'zweite Petrusbekenntnis': zur Rezeption von I Kor 15,3ff in 1 Petr 3,18-22," in Norbert Box, et al., eds., *Anfänge der Theologie*. Graz: Styria, 1987. Pp. 81-99.

1027 A. Satake, "1 Ko 15,3 und das Verhalten von Paulus den Jerusalemern gegenüber," *AJBI* 16 (1990): 100-11.

15:4

1028 B. Prete, "Al terzo giorno," in *Studiorum Paulinorum Congressus, 1961*. 2 vols. Rome: Pontifical Biblical Institute, 1963. 1:403-31.

1029 H. K. McArthur, " 'On the Third Day'," *NTS* 18/1 (1971): 81-86.

1030 Jens Christensen, "And That He Rose on the Third Day according to the Scriptures," *SJOT* 2 (1990): 101-13.

15:5-7

1031 F. Gils, "Pierre et la foi au Christ ressuscité," *ETL* 38 (1962): 5-43.

1032 Rinaldo Fabris, "Figura e ruolo di Giacomo nell'antipaolinismo," in Romano Penna, ed., *Antipaolinismo: Reazioni a Paolo tra il I e il II secolo*. Bologna: Edizioni Dehoniane Bologna, 1989. Pp. 77-92.

1033 Susanne Heine, "Eine Person von Rang und Namen: historische Konturen der Magdalenerin," in Dietrich Koch, et al., eds., *Jesu Rede von Gott und ihre Nachgeschichte im frühen Christendum*. Gütersloh: Gütersloher Verlagshaus Mohn, 1989. Pp. 179-94 .

15:5

1034 William O. Walker, "Acts and the Pauline Corpus Reconsidered," *JSNT* 24 (1985): 3-23.

15:6

1035 E. E. Bishop, "The Risen Christ and the Five Hundred Brethren," *CBQ* 18 (1956): 341-44.

1036 Victor Hasler, "Credo und Auferstehung in Korinth," *TZ* 40/1 (1984): 12-33.

1037 H. U. von Balthasar, "Gottes Reich und die Kirche," *IKaZ* 15 (1986): 124-30.

15:8

1038 P. R. Jones, "1 Corinthians 15:8: Paul the Last Apostle," *TynB* 36 (1985): 3-34.

1039 Ulrich Luck, "Die Bekehrung des Paulus und das paulinische Evangelium: zur Frage der Evidenz in Botschaft und Theologie des Apostels," *ZNW* 76/3-4 (1985): 187-208.

1040 David Stanley, "The Apostle Paul as Saint," *SM* 35 (1986): 71-97.

1041 M. Schaefer, "'Paulus, 'Fehlgeburt' oder 'unvernünftiges Kinds'? Ein Interpretationsvorschlag zu 1 Kor 15,8," *ZNW* 85 (1994): 207-17.

1042 H. W. Hollander and G. E. van de Hout, "Calling Himself an Abortion: 1 Corinthians 15:8 within the Context of 1 Corinthians 15:8-10," *NovT* 38 (1996): 224-36.

15:10

1043 H. von Lips, "Der Apostolat des Paulus - en Charisma: semantische Aspekte zu charis-charisma und anderen Wortpaaren im Sprachgebrauch des Paulus," *Bib* 66/3 (1985): 305-43.

1044 Walter Radl, "Alle Mühe umsonst: Paulus und der Gottesknecht," in Albert Vanhoye, ed., *L'Apôtre Paul: personnalité, style et conception du ministre.* Louvain: Peeters, 1986. Pp. 144-49.

1045 Karl P. Donfried, "The Kingdom of God in Paul," in Wendell Willis, ed., *The Kingdom of God in 20th-Century Interpretation.* Peabody MA: Hendrickson, 1987. Pp. 175-90.

15:12-58

1046 Mark A. Plunkett, "Eschatology at Corinth," in *EGLMBS* 9 (1989): 195-211.

15:12-22

1047 C. Ghidelli, "Notre résurrection dans le Christ," *AsSeign* 96 (1967): 18-30.

15:12-20

1048 Theodor G. Bucher, "Nochmals zur Beweisfuhrung in 1. Korinther 15,12-20," *TZ* 36/3 (1980): 129-52.

1049 C. Zimmer, "Das argumentum resurrectionis 1 Kor 15,12-20," *LB* 65 (1991): 25-36.

15:12-19

1050 Ulrich Luck, "Die Bekehrung des Paulus und das paulinische Evangelium: zur Frage der Evidenz in Botschaft und Theologie des Apostels," *ZNW* 76/3-4 (1985): 187-208.

15:12

1051 Michael Bachmann, "Zur Gedankenfuhrung in 1. Kor. 15:12 ff.," *TZ* 34/5 (1978): 265-76.

1052   Karl A. Plank, "Resurrection Theology: The Corinthian Contro-
       versy Re-Examined," *PRS* 8/1 (1981): 41-54.

1053   Michael Bachmann, "Rezeption von 1 Kor. 15 (v. 12ff) unter
       Logischem und unter Philologischem Aspekt," *LB* 51 (1982):
       79-103.

1054   R. Trevijano Etcheverria, "Los que dicen que no hay resurrección
       (1 Cor 15,12)," *Sal* 33 (1986): 275-302.

1055   Hermann Binder, "Zum geschichtlichen Hintergrund von 1 Kor
       15,12," *TZ* 46/3 (1990): 193-201.

1056   Michael Bachmann, "Zum 'argumentum resurrectionis' von 1 Kor
       15,12ff nach Christoph Zimmer, Augustin und Paulus," *LB* 67
       (1992): 29-39.

15:14

1057   Gordon Dalbey, "Does the Resurrection Happen?" *CC* 102 (1985):
       319-20.

1058   Walter Radl, "Alle Mühe umsonst: Paulus und der Gottesknecht,"
       in Albert Vanhoye, ed., *L'Apôtre Paul: personnalité, style et
       conception du ministre*. Louvain: Peeters, 1986. Pp. 144-49.

15:17-19

1059   Vincent P. Branick, "Apocalyptic Paul?" *CBQ* 47 (1985): 664-75.

15:17

1060   Sigfred Pedersen, "Theologische Uberlegungen zur Isagogik des
       Römerbriefs," *ZNW* 76/1-2 (1985): 47-67.

1061   Walter Radl, "Alle Mühe umsonst: Paulus und der Gottesknecht,"
       in Albert Vanhoye, ed., *L'Apôtre Paul: personnalité, style et
       conception du ministre*. Louvain: Peeters, 1986. Pp. 144-49.

15:20-28

1062   L. Cerfaux, "Le scenario de la Parousie," in *Le Christ dans la
       théologie de saint Paul*. 2nd ed. Paris: Cerf, 1954. Pp. 42-47.

1063   William Dykstra, "1 Corinthians 15:20-28: An Essential Part of
       Paul's Argument against Those Who Deny the Resurrection," *CTJ*
       4/2 (1969): 195-211.

1064 Gerhard Barth, "Erwagungen zu 1. Korinther 15:20-28," *EvT* 30/10 (1970): 515-27.

1065 Wilber B. Wallis, "The Problem of an Intermediate Kingdom in 1 Corinthians 15:20-28," *JETS* 18/4 (1975): 229-42.

1066 D. A. Templeton, "Paul the Parasite. Notes on the Imagery of Corinthians 15:20-28," *HeyJ* 26 (1985): 1-4.

1067 A. J. Chvala-Smith, "The Boundaries of Christology: 1 Corinthians 15:20-28 and Its Exegetical Substructure," doctoral dissertation, Marquette University, Milwalkee WI, 1993.

1068 Walter Schmithals, "The Pre-Pauline Tradition in 1 Corinthians 15:20-28," trans. Clayton N. Jefford, *PRS* 20 (1993): 357-80.

1069 J. Lambrecht, "Paul's Christological Use of Scripture in 1 Cor 15,20-28," in *Pauline Studies: Collected Essays*. Louvain: Peeters, 1994. Pp. 125-49.

1070 C. E. Hill, "Paul's Understanding of Christ's Kingdom in 1 Corinthians 15:20-28," *NovT* 30/4 (1988): 297-320.

15:20-26
1071 E.-B. Allo, "Saint Paul et la 'double résurrection,' corporelle," *RB* 41 (1932): 188-209.

15:20-24
1072 Robert D. Culver, "A Neglected Millennial Passage from Saint Paul," *BSac* 113 (1956): 141-52.

15:20-22
1073 Stanley E. Porter, "The Pauline Concept of Original Sin in Light of Rabbinic Background," *TynB* 41 (1990): 3-30.

15:20
1074 F.-J. Steinmetz and F. Wulf, "Mit Christus auferstanden. Auslegung und Meditation von 1 Kor 15, 20; Eph 2,6 und 2 Tim 2,18," *GeistL* 42 (1969): 146-50.

1075 Timothy N. Boyd, "Paul's Use of Analogy," *BI* 14/2 (1989): 24-28.

15:21-28
> **1076** David L. Turner, "The Continuity of Scripture and Eschatology: Key Hermeneutical Issues," *GTJ* 6/2 (1985): 275-87.

15:21-22
> **1077** R. H. Allaway, "Fall or Fall-short," *ET* 97 (1986): 108-10.

15:22
> **1078** Mark W. Karlberg, "Legitimate Discontinuities between the Testaments," *JETS* 28 (1985): 9-20.

15:23-28
> **1079** Uta Heil, "Theologische Interpretation von 1 Kor 15,23-28," *ZNW* 84/1-2 (1993): 27-35.

> **1080** J. Lambrecht, "Structure and Line of Thought in 1 Cor 15,23-28," in *Pauline Studies: Collected Essays*. Louvain: Peeters, 1994. Pp. 151-59.

15:23-24
> **1081** Frank Pack, "Does 1 Corinthians 15:23-24 Teach a Premillennial Reign of Christ on Earth?" *RQ* 3 (1959): 205-13.

15:23
> **1082** Luis F. Ladaria, "Presente y futuro en la escatología cristiana," *EE* 60 (1985): 351-59.

15:24-28
> **1083** J. Prado, "La Iglesia del futuro, según San Pablo," *EB* 22 (1963): 255-302.

> **1084** W. Thüsing, "Die Übergabe der Herrschaft an den Vater," in *Per Christum in Deum: Studien zum Verhältnis von Christozentrik und Theozentrik in den paulinischen Hauptbriefen*. Münster: Aschendorff, 1965. Pp. 238-54.

> **1085** H. U. von Balthasar, "Gottes Reich und die Kirche," *IKaZ* 15 (1986): 124-30.

> **1086** John F. Jansen, "1 Corinthians 15:24-28 and the Future of Jesus Christ," *SJT* 40/4 (1987): 543-70.

15:24-25

1087 Martin Hengel, "Psalm 110 und die Erhöhung des Auferstandenen zur Rechten Gottes," in Cilliers Breytenbach and Henning Paulsen, eds., *Anfänge der Christologie* (festschrift for Ferdinand Hahn). Göttingen: Vandenhoeck & Ruprecht, 1991. Pp. 43-73.

15:24

1088 J. Leal, "Deinde finis (1 Cor. 15,24a)," *VD* 37 (1959): 225-31.

1089 Karl P. Donfried, "The Kingdom of God in Paul," in Wendell Willis, ed., *The Kingdom of God in 20th-Century Interpretation.* Peabody MA: Hendrickson, 1987. Pp. 175-90.

15:25-27

1090 Wilber B. Wallis, "The Use of Psalm 8 and 110 in 1 Corinthians 15:25-27 and in Hebrews 1 and 2," *JETS* 15/1 (1972): 25-29.

15:25

1091 Roy A. Harrisville, "Paul and the Psalms: A Formal Study," *WW* 5 (1985): 168-79.

15:26

1092 Vincent P. Branick, "Apocalyptic Paul?" *CBQ* 47 (1985): 664-75.

15:27-28

1093 G. Pelland, "Un passage difficile de Novatien sur 1 Cor 15:27-28," *Greg* 66 (1985): 25-52.

15:27

1094 Roy A. Harrisville, "Paul and the Psalms: A Formal Study," *WW* 5 (1985): 168-79.

15:28

1095 Anne-Marie La Bonnardière, "Les deux vies: Marthe et Marie (Luc 10,38-42)," in A.-M. La Bonnardière, ed., *Saint Augustin et la Bible.* Paris: Editions Beauchesne, 1986. Pp. 411-25.

15:29

1096 R. Schnackenburg, "Die (stellvertretende): Taufe 'für die Toten' in Korinth (1 Kor 15,29)," in *Das Heilsgeschehen bei der Taufe nach dem Apostel Paulus.* Münich: Zink, 1950. Pp. 90-98.

1097 B. M. Foschini, "Those Who Are Baptized for the Dead," *CBQ* 12 (1950): 260-76, 379-88; 13 (1951): 46-78, 172-98, 276-83.

1098   K. Stabb, "Kor 15,29 im Lichte der Exegese der griechischen
       Kirche," in *Studiorum Paulinorum Congressus, 1961.* 2 vols.
       Rome: Pontifical Biblical Institute, 1963. 1:443-50.

1099   J. Downey, "1 Cor 15:29 and the Liturgy of Baptism," *ED* 38
       (1985): 23-35.

1100   Ole Wierod, "Daben i 1 Kor 15:29," *DTT* 50/1 (1987): 54-58.

15:31

1101   Donald   S.   Deer,   "Whose   Pride/Rejoicing/Glory(ing)   in
       1 Corinthians 15:31?" *BT* 38/1 (1987): 126-28.

15:31-32

1102   Jerome Murphy-O'Connor, "Interpolations in 1 Corinthians," *CBQ*
       48 (1986): 81-94.

15:32-34

1103   Brendan Byrne, "Eschatologies of Resurrection and Destruction:
       The Ethical Significance of Paul's Dispute with the Corinthians,"
       DR 104/357 (1986): 280-98.

15:32

1104   Robert E. Osborne, "Paul and the Wild Beasts," *JBL* 85/2 (1966):
       225-30.

15:34

1105   Homer A. Kent, "A Fresh Look at 1 Corinthians 15:34: An Appeal
       for Evangelism or a Call to Purity?" *GTJ* 4/1 (1983): 3-14.

1106   T. de Kruijff, " 'Naar de Schriften': De eerste brief van den
       apostel Paulus aan die van Corinthe: 15,34," inD. Akerboom, et
       al., eds., *Broeder Jehoshoea* (festschrift for B. Hemelsoet).
       Kampen: Kok, 1994. Pp. 129-36.

15:35-56

1107   William L. Craig, "The Historicity of the Empty Tomb of Jesus,"
       NTS 31 (1985): 39-67.

15:35-54

1108   Ronald J. Sider, "The Pauline Conception of the Resurrection
       Body in 1 Corinthians 15:35-54," *NTS* 21/3 (1974): 428-39.

15:35-49

1109 M. Teani, *Corporcità e reassertion: L'interpretazione di 1 Corinti 15.35-49 nel Novecento.* Rome: Gregorian University Press, 1994.

15:35-44

1110 Normand Bonneau, "The Logic of Paul's Argument on the Resurrection Body in 1 Cor 15:35-44a," *SE* 45 (1993): 79-92.

15:36

1111 Gerhard Ebeling, "Des Todes Tod: Luthers Theologie der Konfrontation mit dem Tode," *ZTK* 84/2 (1987): 62-94.

15:39-49

1112 A. Miranda, "L' 'uomo spirituale' nella Prima ai Corinzi," *RBib* 43 (1995): 485-519.

15:42-51

1113 Alan F. Segal, "Paul and Ecstasy," *SBLSP* 25 (1986): 555-80.

15:42-44

1114 Vincent P. Branick, "Apocalyptic Paul?" *CBQ* 47 (1985): 664-75.

15:42

1115 Vincenz Buchheit, "Resurrectio carnis bei Prudentius," *VC* 40 (1986): 261-85.

15:44-49

1116 Egon Brandenburger, "Alter und neuer Mensch, erster und letzter Adam-Anthropos," in Walter Strolz, ed., *Vom alten zum neuen Adam.* Freiburg: Herder, 1986. Pp. 182-223.

1117 G. E. Sterling, " 'Wisdom among the Perfect': Creation Traditions in Alexanderian Judaism and Corinthian Christianity," *NovT* 37/4 (1995): 355-84.

15:44-48

1118 Jerome Murphy-O'Connor, "Interpolations in 1 Corinthians," *CBQ* 48 (1986): 81-94.

15:44

1119 Leonard Audet, "Avec quel corps les justes ressusicitent-ils? analyse de 1 Corinthiens 15:44," *SR* 1/3 (1971): 165-77.

15:45-49

1120 M. Trimaille, "Notre résurrection à l'image de Jésus, nouvel Adam," *AsSeign* N.S. 38 (1970): 51-58.

1121 Mark W. Karlberg, "Legitimate Discontinuities between the Testaments," *JETS* 28 (1985): 9-20.

1122 S. P. Botha, "1 Corinthians 15:49b: A Hortative or Future Reading," *HTS* 49 (1993): 760-74.

15:45-47

1123 Rowan A. Greer, "The Man from Heaven: Paul's Last Adam and Apollinaris' Christ," in William S. Babcock, ed., *Paul and the Legacies of Paul*. Dallas: SMU Press, 1990. Pp. 165-82.

1124 Louis Painchard, "Le sommaire anthropogonique de (NH II, 117:38-118:2) à la lumiere de 1 Co 15:45-47," *VC* 44 (1990): 382-93.

15:45

1125 John F. Walvoord, "The Present Work of Christ in Heaven," *BSac* 121 (1964): 195-208, 291-302.

1126 B. Schneider, "The Corporate Meaning and Background of 1 Cor 15,45b," *CBQ* 29 (1967): 450-67.

1127 J. J. Buckley, "An Interpretation of Logion 114 in The Gospel of Thomas," *NovT* 27 (1985): 245-72.

15:50

1128 Antonio Orbe, "Cristo, sacrificio y manjar," *Greg* 66/2 (1985): 185-239.

15:51-57

1129 Walter Harrelson, "Death and Victory in 1 Corinthians 15:51-57: The Transformation of a Prophetic Theme," in John T. Carroll, et al., eds., *Faith and History* (festschrift for Paul W. Meyer). Atlanta: Scholars Press, 1990. Pp. 149-59.

15:51-52

1130 Joël Delobel, "The Fate of the Dead according to 1 Thessalonians 4 and 1 Corinthians 15," in Raymond F. Collins, ed., *The Thessalonian Correspondence*. Louvain: Peeters, 1990. Pp. 340-47.

15:51

1131 P. Oppenheim "1 Kor. 15,51. Eine kritische Untersuchung zur Text und Auffassung bei den Vatern," *TQ* 112 (1931): 92-135.

1132 A. Vaccari, "Il testo 1 Cor. 15,51," *Bib* 13 (1932): 73-76.

1133 A. Romeo, " 'Omnes quid em resurgemus' seu 'Omnes quidem nequaquam dormiemus'," *VD* 14 (1934): 142-48, 250-55, 267-75, 313-20, 328-36, 375-78.

1134 P. Brandhuber, "Die sekundären Lesarten bei 1 Kor. 15,51. Ihre Verbreitung und Entstehung," *Bib* 18 (1937): 303-33, 418-38.

15:54

1135 A. Dirksen, "Desth Is Swallowed in Victory (1 Cor. 15: 54)," *AmER* 96 (1937): 347-56.

15:55

1136 J. C. de Moor, "O Death, Where Is Thy Sting?" in Lyle Eslinger and J. G. Taylor, eds., *Ascribe to the Lord* (festschrift for Peter C. Craigie). Sheffield: JSOT Press, 1988. Pp. 99-107.

15:56

1137 Christophe Senft, "Paul et Jésus," *FV* 84/5 (1985): 49-56.

1138 F. W. Horn, "1 Korinther 15,56—ein exegetischer Stachel," *ZNW* 82 (1991): 88-105

1139 T. Söding, " 'Die Kraft der Sünde ist das Gesetz' (1 Kor 15:56): Anmerkungen zum Hintergrund und zur Pointe einer gesetzeskritischen Sentenz des Apostels Paulus," *ZNW* 83/1-2 (1992): 74-84.

15:57

1140 W. J. McGarry, "Victory through Our Lord (1 Cor. 15:57)," *AmER* 96 (1937): 337-47.

15:58

1141 Walter Radl, "Alle Mühe umsonst: Paulus und der Gottesknecht," in Albert Vanhoye, ed., *L'Apôtre Paul: personnalité, style et conception du ministre.* Louvain: Peeters, 1986. Pp. 144-49.

16:1-4

1142 W. C. Linss, "The First World Hunger Appeal," *CThM* 12 (1985): 211-19.

16:1

1143 Bruce W. Winter, "Secular and Christian Responses to Corinthian Famines," *TynB* 40 (1989): 86-106.

16:9

1144 Richard B. Cunningham, "Wide Open Doors and Many Adversaries (1 Corinthians 16:9; Acts 19)," *RevExp* 89 (1992): 89-98.

16:12

1145 M. C. Griffths, "Today's Missionary, Yesterday's Apostle," *EMQ* 21/2 (1985): 154-65.

16:15-18

1146 A. C. Wire, "Theological and Biblical Perspective: Liberation for Women Calls for a Liberated World," *ChS* 76 (1986): 7-17.

16:15

1147 L. Hertling, "1 Kor, 16,15 und 1 Clem. 42," *Bib* 20 (1939): 276-83.

16:18

1148 Juan Mateos, "Analisis de un campo lexematico: eulogia en el Nuevo Testamento," *FilN* 1 (1988): 5-25.

16:19

1149 Marlis Gielen, "Zur Interpretation der paulinischen Formel He kat' oikon ekklesia," *ZNW* 77 (1986): 109-25.

16:22

1150 John J. O'Rourke, "Question and Answer: Maranatha," *Scr* 13 (1961): 24-32.

1151 W. F. Albright, "Two Texts in 1 Corinthians," *NTS* 16/3 (1970): 271-76.

1152 W. Dunphy, "Maranatha: Development in Early Christianity," *ITQ* 37 (1970): 294-309.

16:23

1153 H. Duesberg, "La proximaté de Dieu dans la liturgy de l'Avent," *BVC* 8 (1954-1955): 16-30.

PART TWO

Citations by Subjects

Abraham, Testament of

1154 Charles W. Fishburne, "1 Cor. 3:10-15 and the Testament of Abraham," *NTS* 17/1 (1970): 109-15.

Acts of Paul & Thecla

1155 W. E. Glenny, "1 Corinthians 7:29-31 and the Teaching of Continence in *The Acts of Paul and Thecla*," *GTJ* 11/1 (1990): 53-70.

anthropology

1156 A. R. C. Leaney, "The Doctrine of Man in 1 Corinthians," *SJT* 15 (1962): 394-99.

1157 John Chryssavgis, "Soma - Sarx: The Body and the Flesh—An Insight into Patristic Anthropology," *Coll* 18/1 (1985): 61-66.

1158 Egon Brandenburger, "Alter und neuer Mensch, erster und letzter Adam-Anthropos," in Walter Strolz, ed., *Vom alten zum neuen Adam*. Freiburg: Herder, 1986. Pp. 182-223.

1159 G. L. Müller, "Fegfeuer: zur Hermeneutik eines umstrittenen Lehrstücks in der Eschatologie," *TQ* 166 (1986): 25-39.

Aphrodite

1160 H. D. Saffrey, "Aphrodite à Corinthe. Réflexions sur une idee recue," *RB* 92 (1985): 359-74.

apologetics

1161 Charles M. Horne, "Toward a Biblical Apologetic," *GTJ* 2 (1961): 14-18.

assurance

1162 Glenn W. Reeves, "The Doctrine of Christian Assurance in the Corinthian Correspondence of Paul," master's thesis, Southern Baptist Theological Seminary, Louisville KY, 1957.

atonement

1163 Christophe Senft, "Paul et Jésus," *FV* 84/5 (1985): 49-56.

authority

1164 Robert A. Kelly, "Luther's Use of 1 Corinthians 14," in James E. Bradley and Richard A. Muller, eds., *Church, Word and Spirit: Historical and Theological Essays* (festschrift for Geoffrey W. Bromiley). Grand Rapids: Eerdmans, 1987. Pp. 123-34.

1165   Inge Mager, "Die theologische Lehrfreiheit in Göttingen und ihre Grenzen: Der Abendmahlskonflikt um Christoph August Heumann," in Bernd Moeller, ed., *Theologie in Göttingen: eine Vorlesungsreihe*. Göttingen: Vandenhoeck & Ruprecht, 1987. Pp. 41-57.

1166   Wendy Cotter, "Women's Authority Roles in Paul's Churches: Countercultural or Conventional?" *NovT* 36 (1994): 350-72.

baptism

1167   Steward C. Petrie, "Observations on Baptism," *Reformed Theological Review* 24 (1965): 33-40.

1168   G. R. Beasley-Murray, "The Holy Spirit, Baptism, and the Body of Christ," *RevExp* 63/2 (1966): 177-85.

1169   G. de Ru, "De Doop Van Israël tussen Egypte en de Sinaï," *NTT* 21/5 (1967): 348-69.

1170   A. T. Hanson, "Was There a Complimentary Rite of Initiation in the First Two Centuries?" *Theology* 75/622 (1972): 190-97.

1171   Ronald E. Cottle, "All Were Baptized," *JETS* 17/2 (1974): 75-80.

1172   D. W. B. Robinson, "Towards a Definition of Baptism," *RTR* 34/1 (1975): 1-15.

1173   J. Downey, "1 Cor 15:29 and the Liturgy of Baptism," *ED* 38 (1985): 23-35.

1174   Vigen Guroian, "Seeing Worship as Ethics: An Orthodox Perspective," *JRE* 13 (1985): 332-59.

1175   Max A. Chevallier, "L'unité plurielle de l'église d'après le Nouveau Testament," *RHPR* 66 (1986): 3-20.

1176   John C. O'Neill, "1 Corinthians 7,14 and Infant Baptism," in Albert Vanhoye, ed., *L'Apôtre Paul: personnalité, style et conception du ministre*. Louvain: Peeters, 1986. Pp. 357-61.

1177   N. R. Petersen, "Pauline Baptism and 'Secondary Burial'," *HTR* 79 (1986): 217-26.

1178 David Wright, "The Origins of Infant Baptism—Child Believers' Baptism," *SJT* 40/1 (1987): 1-23.

1179 William B. Badke, "Baptised into Moses-Baptised into Christ: A Study in Doctrinal Development," *EQ* 60/1 (1988): 23-29.

1180 David Petts, "Baptism of the Spirit in Pauline Thought: A Pentecostal Perspective," *EPTA* 7/3 (1988): 88-95.

1181 Robert W. Jenson, "The Mandate and Promise of Baptism," *Int* 30/3 (1976): 271-87.

body

1182 B. M. Ahern, "The Christian's Union with the Body of Christ in Cor, Gal, and Rom," *CBQ* 23 (1961): 199-209.

1183 John Chryssavgis, "Soma - Sarx: The Body and the Flesh—An Insight into Patristic Anthropology," *Coll* 18/1 (1985): 61-66.

1184 Vincenz Buchheit, "Resurrectio carnis bei Prudentius," *VC* 40 (1986): 261-85.

1185 R. Trevijano Etcheverria, "Los que dicen que no hay resurrección (1 Cor 15,12)," *Salm* 33 (1986): 275-302.

1186 James Benedict, "The Corinthian Problem of 1 Corinthians 5:1-8," *BLT* 32 (1987): 70-73.

1187 N. George Joy, "Is the Body Really to be Destroyed?" *BT* 39/4 (1988): 429-36.

1188 Gerhard Dautzenburg, "Pheugete ten porneian (1 Kor 6,18): eine Fallstudie zur paulinischen Sexualethik in ihrem Verhältnis zur Sexualethik des Frühjudentums," in Helmut Merklein, ed., *Neues Testament und Ethik* (festschrift for Rudolf Schnackenburg). Freiburg: Herder, 1989. Pp. 271-98.

1189 R. Trevijano Etchevrria, "A propósito del incestuoso (1 Cor 5-6)," *Salm* 38/2 (1991): 129-53.

1190 Barth Campbell, "Flesh and Spirit in 1 Cor 5:5: An Exercise in Rhetorical Criticism of the New Testament," *JETS* 36 (1993): 331-42.

celibacy
1191   Piet Farla, "The Two Shall Become One Flesh: Gen 1.27 and 2.24
       in the New Testament Marriage Texts," trans. Richard Rosser in
       Sipke Draisma, ed., *Intertextuality in Biblical Writings* (festschrift
       for Bas van Iersel). Kampen: Kok, 1989. Pp. 67-82.

1192   Gregory W. Dawes, "But If You Can Gain Your Freedom
       (1 Corinthians 7:17-24)," *CBQ* 52 (1990): 681-97.

1193   Vincent L. Wimbush, "The Ascetic Impulse in Early Christianity:
       Methodological Challenges and Opportunities," in Elizabeth A.
       Livingstone, ed., *Studia Patristica, 25: Biblica et Arocrypha.*
       Louvain: Peeters, 1993. Pp. 462-78.

charisma
1194   Norbert Baumert, "Charisma und Amt bei Paulus," in Albert
       Vanhoye, ed., *L'Apôtre Paul: personnalité, style et conception du
       ministre.* Louvain: Peeters, 1986. Pp. 203-28.

1195   Gary W. Charles, "1 Corinthians 12:1-13," *Int* 44/1 (1990): 65-68.

1196   Enrique Nardoni, "Charism in the Early Church since Rudolph
       Sohm: An Ecumenical Challenge," *TS* 53 (1992): 646-62.

chiasmus
1197   Craig Blumberg, "The Structure of 2 Corinthians 1-7," *CTR* 4
       (1989): 3-20.

christology
1198   Schubert M. Ogden, "The Lordship of Jesus Christ," *Enc* 21
       (1960): 408-22.

1199   Francis Martin, "Pauline Trinitarian Formulas and Christian
       Unity," *CBQ* 30/2 (1968): 199-219.

1200   Philip Van Linden, "Paul's Christology in First Corinthians,"
       BibTo 18/6 (1980): 379-86.

1201   Christophe Senft, "Paul et Jésus," *FV* 84/5 (1985): 49-56.

1202   Egon Brandenburger, "Alter und neuer Mensch, erster und letzter
       Adam-Anthropos," in Walter Strolz, ed., *Vom alten zum neuen
       Adam.* Freiburg: Herder, 1986. Pp. 182-223.

1203 Ted Peters, "What Is the Gospel?" *PRS* 13 (1986): 21-43.

1204 Wolfgang Schrage, "Den Juden ein Skandalon: Der Anstoss des Kreuzes nach 1 Kor 1,23," in Edna Brocke and Jürgen Seim, eds., *Gottes Augapfel: Beiträge zur Erbeuerung des Verhältnisses von Christen und Juden*. Neukirchener-Vluyn: Neukirchener Verlag, 1986. Pp. 59-76.

1205 John F. Jansen, "1 Corinthians 15:24-28 and the Future of Jesus Christ," *SJT* 40/4 (1987): 543-70.

1206 Franz Zeilinger, "Das 'zweite Petrusbekenntnis': zur Rezeption von I Kor 15,3ff in 1 Petr 3,18-22," in Norbert Box, et al., eds., *Anfänge der Theologie*. Graz: Styria, 1987. Pp. 81-99.

1207 Jens Christensen, "Opstanden pa den tredje dag efter skrifterne," *DTT* 51/2 (1988): 91-103.

1208 J. Reiling, "Wisdom and the Spirit: An Exegesis of 1 Corinthians 2,6-16," in Tjitze Baarda, ed., *Text and Testimony: Essays on New Testament and Apocryphal Literature* (festschrift for A. F. J. Klijn). Kampen: Kok, 1988. Pp. 200-11.

1209 P. B. Boshoff, "Die reëls en tussen die reëls van die Korintiërbriewe: Walter Schmithals '*Die Gnosis in Korinth*'," *HTS* 45/2 (1989): 302-27.

1210 Victor P. Furnish, "Theology in 1 Corinthians: Initial Soundings," *SBLSP* 28 (1989): 246-64.

1211 Larry Kreitzer, "Christ and Second Adam in Paul," *CVia* 32 (1989): 55-101.

1212 Otto Merk, "Nachahmung Christi: zu ethischen Perspektiven in der paulinischen Theologie," in Helmut Merklein, ed., *Neues Testament und Ethik* (festschrift for Rudolf Schnackenburg). Freiburg: Herder, 1989. Pp. 172-206.

1213 W. L. Willis, "The 'Mind of Christ' in 1 Corinthians 2:16," *Bib* 70/1 (1989): 110-22.

1214 Andrew Chester, "Jewish Messianic Expectations and Mediatorial Figures and Pauline Christology," in Martin Hengel and Ulrich

Heckel, eds., *Paulus und das antike Judentum*. Tübingen: Mohr, 1991. Pp. 17-89.

1215   T. Engberg-Pedersen "Proclaiming the Lord's Death: 1 Corinthians 11:7-34 and the Forms of Paul's Theological Argument," *SBLSP* (1991): 592-617.

1216   Martin Hengel, "Psalm 110 und die Erhöhung des Auferstandenen zur Rechten Gottes," in Cilliers Breytenbach and Henning Paulsen, eds., *Anfänge der Christologie* (festschrift for Ferdinand Hahn). Göttingen: Vandenhoeck & Ruprecht, 1991. Pp. 43-73.

1217   Traugott Holtz, "Paul and the Oral Gospel Tradition," in Henry Wansbrough, ed., *Jesus and the Oral Gospel Tradition*. Sheffield: JSOT Press, 1991. Pp. 380-93.

1218   T. Siding, "Das Geheimnis Gottes im Kreuz Jesu (1 Kor): Die paulinische Christologie im Spannungsfeld von Mythos und Kerygma," *BZ* 38 (1994): 174-94.

church and state

1219   I. L. Grohar, "El 'mundo' en los escritos juanicos: un ensayo de interpretación," *RevB* 47 (1985): 221-27.

1220   Daniel Marguerat, "Paul: un génie théologique et ses limites," *FV* 84/5 (1985): 65-76.

1221   Jean Delumeau, "La difficile émergence de la tolérance," in Roger Zuber and Laurent Theis, eds., *La Révocation de l'Edit de Nantes et le protestantisme français en 1685*. Paris: Société de l'Historie du Protestantisme Français, 1986. Pp. 359-74.

1222   Gunter Klein, "Der Friede Gottes und der Friede der Welt," *ZTK* 83/3 (1986): 325-55.

1223   Mauro Pesce, "Marginalità e sottomissione: la concezione escatologica del potere politico in Paolo," in Paolo Prodi and Luigi Sartori, eds., *Cristianesimo e potere*. Bologna: Centro Editoriale Dehoniano, 1986. Pp. 43-82.

1224   H. U. von Balthasar, "Gottes Reich und die Kirche," *IKaZ* 15 (1986): 124-30.

1225   Henry I. Lederle, "Better the Devil You Know: Seeking a Biblical Basis for the Societal Dimension of Evil and/or the Demonic in the Pauline Concept of the 'Powers'," in Pieter G. R. Villiers, ed., *Like a Roaring Lion: Essays on the Bible, the Church and Demonic Powers*. Pretoria: University of South Africa, 1987. Pp. 102-20.

1226   B. W. Winter, "Civil Litigation in Secular Corinth and the Church. The Forensic Background to 1 Corinthians 6.1-8," *NTS* 37/4 (1991): 559-72.

circumcision
1227   Gregory W. Dawes, "But If You Can Gain Your Freedom (1 Corinthians 7:17-24)," *CBQ* 52 (1990): 681-97.

community
1228   Earl L. Riley, "'Koinonia' in the Corinthian Church," doctoral dissertation, Midwestern Baptist Theological Seminary, Kansas City KN, 1953.

1229   H.-J. Klauck, "Gemeindestrukturen im ersten Korintherbrief," *BK* 40 (1985): 915.

1230   Harm W. Hollander, "The Testing by Fire of the Builders' Works: 1 Corinthians 3:10-15," *NTS* 40 (1994): 89-104.

conscience
1231   Eugene J. Cooper, "Man's Basic Freedom and Freedom of Conscience in the Bible: Reflections on 1 Corinthians 8-10," *ITQ* 42/4 (1975): 272-83.

1232   Jean Delumeau, "La difficile émergence de la tolérance," in Roger Zuber and Laurent Theis, eds., *La Révocation de l'Edit de Nantes et le protestantisme français en1685*. Paris: Société de l'Historie du Protestantisme Français, 1986. Pp. 359-74.

1233   Paul W. Gooch, "Conscience in 1 Corinthians 8 and 10," *NTS* 33/2 (1987): 244-54.

1234   Peter D. Gooch, *Dangerous Food: 1 Corinthians 8-10 in Its Context*. Studies in Christianity and Judaism #5. New York: Edwin Mellen Press, 1993.

Corinth, city of
1235 W. Rees, "Corinth in St. Paul's Time," *Scr* 2 (1947): 71-76, 105-11.

covenants
1236 Martin Karrer, "Der Kelch des neuen Bundes: Erwägungen zum Verständnis des Herrenmahls nach 1 Kor 11:23b-25," *BZ* 34/2 (1990): 198-221.

crucifixion
1237 Gregory M. Corigan, "Paul's Shame for the Gospel," *BTB* 16/1 (1986): 23-27.

death
1238 Chalmer E. Faw, "Death and Resurrection in Paul's Letters," *JBR* 27 (1959): 291-98.

1239 Gerhard Ebeling, "Des Todes Tod: Luthers Theologie der Konfrontation mit dem Tode," *ZTK* 84/2 (1987): 62-94.

1240 Walter Harrelson, "Death and Victory in 1 Corinthians 15:51-57: The Transformation of a Prophetic Theme," in John T. Carroll, et al., eds., *Faith and History* (festschrift for Paul W. Meyer). Atlanta: Scholars Press, 1990. Pp. 149-59.

demonology
1241 Richard H. Hiers, "Binding and 'Loosing': The Matthean Authorizations," *JBL* 104 (1985): 233-50.

devil
1242 James T. South, "A Critique of the 'Curse/Death' Interpretation of 1 Corinthians 5:1-8," *NTS* 39 (1993): 539-61.

discipline
1243 David G. Hause, "The Doctrine of Church Discipline According to Paul," master's thesis, Midwestern Baptist Theological Seminary, Kansas City KN, 1946.

1244 N. George Joy, "Is the Body Really to be Destroyed?" *BT* 39/4 (1988): 429-36.

1245 Colin G. Kruse, "The Offender and the Offence in 2 Corinthians 2:5 and 7:12," *EQ* 60 (1988): 129-39.

1246 Elsie Anne McKee, "Calvin, Discipline and Exegesis: The Interpretation of Mt 18,17 and 1 Cor 5,1ff in the Sixteenth Century," in Irena Backus and Francis Higman, eds., *Théorie et pratique de l'exégèse*. Geneva: Librarie Droz, 1990. Pp. 319-27.

1247 G. Harris, "The Beginnings of Church Discipline: 1 Corinthians 5," *NTS* 37/1 (1991): 1-21.

1248 J. W. MacGorman, "The Discipline of the Church," in Paul Basden and David Dockery, eds., *The People of God*. Nashville: Broadman Press, 1991. Pp. 74-84.

1249 Brian S. Rosner, "Temple and Holiness in 1 Corinthians 5," *TynB* 42/1 (1991): 137-45.

1250 Simon J. Kistemaker, " 'Deliver This Man to Satan': A Case Study in Church Discipline," *McMJT* 3 (1992): 33-46.

discourse analysis

1251 Olivette Genest, "L'interprétation de la mort de Jésus en situation discursive: un cas-type: l'articulation des figures de cette mort in 1-2 Corinthiens," *NTS* 34/4 (1988): 506-35.

1252 Kathleen Callow, "Patterns of Thematic Development in 1 Corinthians 5:1-13," in David A. Black, et al., eds., *Linguistics and New Testament Interpretation: Essays on Discourse Analysis*. Nashville: Broadman Press, 1992. Pp. 194-206.

divorce/marriage

1253 John J. Bandy, "Paul's Teaching Concerning Marriage in 1 Corinthians 7:1-16," master's thesis, Southern Baptist Theological Seminary, Louisville KY, 1952.

1254 Robert C. Campbell, "Teachings of Paul Concerning Divorce," *Found* 6 (1963): 362-66.

1255 Walter J. Bartling, "Sexuality, Marriage, and Divorce in 1 Corinthians 6:12-7:16," *CTM* 39/6 (1968): 355-66.

1256 H. G. Coiner, "Those 'Divorce and Remarriage' Passages," *CTM* 39/6 (1968): 367-84.

1257 M. L. Barré, "To Marry or to Burn: Purousthai in 1 Cor. 7:9,"
      CBQ 36/2 (1974): 193-202.

1258 David R. Catchpole, "The Synoptic Divorce Material as a
      Traditio-Historical Problem," *BJRL* 57/1 (1974): 92-127.

1259 James A. Fischer, "1 Cor. 7:8-24. Marriage and Divorce," *BR* 23
      (1978): 26-35.

1260 J. Cambier, "Doctrine Paulinienne du Mariage Chrétien. Etude
      Critique de 1 Co 7 et d'Ep 5, 21-33 et Essai de Leur Traduction
      Actuelle," *EgT* 10/1 (1979): 13-59.

1261 Charles C. Ryrie, "Biblical Teaching on Divorce and Remarriage,"
      GTJ 3/2 (1982): 177-92.

1262 B. N. Wambacq, "Matthieu 5, 31-32. Possibilite De Divorce ou
      Obligation De Rompre Une Union Illigitime," *NRT* 104/1 (1982):
      34-49.

1263 Lisa Sowle Cahill, "Sex, Marriage, and Community in Christian
      Ethics," *Thought* 58/228 (1983): 72-81.

1264 David E. Garland, "The Christian's Posture Toward Marriage and
      Celibacy: 1 Corinthians 7," *RevExp* 80/3 (1983): 351-62.

1265 G. Greenfield, "Paul and Eschatological Marriage," *SouJT* 26/1
      (1983): 32-48.

1266 John R. W. Stott, "Homosexual Marriage: Why Same Sex
      Partnerships Are Not a Christian Option," *CT* 29/17 (1985): 21-28.

1267 Edward Dobson, "Divorce and the Teaching of Paul; pt 7," *FundJ*
      5 (1986): 26-27.

1268 William A. Heth, "Matthew's 'Eunuch Saying' (19:12) and Its
      Relationship to Paul's Teaching on Singleness in 1 Corinthians 7,"
      doctoral dissertation, Dallas Theological Seminary, Dallas TX,
      1986.

1269 Frans Neirynck, "Paul and the Sayings of Jesus," in Albert
      Vanhoye, ed., *L'Apôtre Paul: personnalité, style et conception du
      ministre*. Louvain: Peeters, 1986. Pp. 265-321.

1270 John C. O'Neill, "1 Corinthians 7,14 and Infant Baptism," in Albert Vanhoye, ed., *L'Apôtre Paul: personnalité, style et conception du ministre*. Louvain: Peeters, 1986. Pp. 357-61.

1271 Wolfgang Trilling, "Zum Thema: Ehe und Ehescheidung im Neuen Testament," in Joachim Rogge and Gottfried Schille, eds., *Theologische Versuche, 16*. Berlin: Evangelische Verlagsanstalt, 1986. Pp. 73-84.

1272 William A. Heth, "Unmarried 'for the Sake of the Kingdom' in the Early Church," *GTJ* 8 (1987): 55-88.

1273 Gerhard Dautzenburg, "Pheugete ten porneian (1 Kor 6,18): eine Fallstudie zur paulinischen Sexualethik in ihrem Verhältnis zur Sexualethik des Frühjudentums," in Helmut Merklein, ed., *Neues Testament und Ethik* (festschrift for Rudolf Schnackenburg). Freiburg: Herder, 1989. Pp. 271-98.

1274 Piet Farla, "The Two Shall Become One Flesh: Gen 1.27 and 2.24 in the New Testament Marriage Texts," trans. Richard Rosser in Sipke Draisma, ed., *Intertextuality in Biblical Writings* (festschrift for Bas van Iersel). Kampen: Kok, 1989. Pp. 67-82.

1275 Gregory W. Dawes, "But If You Can Gain Your Freedom (1 Corinthians 7:17-24)," *CBQ* 52 (1990): 681-97.

1276 Bruce N. Kaye, "One Flesh and Marriage," *CANZTR* 22 (1990): 46-57.

1277 Vincent L. Wimbush, "The Ascetic Impulse in Early Christianity: Methodological Challenges and Opportunities," in Elizabeth A. Livingstone, ed., *Studia Patristica, 25: Biblica et Arocrypha*. Louvain: Peeters, 1993. Pp. 462-78.

early church

1278 Leonard Audet, "L'organisation des Communautes Chrétiennes selon les gran des epîtres pauliniennes," *SR* 2/3 (1972): 235-50.

1279 Leonidas Kalugila, "Women in the Ministry of Priesthood in the Early Church: An Inquiry," *AfTJ* 14/1 (1985): 35-45.

1280 E. Mazza, "L'Eucaristia di 1 Corinti 10:16-17 in rapporto a Didache 9-10," *EphL* 100 (1986): 193-223.

1281 Ted Peters, "What Is the Gospel?" *PRS* 13 (1986): 21-43.

1282 J. Louis Martyn, "Paul and His Jewish-Christian Interpreters," *USQR* 42/1-2 (1988): 1-15.

1283 Rinaldo Fabris, "Figura e ruolo di Giacomo nell'antipaolinismo," in Romano Penna, ed., *Antipaolinismo: Reazioni a Paolo tra il I e il II secolo*. Bologna: Edizioni Dehoniane Bologna, 1989. Pp. 77-92.

1284 T. J. van Bavel, "Women as the Image of God in Augustine's De trinitate XII," in *Signum pietatis* (festschrift for Cornelius P. Mayer). Würzburg: Augustinus- Verlag, 1989. Pp. 267-88.

1285 Margaret Y. MacDonald, "Women Holy in Body and Spirit: The Social Setting of 1 Corinthians 7," *NTS* 36/2 (1990): 161-81.

1286 Donald A. Donald, "Silent in the Churches: On the Role of Women in 1 Corinthians 14:33b-36," in John Piper and Wayne Grudem, eds., *Recovering Biblical Manhood and Womanhood*. Wheaton IL: Crossway Books, 1991. Pp. 140-53, 487-90.

1287 Lone Fatum, "Image of God and Glory of Man: Women in the Pauline Congregations," in Karl E. Borresen, ed., *Image of God and Gender Models*. Oslo: Solum Forlag, 1991. Pp. 56-137.

ecclesiology
1288 Robert L. Lee, "The Basic Church Problem Reflected in the Corinthian Letters," doctoral dissertation, New Orleans Baptist Theological Seminary, New Orleans LA, 1951.

1289 John F. Walvoord, "Premillennialism and the Church as Mystery," *BSac* 111 (1954): 97-104.

1290 Joseph Clifford Fenton, "The New Testament Designation of the True Church As God's Temple," *AmER* 140 (1959): 103-17.

1291 Everett Ferguson, "The Church at Corinth Outside the New Testament," *RQ* 3 (1959): 169-72.

1292 John F. Walvoord, "The Church in Heaven," *BSac* 123 (1966) 99-103.

1293 M. M. Bourke, "Reflections on Church Order in the New Testament," *CBQ* 30/4 (1968): 493-511.

1294 Luther L. Grubb, "The Church Reaching Tomorrow's World," *GTJ* 12/3 (1971): 13-22.

1295 A. J. M. Wedderburn, "The Body of Christ and Related Concepts in 1 Corinthians," *SJT* 24/1 (1971): 74-96.

1296 M. C. Griffths, "Today's Missionary, Yesterday's Apostle," *EMQ* 21/2 (1985): 154-65.

1297 Paul D. Hanson, "The Identity and Purpose of the Church," *TT* 42 (1985): 342-52.

1298 George W. Knight, "Two Offices and Two Orders of Elders: A New Testament Study," *Pres* 11/1 (1985): 1-12.

1299 David W. Miller, "The Uniqueness of New Testament Church Eldership," *GTJ* 6/2 (1985): 315-27.

1300 A. P. Spilly, "The Church in Corinth," *CS* 24/3 (1985): 307-22.

1301 Jean-Noël Aletti, "L'autorité apostolique de Paul: théorie et pratique," in Albert Vanhoye, ed., *L'Apôtre Paul: personnalité, style et conception du ministre.*Louvain: Peeters, 1986. Pp. 229-46.

1302 Norbert Baumert, "Charisma und Amt bei Paulus," in Albert Vanhoye, ed., *L'Apôtre Paul: personnalité, style et conception du ministre.* Louvain: Peeters, 1986. Pp. 203-28.

1303 J. C. Breytenbach, "The Corinthian Church In the First Century, A.D.—A Living Church?" *Missionalia* 14/1 (1986): 3-13.

1304 James E. Carter, "Paul's View of Church Administration," *BI* 12/3 (1986): 77-79.

1305 Max A. Chevallier, "L'unité plurielle de l'église d'après le Nouveau Testament," *RHPR* 66 (1986): 3-20.

1306 Marlis Gielen, "Zur Interpretation der paulinischen Formel He kat' oikon ekklesia," *ZNW* 77 (1986): 109-25.

1307 H. U. von Balthasar, "Gottes Reich und die Kirche," *IKaZ* 15 (1986): 124-30.

1308 Gail P. Corrington, "The Beloved Community: A Roycean Interpretation of Paul," *EGLMBS* 7 (1987): 27-38.

1309 Robert A. Kelly, "Luther's Use of 1 Corinthians 14," in James E. Bradley and Richard A. Muller, eds., *Church, Word and Spirit: Historical and Theological Essays* (festschrift for Geoffrey W. Bromiley). Grand Rapids: Eerdmans, 1987. Pp. 123-34.

1310 Peter T. O'Brien, "The Church as a Heavenly and Eschatological Entity," in Don A Carson, ed., *The Church in the Bible and the World.* Exeter: Paternoster Press, 1987. Pp. 88-119.

1311 F. J. Moritz, "Church as Body," *CBTJ* 4/1 (1988): 1-24.

1312 Jay Shanor, "Paul as Master Builder: Construction Terms in First Corinthians," *NTS* 34/3 (1988): 461-71.

1313 Albert Vanhoye, "Nécessité de la diversité dans l'unité selon 1 Co 12 et Rom 12," in J. E. Martins Terra, et al., eds., *Unité et diversité dans l'église.* Vatican City: Libreria Editrice Vaticana, 1989. Pp. 143-56.

1314 Elsie Anne McKee, "Calvin, Discipline and Exegesis: The Interpretation of Mt 18,17 and 1 Cor 5,1ff in the Sixteenth Century," in Irena Backus and Francis Higman, eds., *Théorie et pratique de l'exégèse.* Geneva: Librarue Droz, 1990. Pp. 319-27.

1315 Douglas R. de Lacey, "ohitines este Hymeis: The Function of a Metaphor in St. Paul," in William Horbury, ed., *Templum Amicitiae: Essays on the Second Temple* (festschrift for Ernst Bammel). Sheffield: JSOT Press, 1991. Pp. 391-409

1316 J. D. M. Derrett, "Judgement and 1 Corinthians 6," *NTS* 37/1 (1991): 22-36.

1317 G. Harris, "The Beginnings of Church Discipline: 1 Corinthians 5," *NTS* 37/1 (1991): 1-21.

1318 J. W. MacGorman, "The Discipline of the Church," in Paul Basden and David Dockery, eds., *The People of God*. Nashville: Broadman Press, 1991. Pp. 74-84.

1319 K. Romaniuk, "... wie ein guter Baumeister ...." in J. J. Degenhardt, ed., *Die Freude an Gott - unsere Kraft* (festschrift for Otto B. Knoch). Stuttgart: Verlag Katholisches Bibelwerk, 1991. Pp. 164-69.

1320 Enrique Nardoni, "Charism in the Early Church since Rudolph Sohm: An Ecumenical Challenge," *TS* 53 (1992): 646-62.

1321 Fika van Rensburg, "The Church as the Body of Christ," in Paul G. Schrotenboer, ed., *Catholicity and Secession: A Dilemma*. Kampen: Kok, 1992. Pp. 28-44.

1322 Ola Tjorhom, "Enhet og mangfold innenfor Kristi legeme i 1 Kor 12—og i dag," *NTT* 94/4 (1993): 247-63.

ecstasy

1323 Terrance Callan, "Prophecy and Ecstasy in Greco-Roman Religion and in 1 Corinthians," *NovT* 27/2 (1985): 125-40.

1324 Alan F. Segal, "Paul and Ecstasy," *SBLSP* 25 (1986): 555-80.

eschatology

1325 Frank Pack, "Does 1 Corinthians 15:23-24 Teach a Premillennial Reign of Christ on Earth?" *RQ* 3 (1959): 205-13.

1326 K. Müller, "1 Kor 1:18-25. Die eschatologisch-kritische Funktion der Verkündigung des Kreuzes," *BZ* 10 (1966): 246-72.

1327 Otfried Hofius, "Bis Dass Kommt: 1 Kor. xi. 26," *NTS* 14/3 (1968) 439-41.

1328 John G. Gager, "Functional Diversity in Paul's Use of End-Time Language," *JBL* 89/3 (1970): 325-37.

1329 Darrell Doughty, "The Presence and Future of Salvation in Corinth," *ZNW* 66/1-2 (1975): 61-90.

1330 Wilber B. Wallis, "The Problem of an Intermediate Kingdom in 1 Corinthians 15:20-28," *JETS* 18/4 (1975): 229-42.

1331   Karl P. Donfried, "Justification and Last Judgment in Paul," *Int* 30/2 (1976): 140-52.

1332   P. von der Osten-Sacken, "Gottes treue bis zur Parusie: Formgeschichtliche Beobachtungen zu 1 Kor. 1:7b-9," *ZNW* 68/3-4 (1977): 176-99.

1333   A. C. Thiselton, "Realized Eschatology at Corinth," *NTS* 24/4 (1978): 510-26.

1334   C. L. Mearns, "Early Eschatological Development in Paul: The Evidence of 1 Corinthians," *JSNT* 22 (1984): 19-35.

1335   Vincent P. Branick, "Apocalyptic Paul?" *CBQ* 47 (1985): 664-75.

1336   Peter E. Fink, "The Challenge of God's Koinonia," *Worship* 59 (1985): 386-403.

1337   Walter Kasper, "Die Hoffnung auf die endgültige Ankunft Jesu Christi in Herrlichkeit," *IKaZ* 14/1 (1985): 1-14.

1338   Luis F. Ladaria, "Presente y futuro en la escatología cristiana," *EE* 60 (1985): 351-59.

1339   David L. Turner, "The Continuity of Scripture and Eschatology: Key Hermeneutical Issues," *GTJ* 6/2 (1985): 275-87.

1340   Brendan Byrne, "Eschatologies of Resurrection and Destruction: The Ethical Significance of Paul's Dispute with the Corinthians," *DR* 104/357 (1986): 280-98.

1341   Günter Haufe, "Individuelle Eschatologie des Neuen Testaments," *ZTK* 83/4 (1986): 436-63.

1342   Anne-Marie La Bonnardière, "Les deux vies: Marthe et Marie (Luc 10,38-42)," in A.-M. La Bonnardière, ed., *Saint Augustin et la Bible*. Paris: Editions Beauchesne, 1986. Pp. 411-25.

1343   G. L. Müller, "Fegfeuer: zur Hermeneutik eines umstrittenen Lehrstücks in der Eschatologie," *TQ* 166 (1986): 25-39.

1344   G. M. M. Pelser, "Resurrection and Eschatology in Paul's Letters," *Neo* 20 (1986): 37-46.

1345 Mauro Pesce, "Marginalità e sottomissione: la concezione escatologica del potere politico in Paolo," in Paolo Prodi and Luigi Sartori, eds., *Cristianesimo e potere*. Bologna: Centro Editoriale Dehoniano, 1986. Pp. 43-82.

1346 Karl P. Donfried, "The Kingdom of God in Paul," in Wendell Willis, ed., *The Kingdom of God in 20th-Century Interpretation*. Peabody MA: Hendrickson, 1987. Pp. 175-90.

1347 Peter T. O'Brien, "The Church as a Heavenly and Eschatological Entity," in Don A Carson, ed., *The Church in the Bible and the World*. Exeter: Paternoster Press, 1987. Pp. 88-119.

1348 P. H. Towner, "Gnosis and Realized Eschatology in Ephesus (of the Pastoral Epistles) and the Corinthian Enthusiasm," *JSNT* 31 (1987): 95-124.

1349 Judith L. Kovacs, "The Archons, the Spirit, and the Death of Christ: Do We Need the Hypothesis of Gnostic Opponents to Explain 1 Corinthians 2:6-16?" in Joel Marcus and Marion L. Soards, eds., *Apocalyptic and the New Testament* (festschrift J. Louis Martyn). Sheffield: JSOT Press, 1989. Pp. 217-36.

1350 Stephen Motyer, "The Relationship between Paul's Gospel of 'All One in Christ Jesus' and the 'Household Codes'," *VoxE* 19 (1989): 33-48.

1351 David R. Nichols, "The Problem of Two-Level Christianity at Corinth," *Pneuma* 11 (1989): 99-112.

1352 A. C. Perriman, "Paul and the Parousia: 1 Corinthians 15:50-57 and 2 Corinthians 5:1-5," *NTS* 35/4 (1989): 512-21.

1353 Mark A. Plunkett, "Eschatology at Corinth," in *EGLMBS* 9 (1989): 195-211.

1354 Martin Hengel, "Psalm 110 und die Erhöhung des Auferstandenen zur Rechten Gottes," in Cilliers Breytenbach and Henning Paulsen, eds., *Anfänge der Christologie* (festschrift for Ferdinand Hahn). Göttingen: Vandenhoeck & Ruprecht, 1991. Pp. 43-73.

1355 Roman Garrison, "Paul's Use of the Athlete Metaphor in 1 Corinthians 9," *SR* 22/2 (1993): 209-17.

1356 Harm W. Hollander, "Revelation by Fire: 1 Corinthians 3:13," *BT* 44 (1993): 242-44.

1357 Harm W. Hollander, "The Testing by Fire of the Builders' Works: 1 Corinthians 3:10-15," *NTS* 40 (1994): 89-104.

1358 C. E. Hill, "Paul's Understanding of Christ's Kingdom in 1 Corinthians 15:20-28," *NovT* 30/4 (1988): 297-320.

ethics

1359 W. M. Alwynse, "The Ethical Principles of Paul in the Corinthian Epistles," doctoral dissertation, Southern Baptist Theological Seminary, Louisville KY, 1934.

1360 Robert C. Campbell, "Teachings of Paul Concerning Divorce," *Found* 6 (1963): 362-66.

1361 H. G. Coiner, "Those 'Divorce and Remarriage' Passages," *CTM* 39/6 (1968): 367-84.

1362 Donald C. Houts, "Sensitivity, Theology, and Change: Pastoral Care in the Corinthian Letters," *PPsy*20/193 (1969): 25-29, 30-32, 34.

1363 David R. Cartlidge, "1 Corinthians 7 as a Foundation for a Christian Sex Ethic," *JR* 55/2 (1975): 220-34.

1364 Paul W. Gooch, "The Ethics of Accommodation: A Study in Paul," *TynB* 29 (1978): 93-117.

1365 J. Cambier, "Doctrine Paulinienne du Mariage Chrétien. Etude Critique de 1 Co 7 et d'Ep 5, 21-33 et Essai de Leur Traduction Actuelle," *EgT* 10/1 (1979): 13-59.

1366 Brendan Byrne, "Sinning Against One's Own Body: Paul's Understanding of the Sexual Relationship in 1 Corinthians 6:18," *CBQ* 45/4 (1983): 608-16.

1367 J.-J. Suurmond, "The Ethical Influence of the Spirit of God: An Exegetical and Theological Study with Special Reference to 1 Corinthians, Romans 7:14-8:30, and the Johannine Literature," doctoral dissertation, Fuller Theological Seminary, Pasadena CA, 1983.

1368   Paul D. Feinberg, "Homosexuality and the Bible," *FundJ* 4/3 (1985): 17-19.

1369   Vigen Guroian, "Seeing Worship as Ethics: An Orthodox Perspective," *JRE* 13 (1985): 332-59.

1370   Morna D. Hooker, "Interchange in Christ and Ethics," *JSNT* 25 (1985): 3-17.

1371   W. C. Linss, "The First World Hunger Appeal," *CThM* 12 (1985): 211-19.

1372   Randolph A. Nelson, "Homosexuality and Social Ethics," *WW* 5 (1985): 380-94.

1373   Terrance Callan, "Toward a Psychological Interpretation of Paul's Sexual Ethic," *EGLMBS* 6 (1986): 57-71.

1374   Arthur J. Dewey, "Paulos Pornographos: The Mapping of Sacred Space," *EGLMBS* 6 (1986): 104-13.

1375   Edward Dobson, "Divorce and the Teaching of Paul; pt 7," *FundJ* 5 (1986): 26-27.

1376   Richard B. Hays, "Relations Natural and Unnatural: A Response to J. Boswell's Exegesis of Rom 1," *JREth* 14 (1986): 184-215.

1377   William R. Herzog, "The New Testament and the Question of Racial Injustice," *ABQ* 5 (1986): 12-32.

1378   Andreas Lindemann, "Die biblischen Toragebote und die paulinische Ethik," in Wolfgand Schrage *Studien zum Text und zur Ethik des Neuen Testaments* (festschrift for Heinrich Greeven). Berlin: de Gruyter, 1986. Pp. 242-65.

1379   V. George Shillington, "People of God in the Courts of the World: A Study of 1 Corinthians 6:1-11," *Dir* 15 (1986): 40-50.

1380   Roy B. Ward, "Porneia and Paul," *EGLMBS* 6 (1986): 219-28.

1381   Horst Balz, "Biblische Aussagen zur Homosexualität," *ZEE* 31/1 (1987): 60-72.

1382   Jürgen Becker, "Zum Problem der Homosexualität in der Bibel,"
         ZEE 31/1 (1987): 36-59.

1383   Henry I. Lederle, "Better the Devil You Know: Seeking a Biblical
         Basis for the Societal Dimension of Evil and/or the Demonic in the
         Pauline Concept of the 'Powers'," in Pieter G. R. Villiers, ed.,
         *Like a Roaring Lion: Essays on the Bible, the Church and Demonic
         Powers.* Pretoria: University of South Africa, 1987. Pp. 102-20.

1384   James A. Davis, "The Interaction Between Individual Ethical
         Conscience   and   Community   Ethical   Consciousness   in
         1 Corinthians," *Horizons in Biblical Theology* 10/2 (1988): 1-18.

1385   Jonathan J. Bonk, "Doing Mission out of Affluence: Reflections on
         Recruiting 'End of the Procession' Missionaries from 'Front of the
         Procession' Churches," *Miss* 17/4 (1989): 427-52.

1386   Gerhard Dautzenburg, "Pheugete ten porneian (1 Kor 6,18): eine
         Fallstudie zur paulinischen Sexualethik in ihrem Verhältnis zur
         Sexualethik des Frühjudentums," in Helmut Merklein, ed., *Neues
         Testament und Ethik* (festschrift for Rudolf Schnackenburg).
         Freiburg: Herder, 1989. Pp. 271-98.

1387   Piet Farla, "The Two Shall Become One Flesh: Gen 1.27 and 2.24
         in the New Testament Marriage Texts," trans. Richard Rosser in
         Sipke Draisma, ed., *Intertextuality in Biblical Writings* (festschrift
         for Bas van Iersel). Kampen: Kok, 1989. Pp. 67-82.

1388   Bruce Fisk, "Eating Meat Offered to Idols: Corinthian Behavior
         and Pauline Response in 1 Corinthians 8-10," *TriJ* 10/1 (1989):
         49-70.

1389   Otto Merk, "Nachahmung Christi: zu ethischen Perspektiven in der
         paulinischen Theologie," in Helmut Merklein, ed., *Neues
         Testament und Ethik* (festschrift for Rudolf Schnackenburg).
         Freiburg: Herder, 1989. Pp. 172-206.

1390   Gregory W. Dawes, "But If You Can Gain Your Freedom
         (1 Corinthians 7:17-24)," *CBQ* 52 (1990): 681-97.

1391   Stanley K. Stanley, "Paul on the Use and Abuse of Reason," in
         David L. Balch, et al., eds., *Greeks, Romans, and Christians*

(festschrift for Abraham J. Malherbe). Minneapolis: Fortress Press, 1990. Pp. 253-86.

1392   J. D. M. Derrett, "Judgement and 1 Corinthians 6," *NTS* 37/1 (1991): 22-36.

1393   G. Harris, "The Beginnings of Church Discipline: 1 Corinthians 5," *NTS* 37/1 (1991): 1-21.

1394   U. R. Onunwa, "Paul, Social Issues and Future Salvation: Challenge to the Modern Church," *BB* 17/1 (1991): 5-13.

1395   R. Trevijano Etchevrria, "A propósito del incestuoso (1 Cor 5-6)," *Salm* 38/2 (1991): 129-53.

1396   James B. de Young, "The Source and NT Meaning of arsenokoitai, with Implications for Christian Ethics and Ministry," *MSJ* 3 (1992): 191-215.

1397   P. Genton, "1 Corinthiens 7/25-40. Notes exégétiques," *ÉTR* 67/2 (1992): 249-53.

1398   F. W. Horn, "Wandel im Geist: zur pneumatologischen Begründung der Ethik bei Paulus," *KD* 38 (1992): 149-70.

1399   Charles D. Myers, "What the Bible Really Says about Homosexuality," *Anima* 19 (1992): 47-56.

1400   R. B. Hays, "Ecclesiology and Ethics in 1 Corinthians," *ExA* 10 (1994): 31-43.

1401   J. J. Meggitt, "Meat Consumption and Social Conflict in Corinth," *JTS* 45 (1994): 137-41.

1402   Brian S. Rosner, *Paul, Scripture and Ethics: A Study of 1 Corinthians 5-7.* Leiden: Brill, 1994.

1403   T. Söding, "Starke und Schwache: Der Götzenopferstreit in 1 Kor 8-10 als Paradigma paulinischer Ethik," *ZNW* 85 (1994): 69-92.

faith

1404   Richard Morgan, "Faith, Hope and Love Abide," *Ch* 101/2 (1987): 128-39.

1405 Thomas A. Jackson, "Concerning Spiritual Gifts: A Study of 1 Corinthians 12," *FM* 7/1 (1989): 61-69.

form criticism
1406 Byung-Mu Ahn, "The Body of Jesus-Event Tradition," *EAJT* 3/2 (1985): 293-309.

freedom
1407 David K. Lowery, "The Head Covering and the Lord's Supper in 1 Corinthians 11:2-34," *BSac* 143 (1986): 155-63.

1408 Inge Mager, "Die theologische Lehrfreiheit in Göttingen und ihre Grenzen: Der Abendmahlskonflikt um Christoph August Heumann," in Bernd Moeller, ed., *Theologie in Göttingen: eine Vorlesungsreihe.* Göttingen: Vandenhoeck & Ruprecht, 1987. Pp. 41-57.

1409 Kenneth V. Neller, "A Model for Those Who Seek to Win Souls: 1 Corinthians 9:19-23," *RQ* 29/3 (1987): 129-42.

genre
1410 J. G. Sigountos, "The Genre of 1 Connthians 13," *NTS* 40 (1994): 246-60.

gentiles
1411 William L. Lane, "Covenant: The Key to Paul's Conflict with Corinth," *TynB* 33 (1982): 3-29.

1412 Gail P. Corrington, "Paul and the Two Wisdoms: 1 Corinthians 1:18-31 and the Hellenistic Mission," *EGLMBS* 6 (1986): 72-84.

1413 Ted Peters, "What Is the Gospel?" *PRS* 13 (1986): 21-43.

glossolalia
1414 Nat Tracy, "Speaking in Tongues," doctoral dissertation, New Orleans Baptist Theological Seminary, New Orleans LA, 1936.

1415 S. Lewis Johnson, "The Gift of Tongues and the Book of Acts," *BSac* 120 (1963): 309-11.

1416 Stanley D. Toussaint, "First Corinthians Thirteen and the Tongues Question," *BSac* 120 (1963): 311-16.

1417 Watson E. Mills, "A Theological Interpretation of Tongues in Acts and 1 Corinthians," doctoral dissertation, Southern Baptist Theological Seminary, Louisville KY, 1968.

1418 J. M. Ford, "Toward a Theology of 'Speaking in Tongues'," *TS* 32/1 (1971): 3-29.

1419 Gilbert B. Weaver, "Tongues Shall Cease," *GTJ* 14/1 (1973): 12-24.

1420 D. Moody Smith, "Glossolalia and Other Spiritual Gifts in a New Testament Perspective," *Int* 28/3 (1974): 307-20.

1421 Robert L. Thomas, " 'Tongues. . . Will Cease'," *JETS* 17/2 (1974): 81-89.

1422 Francis A. Sullivan, "Speaking In Tongues," *LV* 31/2 (1976): 145-70.

1423 Vern S. Poythress, "The Nature of Corinthian Glossolalia: Possible Options," *WTJ* 40/1 (1977): 130-35.

1424 A. C. Thiselton, "The Interpretation of Tongues: A New Suggestion in the Light of Greek Usage in Philo and Josephus," *JTS* 30/1 (1979): 15-36.

1425 H. Wayne House, "Tongues and the Mystery Religions of Corinth," *BSac* 140 (1983): 134-50.

1426 Charles H. Talbert, "Paul's Understanding of the Holy Spirit: The Evidence of 1 Corinthians 12-14," *PRS* 11/4 (1984): 95-108.

1427 G. L. Lasebikan, "Glossolalia: Its Relationship with Speech Disabilities and Personality Disorders," *AfTJ* 14/2 (1985): 111-20.

1428 W. E. Richardson, "Liturgical Order and Glossolalia: 1 Corinthians 14:26c-33a and Its Implications," *AUSS* 24 (1986): 47-48.

1429 John F. Walvoord, "The Holy Spirit and Spiritual Gifts," *BSac* 143 (1986): 109-22.

1430 R. K. Levang, "The Content of an Utterance in Tongues," *Para* 23/1 (1989): 14-20.

1431 D. E. Lanier, "With Stammering Lips and Another Tongue: 1 Cor 14:20-22 and Isa 28:11-12," *CTR* 5/2 (1991): 259-85.

1432 G. D. Fee, "Toward a Pauline Theology of Glossolalia," *Crux* 31 (1995): 22-23; 26-31.

gnosis

1433 J. Dupont, "Gnose et liberte," in *Gnosis: La connaissance religieuse dans les épîtres de saint Paul*. Louvain: Nauwlaerts, 1949. Pp. 266-377.

1434 J. Dupont, "Le charisma de gnose," in *Gnosis: La connaissance religieuse dans les épîtres de saint Paul*. Louvain: Nauwlaerts, 1949.Pp. 151-263.

1435 J. Dupont, "Gnose et liberte," in *Gnosis: La connaissance religieuse dans les épîtres de saint Paul*. Louvain: Nauwlaerts, 1949. Pp. 266-377.

1436 S. Arai, "Die Gegner des Paulus im 1. Korintherbrief und das Problem der Gnosis," *NTS* 19/4 (1973): 430-37.

gnosticism

1437 W. Stephen Sabom, "The Gnostic World of Anorexia Nervosa," *JPT* 13 (1985): 243-54.

1438 P. B. Boshoff, "Die reëls en tussen die reëls van die Korintiërbriewe: Walter Schmithals '*Die Gnosis in Korinth*'," *HTS* 45/2 (1989): 302-27.

1439 Judith L. Kovacs, "The Archons, the Spirit, and the Death of Christ: Do We Need the Hypothesis of Gnostic Opponents to Explain 1 Corinthians 2:6-16?" in Joel Marcus and Marion L. Soards, eds., *Apocalyptic and the New Testament* (festschrift J. Louis Martyn). Sheffield: JSOT Press, 1989. Pp. 217-36.

Gospel of Thomas

1440 Takashi Onuki, "Traditionsgeschichte von Thomas 17 und ihre christologische Relevanz," in Cilliers Breytenbach and Henning Paulsen, eds., *Anfänge der Christologie* (festschrift for Ferdinand Hahn). Göttingen: Vandenhoeck & Ruprecht, 1991. Pp. 399-415.

1441   R. Trevijano Etcheverría, "La valoración de los dichos no canónicos: el caso de 1 Cor 2.9 y Ev Tom log 17," in Elizabeth A. Livingstone, ed., *Studia Patristica, 24: Historica, Theologica et Philosophica*. Louvain: Peeters, 1993. Pp. 406-14.

grace

1442   Knox Chamblin, "Revelation and Tradition in the Pauline Euangelion," *WTJ* 48 (1986): 1-16.

hellenism

1443   Hans D. Betz, "The Problem of Rhetoric and Theology according to the Apostle Paul," in Albert Vanhoye, ed., *L'Apôtre Paul: personnalité, style et conception du ministre*. Louvain: Peeters, 1986. Pp. 16-48.

1444   Benoît Standaert, "La rhétorique ancienne dans saint Paul," in Albert Vanhoye, ed., *L'Apôtre Paul: personnalité, style et conception du ministre*. Louvain: Peeters, 1986. Pp. 78-92.

1445   Charles A. Kennedy, "The Cult of the Dead in Corinth," in *Love and Death in the Ancient Near East* (festschrift for Marvin H. Pope). Guillford CN: Four Quarters Publishinh Company, 1987. Pp. 227-36.

1446   Duane F. Watson, "1 Corinthians 10:23-11:1 in the Light of Greco-Roman Rhetoric," *JBL* 108/2 (1989): 301-18.

1447   Jens Christensen, "Paulus livsfornaegteren? For og imod Vilhelm Gronbechs Paulustolkning," *DTT* 53/1 (1990): 1-18.

1448   Stanley K. Stanley, "Paul on the Use and Abuse of Reason," in David L. Balch, et al., eds., *Greeks, Romans, and Christians* (festschrift for Abraham J. Malherbe). Minneapolis: Fortress Press, 1990. Pp. 253-86.

1449   Peter Lampe, "Das korinthische Herrenmahl im Schnittpunkt hellenistisch-römischer Mahlpraxis und paulinischer Theologia Crucis (1Kor 11,17-34)," *ZNW* 82/3-4 (1991): 183-213.

1450   M. Lautenschlager, "Abschied vom Disputierer. Zur Bedeutung von συζητητὴς in Kor 1,20," *ZNW* 83/3-4 (1992): 276-85.

1451   Peter Lampe, "The Eucharist: Identifying with Christ on the
           Cross," *Int* 48 (1994): 36-49.

holiness code
   1452   Brian S. Rosner, "Temple and Holiness in 1 Corinthians 5," *TynB*
              42/1 (1991): 137-45.

holy spirit
   1453   Robin Scroggs, "The Exaltation of the Spirit by Some Early
              Christians," *JBL* 84 (1965): 359-73.

   1454   G. R. Beasley-Murray, "The Holy Spirit, Baptism, and the Body
              of Christ," *RevExp* 63/2 (1966): 177-85.

   1455   D. W. B. Robinson, "Charismata Versus Pneumatika: Paul's
              Method of Discussion," *RTR* 31/2 (1972): 49-55.

   1456   Glenn O'Neal, "The Pastor and the Holy Spirit," *GTJ* 14/3 (1973):
              26-32.

   1457   John H. Schütz, "Charisma and Social Reality in Primitive
              Christianity," *JR* 54/1 (1974): 51-70.

   1458   Paul W. Meyer, "The Holy Spirit in the Pauline Letters: A
              Contextual Exploration," *Int* 33/1 (1979): 3-18.

   1459   Michael W. Duggan, "The Spirit in the Body in First
              Corinthians," *BibTo* 18/6 (1980): 388-93.

   1460   Mauro Pesce, "L'Apostolo di Fronte Alla Crescita Pneumatica dei
              Corinti," *CrNSt* 3/1 (1982): 1-39.

   1461   Gerhard Sellin, "Das 'Beheimins' der Weisheit und das Ratsel der
              'Christtuspartei'," *ZNW* 73/1-2 (1982): 69-96.

   1462   Charles H. Talbert, "Paul's Understanding of the Holy Spirit: The
              Evidence of 1 Corinthians 12-14," *PRS* 11/4 (1984): 95-108.

   1463   M. A. G. Haykin, " 'In the Cloud and in the Sea': Basil of
              Caesarea and the Exegesis of 1 Cor 10:2," *VC* 40 (1986): 135-44.

   1464   W. E. Richardson, "Liturgical Order and Glossolalia in
              1 Corinthians 14.26c-33a," *NTS* 32 (1986): 144-53.

1465 John F. Walvoord, "The Holy Spirit and Spiritual Gifts," *BSac* 143 (1986): 109-22.

1466 Jonathan A. Draper, "The Tip of an Ice-Berg: The Temple of the Holy Spirit," *JTSA* 59 (1987): 57-65.

1467 Walter Kirchschläger, "Das Geistwirken in der Sicht des Neuen Testaments: dargestellt an seinen Hauptzeugen," in Walter Kirchschläger, et al., eds. *Pneumatologie und Spiritualität.* Zürich: Benziger Verlag, 1987. Pp. 15-52.

1468 David Petts, "Baptism of the Spirit in Pauline Thought: A Pentecostal Perspective," *EPTA* 7/3 (1988): 88-95.

1469 A. Miranda, "L' 'uomo spirituale' nella Prima ai Corinzi," *RBib* 43 (1995): 485-519.

1470 Andrew G. Hadden, "Gifts of the Spirit in Assemblies of God Writings," *Para* 24 (1990): 20-32.

1471 E. J. Vledder and A. G. van Aarde, "A Holistic View of the Holy Spirit as Agent of Ethical Responsibility," *HTS* 47 (1991): 503-25.

1472 F. W. Horn, "Wandel im Geist: zur pneumatologischen Begründung der Ethik bei Paulus," *KD* 38 (1992): 149-70.

1473 John J. Kilgallen, "Reflections on Charisma(ta) in the New Testament," *SM* 41 (1992): 289-323.

1474 David S. Lim, "Many Gifts, One Spirit," *Para* 26 (1992): 3-7.

1475 W. C. van Unnik, "The Meaning of 1 Corinthians 12:31," *NovT* 35 (1993): 142-59.

homosexuality

1476 Richard C. Devor, "Homosexuality and St. Paul," *PPsy* 23/224 (1972): 50-58.

1477 P. Michael Ukleja, "The Bible and Homosexuality. Part 2: Homosexuality in the New Testament," *BSac* 140/560 (1983): 350-58.

1478   Paul D. Feinberg, "Homosexuality and the Bible," *FundJ* 4/3 (1985): 17-19.

1479   Randolph A. Nelson, "Homosexuality and Social Ethics," *WW* 5 (1985): 380-94.

1480   John R. W. Stott, "Homosexual Marriage: Why Same Sex Partnerships Are Not a Christian Option," *CT* 29/17 (1985): 21-28.

1481   Richard B. Hays, "Relations Natural and Unnatural: A Response to J. Boswell's Exegesis of Rom 1," *JREth* 14 (1986): 184-215.

1482   W. L. Petersen, "Can ἀρσενοκοῖται Be Translated by 'Homosexuals'?" *VC* 40 (1986): 187-91.

1483   P. von der Osten-Sacken, "Paulinisches Evangelium und Homosexualität," *BTZ* 3 (1986): 28-49.

1484   Horst Balz, "Biblische Aussagen zur Homosexualität," *ZEE* 31/1 (1987): 60-72.

1485   Jürgen Becker, "Zum Problem der Homosexualität in der Bibel," *ZEE* 31/1 (1987): 36-59.

1486   David F. Wright, "Translating Arsenokoitai," *VC* 41/4 (1987): 396-98.

1487   Darrell H. Lance, "The Bible and Homosexuality," *ABQ* 8/2 (1989): 140-51.

1488   David F. Wright, "Homosexuality: The Relevance of the Bible," *EQ* 61/4 (1989): 291-300.

1489   David L. Tiede, "Will Idolaters, Sodomizers, or the Greedy Inherit the Kingdom of God? A Pastoral Exposition of 1 Cor 6:9-10," *WW* 10 (1990): 147-55.

1490   Abraham Smith, "The New Testament and Homosexuality," *QR* 11 (1991): 18-32.

1491   James B. de Young, "The Source and NT Meaning of arsenokoitai, with Implications for Christian Ethics and Ministry," *MSJ* 3 (1992): 191-215.

1492 Charles D. Myers, "What the Bible Really Says about Homosexuality," *Anima* 19 (1992): 47-56.

1493 David E. Malick, "The Condemnation of Homosexuality in 1 Corinthians 6:9," *BSac* 150 (1993): 479-92.

hope

1494 Walter Kasper, "Die Hoffnung auf die endgültige Ankunft Jesu Christi in Herrlichkeit," *IKaZ* 14/1 (1985): 1-14.

1495 Richard Morgan, "Faith, Hope and Love Abide," *Ch* 101/2 (1987): 128-39.

idol meat

1496 W. L. Willis, "Paul's Instructions to the Corinthian Church on the Eating of Idol Meat," doctoral dissertation, Southern Methodist University, Dallas TX, 1982.

1497 John C. Brunt, "Rejected, Ignored, or Misunderstood? The Fate of Paul's Approach to the Problem of Food Offered to Idols in Early Christianity," *NTS* 31/1 (1985): 113-24.

idolatry

1498 Bruce Fisk, "Eating Meat Offered to Idols: Corinthian Behavior and Pauline Response in 1 Corinthians 8-10," *TriJ* 10/1 (1989): 49-70.

1499 Terrance Callan, "Paul and the Golden Calf," *EGLMBS* 10 (1990): 1-17.

1500 Brian S. Rosner, " 'Stronger Than He?' The Strength of 1 Corinthians 10:22b," *TynB* 43/1 (1992): 171-79.

immortality

1501 Ernst Haag, "Seele und Unsterblichkeit in biblischer Sicht," in Wilhelm Breuning, ed., *Seele: Problembegriff christlicher Eschatologie.* Freiburg: Herder, 1986. Pp. 31-93.

incest

1502 R. Trevijano Etchevrria, "A propósito del incestuoso (1 Cor 5-6)," *Salm* 38/2 (1991): 129-53.

introduction
> **1503** Henry J. Cadbury, "The Macellum of Corinth," *JBL* 53 (1934): 134-41.

> **1504** K. Prümm, "Der pastorale Einheit des ersten Korintherbriefes," *ZKT* 64 (1940): 202-14.

> **1505** W. H. M. Walton, "St. Paul's Movements between the Writing of 1 and 2 Corinthians, *ET* 56 (1944-1945): 136-38.

> **1506** R. F. Robbins, "Some Factors Which Contributed to the Distinctiveness of the Corinthian Church," doctoral dissertation, Southern Baptist Theological Seminary, Louisville KY, 1945.

> **1507** L. P. Pherigo, "Paul and the Corinthian Church," *JBL* 68 (1949): 341-51.

> **1508** Oscar Broneer, "Corinth, Center of St. Paul's Missionary Work in Greece," *BA* 14 (1951): 78-96.

> **1509** Beverly B. Tinnin, "The Mystery Religions as Reflected in the Corinthian Correspondence," doctoral dissertation, New Orleans Baptist Theological Seminary, New Orleans LA, 1952.

> **1510** Henry J. Cadbury, "A Qumran Parallel to Paul," *HTR* 51 (1958): 1-2.

> **1511** Neil R. Lightfoot, "Doctrinal and Exegetical Notes on Selected Passages in 1 Corinthians," *RQ* 3 (1959): 173-82.

> **1512** Abraham J. Malherbe, "The Corinthian Contribution," *RQ* 3 (1959): 221-33.

> **1513** Robert H. Mounce, "Continuity of the Primitive Tradition," *Int* 13 (1959): 417-424.

> **1514** Roy B. Ward, "Paul and Corinth: His Visits and Letters," *RQ* 3 (1959): 158-68.

> **1515** Milton Ferguson, "The Theology of First Corinthians," *SouJT* 3 (1960): 25-38.

1516 G. Munn, "The Historical Background of First Corinthians," *SouJT* 3 (1960): 5-14.

1517 Frank Stagg, "The Motif of First Corinthians," *SouJT* 3 (1960): 15-24,

1518 C. K. Barrett, "Christianity at Corinth," *BJRL* 46 (1964): 269-97.

1519 J. M. Ford, "The First Epistle to the Corinthians or the First Epistle to the Hebrews?" *CBQ* 28 (1966): 402-16.

1520 Leonard Goppelt, "Paul and Heilsgeschichte," *Int* 21/3 (1967): 315-26.

1521 Birger A. Pearson, "Did the Gnostics Curse Jesus?" *JBL* 86/3 (1967): 301-305.

1522 Edwrad M. Panosian, et al., "Focus on 1 Corinthians," *BibView* 7/2 (1973): 89-154.

1523 Walter Schmithals, "Die Korintherbriefe als Briefsammlung," *ZNW* 64/3-4 (1973): 263-88.

1524 Oscar Broneer, "Twenty Five Years Ago on Cults at St. Paul's Corinth," *BA* 39/4 (1976): 158-59.

1525 Thomas W. Gillespie, "A Pattern of Prophetic Speech in First Corinthians," *JBL* 97/1 (1978): 74-95.

1526 Barbara L. Johnson, "Corinthian Relief Bowls from Northern Sinai," *IEJ* 29/3-4 (1979): 171-74.

1527 Nikolaus Waiter, "Christusglaube und Heidnische Religiositat in Paulinischen Gemeinden," *NTS* 25/4 (1979): 422-42.

1528 J. Kaplan, "A Samaritan Amulet from Corinth," *IEJ* 30/3-4 (1980): 196-98.

1529 Eugene A. LaVerdiere, "Paul's First Letter to the Corinthians," *BibTo* 18/6 (1980): 371-78.

1530 Michael Neary, "The Cosmic Emphasis of Paul," *ITQ* 48/1-2 (1981): 1-26.

1531 P. J. Cahill, "Hermeneutical Implications of Typology," *CBQ* 44/2 (1982): 266-81.

1532 J. Bradley Chance, "Paul's Apology to the Corinthians," *PRS* 9/2 (1982): 145-55.

1533 Ronald W. Graham, "Paul's Pastorate in Corinth: A Keyhole View of His Ministry," *LTQ* 17/2 (1982): 45-58.

1534 A. E. Harvey, " 'The Workman Is Worthy of his Hire': Fortunes of a Proverb in the Early Church," *NovT* 24/3 (1982): 209-21.

1535 Sherman E. Johnson, "Paul in the Wicked City of Corinth," *LTQ* 17/2 (1982): 59-67.

1536 James L. Blevins, "Introduction to 1 Corinthians," *RevExp* 80/3 (1983): 315-24.

1537 Edouard Delebecque, "Les deux Versions du Voyage de Saint Paul de Corinthe à Troas (AC 20:3-6)," *Bib* 64/4 (1983): 556-64.

1538 John Morgan-Wynne, "Introduction to 1 Corinthians," *SouJT* 26/1 (1983): 4-15.

1539 Jerome Murphy-O'Connor, "Corinthian Bronze," *RB* 90/1 (1983): 80-93.

1540 Roger L. Omanson, "Some Comments about Style and Meaning: 1 Corinthians 9:15 and 7:10," *BT* 34/1 (1983): 135-39.

1541 C. M. Tuckett, "1 Corinthians and Q," *JBL* 102/4 (1983): 607-19.

1542 J. D. G. Dunn, "In Defense of a Methodology" *ET* 95/10 (1984): 295-99.

1543 Victor Hasler, "Evangelist des Paulus in Korinth: Erwagungen zur Hermeneutik," *NTS* 30/1 (1984): 109-29.

1544 Jerome Murphy-O'Connor, "The Corinth that Saint Paul Saw,"*BA* 47/3 (1984): 147-59.

1545 Richard A. Norris, "The Beginnings of Christian Priesthood," *ATR* 66 (Supp. 9) (1984): 18-32.

1546 John Fischer, "Paul in His Jewish Context," *EQ* 57/3 (1985): 211-36.

1547 Robert A. Wild, "Portrait of Paul Created by His Early Christian Admirers," *CS* 24/3 (1985): 273-90.

1548 J. A. Ziesler, "Which is the Best Commentary? III. 1 Corinthians," *ET* 97 (1985-1986): 263-67.

1549 K. Adloff, "Die missionarische Existenz des Apostels Paulus nach dem Zweiten Korintherbrief," *BTZ* 3 (1986): 11-27.

1550 Stephen C. Barton, "Paul's Sense of Place: An Anthropological Approach to Community Formation in Corinth," *NTS* 32/2 (1986): 225-46.

1551 E. Earle Ellis, "Traditions in 1 Corinthians," *NTS* 32/4 (1986): 481-502.

1552 Moshe Fischer, "The Corinthian Capitals of the Capernaum Synagogue: A Revision," *Levant* 18 (1986): 131-42.

1553 C. Forbes, "Comparison, Self-Praise and Irony: Paul's Boasting and the Conventions of Hellenistic Rhetoric," *NTS* 32 (1986): 1-30.

1554 Christopher B. Kaiser, "Calvin, Copernicus and Castellio," *CTJ* 21/1 (1986): 5-31.

1555 Jerome H. Neyrey, "Body Language in 1 Corinthians: The Use of Anthropological Models for Understanding Paul and his Opponents," *Semeia* 35 (1986): 129-70.

1556 Elisabeth Fiorenza, "Rhetorical Situation and Historical Reconstruction in 1 Corinthians," *NTS* 33/3 (1987): 386-403.

1557 Victor P. Furnish, "Corinth in Paul's Time—What Can Archaeology Tell Us?" *BAR* 14/3 (1988): 14-27.

1558 J. M. Gilchrist, "Paul and the Corinthians—The Sequence of Letters and Visits," *JSNT* 47/69 (1988): 34.

1559 Michael Parsons, "Being Precedes Act: Indicative and Imperative in Paul's Writing," *EQ* 60/2 (1988): 99-127.

1560   Larry McGraw, "The City of Corinth," *SouJT* 32/1 (1989): 5-10.

1561   Fred B. Craddock, "Preaching to Corinthians," *Int* 44/2 (1990): 158-68.

1562   Larry Kreitzer, "Notations on First and Second Corinthians in Albert Schweitzer's 1929 New Testament," *AUSS* 28/3 (1990): 219-35.

1563   E. de la Serna, "Los orígenes de 1 Corintios," *Bib* 72/2 (1991): 192-216.

1564   D. L. Gragg, "Discourse Ananlysis of 1 Corinthians 1:10-2:5," *LB* 65 (1991): 37-57.

1565   M. R. Hillmer, "Knowledge: New Age, Gnosticism and First Corinthians," *McMJT* 3/1 (1991): 18-38.

1566   John M. G. Barclay, "Thessalonica and Corinth: Social Contrasts in Pauline Christianity," *JSNT* 47 (1992): 49-74.

1567   David W. J. Gill, "The Meat-Market at Corinth," *TynBll* 43/2 (1992): 389-93.

1568   M. C. de Boer, "The Composition of 1 Corinthians," *NTS* 40 (1994): 229-45.

1569   J. C. Hurd, "Good News and the Integrity of 1 Corinthians," in L. A. Jervis and P. Richardson, eds., *Gospel in Paul: Studies on Corinthians, Galatians, and Romans* (festschrift for R. N. Longenecker). Sheffield: Academic Press, 1994. Pp. 38-62.

1570   K. Quast, *Reading the Corinthian Correspondence: An Introduction.* New York: Paulist, 1994.

1571   Walter Schmithals, "Methodische Erwägungen zur Literarkritik der Paulusbriefe," *ZNW* 87 (1996): 51-82.

James

1572   Rinaldo Fabris, "Figura e ruolo di Giacomo nell'antipaolinismo," in Romano Penna, ed., *Antipaolinismo: Reazioni a Paolo tra il I e il II secolo.* Bologna: Edizioni Dehoniane Bologna, 1989. Pp. 77-92.

Joseph and Asenath

1573   C. Burchard, "The Importance of Joseph and Aseneth for the Study of the New Testament: A General Survey and a Fresh Look at the Lord's Supper," *NTS* 33/1 (1987): 102-34.

Judaizers

1574   P. W. Barnett, "Opposition in Corinth," *JSNT* 22 (1984): 3-17.

judgment

1575   G. L. Müller, "Fegfeuer: zur Hermeneutik eines umstrittenen Lehrstücks in der Eschatologie," *TQ* 166 (1986): 25-39.

1576   J. D. M. Derrett, "Judgement and 1 Corinthians 6," *NTS* 37/1 (1991): 22-36.

1577   John Proctor, "Fire in God's House: Influence of Malachi 3 in the NT," *JETS* 36 (1993): 9-14.

1578   Harm W. Hollander, "The Testing by Fire of the Builders' Works: 1 Corinthians 3:10-15," *NTS* 40 (1994): 89-104.

justification

1579   Karl P. Donfried, "Justification and Last Judgment in Paul," *Int* 30/2 (1976): 140-52.

1580   Paul W. Gooch, "Authority and Justification in Theological Ethics: A Study in 1 Corinthians 7," *JREth* 11/1 (1983): 62-74.

1581   Heikki Räisänen, "Galatians 2:16 and Paul's Break with Judaism," *NTS* 31 (1985): 543-53.

1582   Ted Peters, "What Is the Gospel?" *PRS* 13 (1986): 21-43.

1583   Charles H. Cosgrove, "Justification in Paul: A Linguistic and Theological Reflection," *JBL* 106/4 (1987): 653-70.

1584   James E. Rosscup, "A New Look at 1 Corinthians 3:12—'Gold, Silver, Precious Stones'," *MSJ* 1 (1990): 21-51.

knowledge

1585   E.-B. Allo, "Sagesse et Pneuma dans 1 Cor.," *RB* 43 (1934): 321-46.

law

1586 Jerome Hall, "Paul, the Lawyer, on Law," *JLR* 3/2 (1985): 331-79.

1587 William Klassen, "The King as 'Living Law' with Particular Reference to Musonius Rufus," *SR* 14/1 (1985): 63-71.

1588 Reginald H. Fuller, "An Exegetical Paper: 1 Corinthians 6:1-11," *ExA* 2 (1986): 96-104.

1589 Andreas Lindemann, "Die biblischen Toragebote und die paulinische Ethik," in Wolfgand Schrage *Studien zum Text und zur Ethik des Neuen Testaments* (festschrift for Heinrich Greeven). Berlin: de Gruyter, 1986. Pp. 242-65.

1590 Robert D. Taylor, "Toward a Biblical Theology of Litigation: A Law Professor Looks at 1 Corinthians 6:1-11," *ExA* 2 (1986): 105-16.

law and gospel

1591 J. D. G. Dunn, "Works of the Law and the Curse of the Law," *NTS* 31 (1985): 523-42.

1592 Morna D. Hooker, "Interchange in Christ and Ethics," *JSNT* 25 (1985) 3-17.

1593 Mark W. Karlberg, "Legitimate Discontinuities between the Testaments," *JETS* 28 (1985): 9-20.

1594 Heikki Räisänen, "Galatians 2:16 and Paul's Break with Judaism," *NTS* 3˙ (1985): 543-53.

1595 Françcis Refoulé, "Note sur Romains 9:30-33," *RB* 92 (1985): 161-86.

1596 Norman H. Young, "Paidagogos: The Social Setting of a Pauline Metaphor," *NovT* 29 (1987): 150-76.

1597 Rinaldo Fabris, "Figura e ruolo di Giacomo nell'antipaolinismo," in Romano Penna, ed., *Antipaolinismo: Reazioni a Paolo tra il I e il II secolo*. Bologna: Edizioni Dehoniane Bologna, 1989. Pp. 77-92.

1598 T. Söding, " 'Die Kraft der Sünde ist das Gesetz' (1 Kor 15:56): Anmerkungen zum Hintergrund und zur Pointe einer gesetzeskritischen Sentenz des Apostels Paulus," *ZNW* 83/1-2 (1992): 74-84.

law, Roman

1599 B. W. Winter, "Civil Litigation in Secular Corinth and the Church. The Forensic Background to 1 Corinthians 6.1-8," *NTS* 37/4 (1991): 559-72.

literary criticism

1600 R. G. Hamerton-Kelly, "A Girardian Interpretation of Paul: Rivalry, Mimesis and Victimage in the Corinthian Correspondence," *Semeia* 33 (1985): 65-81.

1601 Peter Richardson and Peter Gooch, "Logia of Jesus in 1 Corinthians," in David Wenham, ed., *The Jesus Tradition outside the Gospels*. Sheffiled: JSOT Press, 1985. Pp. 39-62

1602 Timothy H. Lim, "Not in Persuasive Words of Wisdom but in the Demonstration of the Spirit and Power," *NovT* 29/2 (1987): 137-49.

1603 Walter Schmithals, "The Pre-Pauline Tradition in 1 Corinthians 15:20-28," trans. Clayton N. Jefford, *PRS* 20 (1993): 357-80.

lord's supper

1604 Fred D. Howard, "An Interpretation of the Lord's Supper in the Teaching of the New Testament," doctoral dissertation, New Orleans Baptist Theological Seminary, New Orleans LA, 1957.

1605 Jakob J. Petuchowski, "Do This In Remembrance of Me (1 Cor. 11:24)," *JBL* 76 (1957): 293-98.

1606 K. C. Mathew, "Do This In Remembrance of Me," *IJT* 9 (1960): 4-7.

1607 Sverre Allen, "Das Abendmahl als Offermahl in Neuen Testament," *MeliT* 6 (1963): 128-52.

1608 M. M. Bourke, "The Eucharist and Wisdom in First Corinthians," in *Studiorum Paulinorum Congressus, 1961*. 2 vols. Rome: Pontifical Biblical Institute, 1963. 1:367-81.

1609 Frank Stagg, "The Lord's Supper in the New Testament," *RevExp* 66/1 (1969): 5-14.

1610 Gerd Theissen, "Soziale Schichtung in der Korinthischen Gemeinde," *ZNW* 65/3-4 (1974): 232-72.

1611 Elmer Prout, "One Loaf. One Body," *RQ* 25/2 (1982): 78-81.

1612 Beverly R. Gaventa, " 'You Proclaim the Lord's Death': 1Corinthians 11:26 and Paul's Understanding of Worship," *RevExp* 80/3 (1983): 377-87.

1613 Guillermo J. Garlatti, "La eucaristia como memoria y proclamacion de la muerte del Señor: aspectos de la cena del Señor según San Pablo [2 pts]," *RevB* 46/4 (1984): 321-41; (1984) 47/1-2 (1985): 1-25.

1614 J. Timothy Coyle, "The Agape/Eucharist Relationship in 1 Corinthians 11," *GTJ* 6/2 (1985): 411-24.

1615 James Custer, "When is Communion Communion," *GTJ* 6 (1985): 403-10.

1616 Donald Farner, "The Lord's Supper until He Comes," *GTJ* 6/2 (1985): 391-401.

1617 Peter E. Fink, "The Challenge of God's Koinonia," *Worship* 59 (1985): 386-403.

1618 Vigen Guroian, "Seeing Worship as Ethics: An Orthodox Perspective," *JRE* 13 (1985): 332-59.

1619 Peter Henrici, "Do This in Remembrance of Me: The Sacrifice of Christ and the Sacrifice of the Faithful," *CICR* 12 (1985): 146-57.

1620 Walter Kasper, "The Unity and Multiplicity of Aspects in the Eucharist," *CICR* 12 (1985): 115-38.

1621 G. Macy, "Some Examples of the Influence of Exegesis on the Theology of the Eucharist in the Eleventh and Twelfth Centuries," *RTAM* 52 (1985): 64-77.

1622   Antonio Orbe, "Cristo, sacrificio y manjar," *Greg* 66/2 (1985): 185-239.

1623   H. U. von Balthasar, "The Holy Church and the Eucharistic Sacrifice," *CICR* 12 (1985): 139-45.

1624   Peder Borgen, "Nattverdtradisjonen i 1.Kor. 10 og 11 som evangelietradisjon," *SEÅ* 51-52 (1985-1986): 32-39.

1625   Michel Albaric, "Une catéchèse eucharistique: le sermon 227," in A.-M. La Bonnardière, ed., *Saint Augustin et la Bible*. Paris: Editions Beauchesne, 1986. Pp. 87-98.

1626   Max A. Chevallier, "L'unité plurielle de l'église d'après le Nouveau Testament," *RHPR* 66 (1986): 3-20.

1627   Ray C. Jones, "The Lord's Supper and the Concept of Anamnesis," *WW* 6 (1986): 434-45.

1628   H.-J. Klauck, "Eucharistie und Kirchengemeinschaft bei Paulus," *WuW* 49 (1986): 1-14.

1629   John D. Lawrence, "The Eucharist as the Imitation of Christ," *TS* 47 (1986): 286-96.

1630   David K. Lowery, "The Head Covering and the Lord's Supper in 1 Corinthians 11:2-34," *BSac* 143 (1986): 155-63.

1631   E. Mazza, "L'Eucaristia di 1 Corinti 10:16-17 in rapporto a Didache 9-10," *EphL* 100 (1986): 193-223.

1632   G. C. Nicholson, "Houses for Hospitality: 1 Cor 11:17-34," *CANZTR* 19 (1986): 1-6.

1633   P. C. Potgieter, "The Influence of Zwingli on Calvin concerning the Lord's Supper," in B. J. van der Walt, et al., eds., *John Calvin's Institutes*. Potcherstroom: Institute for Reformational Studies, 1986. Pp. 148-62.

1634   John N. Suggit, "The Perils of Bible Translation: An Examination of the Latin Versions of the Words of Institution of the Eucharist," in K. J. H. Petzer and Patrick Hartin, eds., *A South African*

Perspective on New Testament (festschrift for Bruce Metgzer). Leiden: Brill, 1986. Pp. 54-61.

1635   Robert Taft, ''The Dialogue before the Anaphora in the Byzantine Eucharistic Liturgy; pt 1: The Opening Greeting,'' *OCP* 52/2 (1986): 299-324.

1636   Niels Hyldahl, ''Meta to deipnesai, 1 Kor 11,25 (og Luk 22, 20),'' *SEÅ* 51/52 (1986-1987): 100-107.

1637   C. Burchard, ''The Importance of Joseph and Aseneth for the Study of the New Testament: A General Survey and a Fresh Look at the Lord's Supper,'' *NTS* 33/1 (1987): 102-34.

1638   William R. Farmer, ''Peter and Paul, and the Tradition concerning 'the Lord's Supper' in 1 Corinthians 11:23-26,'' *CTR* 2 (1987): 119-40.

1639   Inge Mager, ''Die theologische Lehrfreiheit in Göttingen und ihre Grenzen: Der Abendmahlskonflikt um Christoph August Heumann,'' in Bernd Moeller, ed., *Theologie in Göttingen: eine Vorlesungsreihe.* Göttingen: Vandenhoeck & Ruprecht, 1987. Pp. 41-57.

1640   Peter Stuhlmacher, ''Das neutestamentliche Zeugnis vom Herrenmahl,'' *ZTK* 84/1 (1987): 1-35.

1641   Otfried Hofius, ''Herrenmahl und Herrenmahlsparadosis,'' *ZTK* 85/4 (1988): 371-408.

1642   H.-J. Klauck, ''Eucharist and Church Community in Paul,'' *TD* 35/1 (1988): 19-24.

1643   Reinhard Schwarz, ''Das Abendmahl - die Testamentshandlung Jesu,'' *Luther* 59/1 (1988): 13-25.

1644   Bonnie B. Thurston, ''Do This: A Study on the Institution of the Lord's Supper,'' *RQ* 30/4 (1988): 207-17.

1645   David T. Adamo, ''The Lord's Supper in 1 Cor. 10:14-22; 11:17-34,'' *AfTJ* 18/1 (1989): 36-48.

1646 Joe O. Lewis, "Paul and the Lord's Supper," *BI* 14/2 (1989): 73-75.

1647 Calvin Porter, "An Interpretation of Paul's Lord's Supper Texts: 1 Corinthians 10:14-22 and 11:17-34," *Enc* 50/1 (1989): 29-45.

1648 Martin Karrer, "Der Kelch des neuen Bundes: Erwägungen zum Verständnis des Herrenmahls nach 1 Kor 11:23b-25," *BZ* 34/2 (1990): 198-221.

1649 Mauro Pesce, "Manigiare e bere il proprio giudizio. Una concezione culturale comune a 1 Cor e a So[dot under]ta?" *RBib* 38/4 (1990): 495-513.

1650 B. B. Blue, "The House Church at Corinth and the Lord's Supper: Famine, Food Supply, and the *Present Distress*," *CTR* 5/2 (1991): 221-39.

1651 R. A. Campbell, "Does Paul Acquiesce in Divisions at the Lord's Supper?" *NovT* 33/1 (1991): 61-70.

1652 Peter Lampe, "The Corinthian Eucharistic Dinner Party: Exegesis of a Cultural Context," *Affirm* 4/2 (1991): 1-15.

1653 T. Engberg-Pedersen "Proclaiming the Lord's Death: 1 Corinthians 11:7-34 and the Forms of Paul's Theological Argument," *SBLSP* (1991): 592-617.

1654 Peter Lampe, "Das korinthische Herrenmahl im Schnittpunkt hellenistisch-römischer Mahlpraxis und paulinischer Theologia Crucis (1Kor 11,17-34)," *ZNW* 82/3-4 (1991): 183-213.

1655 H. Maccoby, "Paul and the Eucharist," *NTS* 37/2 (1991): 247-67.

1656 V. C. Pfitzner, "Proclaiming the Name: Cultic Narrative and Eucharistic Proclamation in First Corinthians," *LTJ* 25/1 (1991): 15-25.

1657 Jesús Sancho Bielsa, "El comentario de Santo Tomás a 1 Cor 11,27-29," in Antonio Piolanti, ed., *Atti del IX Congresso tomistico internazionale, 6.* Vatican City: Libreria Editrice Vaticana, 1991. Pp. 66-77.

1658 N. Kobayashi, "The Meaning of Jesus' Death in the 'Last Supper' Traditions," *TJT* 8/1 (1992): 95-105.

1659 R. A. D. Clancy, "The Old Testament Roots of Remembrance in the Lord's Supper," *CJ* 19/1 (1993): 35-50.

1660 H.-J. Klauck and Barry D. Smith, "Presence in the Lord's Supper: 1 Corinthians 11:23-26 in the Context of Hellenistic Religious History," in Ben F. Meyer, ed., *One Loaf, One Cup: Ecumenical Studies of 1 Cor 11 and Other Eucharistic Texts: The Cambridge Conference on the Eucharist, August 1988.* Macon GA: Mercer University Press, 1993. Pp. 57-74

1661 Ben F. Meyer, ed., *One Loaf, One Cup: Ecumenical Studies of 1 Cor 11 and Other Eucharistic Texts: The Cambridge Conference on the Eucharist, August 1988.* Macon GA: Mercer University Press, 1993.

1662 Peter Lampe, "The Eucharist: Identifying with Christ on the Cross," *Int* 48 (1994): 36-49.

1663 J. A. Gibbs, "An Exegetical Case for Close(d) Communion," *ConcJourn* 21 (1995): 149-63.

1664 D. Horrell, "Lord's Supper at Corinth and in the Church Today," *Theology* 98 (1995): 196-202.

1665 A. McGowan, " 'First Regarding the Cup . . .': Papias and the Diversity of Early Eucharistic Practice," *JTS* 46 (1995): 551-55.

love

1666 Paul D. Fueter, "The Therapeutic Language of the Bible," *IRM* 75 (1986): 211-21.

1667 David K. Lowery, "The Head Covering and the Lord's Supper in 1 Corinthians 11:2-34," *BSac* 143 (1986): 155-63.

1668 Horst Balz, "Biblische Aussagen zur Homosexualität," *ZEE* 31/1 (1987): 60-72.

1669 Donald Gee, "The Gifts and Fruit of the Spirit," *Para* 21 (1987): 21-26.

1670   Richard Morgan, "Faith, Hope and Love Abide," *Ch* 101/2 (1987): 128-39.

1671   Oda Wischmeyer, "Theon agapan bei Paulus: eine traditionsgeschichtliche Miszelle," *ZNW* 78/1-2 (1987): 141-44.

1672   Michael Johnson, "Face to Face," *EGLMBS* 11 (1991): 222-37.

marriage/divorce

1673   John J. Bandy, "Paul's Teaching Concerning Marriage in 1 Corinthians 7:1-16," master's thesis, Southern Baptist Theological Seminary, Louisville KY, 1952.

1674   Robert C. Campbell, "Teachings of Paul Concerning Divorce," *Found* 6 (1963): 362-66.

1675   Walter J. Bartling, "Sexuality, Marriage, and Divorce in 1 Corinthians 6:12-7:16," *CTM* 39/6 (1968): 355-66.

1676   H. G. Coiner, "Those 'Divorce and Remarriage' Passages," *CTM* 39/6 (1968): 367-84.

1677   M. L. Barré, "To Marry or to Burn: Purousthai in 1 Cor. 7:9," *CBQ* 36/2 (1974): 193-202.

1678   David R. Catchpole, "The Synoptic Divorce Material as a Traditio-Historical Problem," *BJRL* 57/1 (1974): 92-127.

1679   James A. Fischer, "1 Cor. 7:8-24. Marriage and Divorce," *BR* 23 (1978): 26-35.

1680   J. Cambier, "Doctrine Paulinienne du Mariage Chrétien. Etude Critique de 1 Co 7 et d'Ep 5, 21-33 et Essai de Leur Traduction Actuelle," *EgT* 10/1 (1979): 13-59.

1681   Charles C. Ryrie, "Biblical Teaching on Divorce and Remarriage," *GTJ* 3/2 (1982): 177-92.

1682   B. N. Wambacq, "Matthieu 5,31-32. Possibilite De Divorce ou Obligation De Rompre Une Union Illigitime," *NRT* 104/1 (1982): 34-49.

1683 Lisa Sowle Cahill, "Sex, Marriage, and Community in Christian Ethics," *Thought* 58/228 (1983): 72-81.

1684 David E. Garland, "The Christian's Posture Toward Marriage and Celibacy: 1 Corinthians 7," *RevExp* 80/3 (1983): 351-62.

1685 G. Greenfield, "Paul and Eschatological Marriage," *SouJT* 26/1 (1983): 32-48.

1686 John R. W. Stott, "Homosexual Marriage: Why Same Sex Partnerships Are Not a Christian Option," *CT* 29/17 (1985): 21-28.

1687 Edward Dobson, "Divorce and the Teaching of Paul; pt 7," *FundJ* 5 (1986): 26-27.

1688 William A. Heth, "Matthew's 'Eunuch Saying' (19:12) and Its Relationship to Paul's Teaching on Singleness in 1 Corinthians 7," doctoral dissertation, Dallas Theological Seminary, Dallas TX, 1986.

1689 Frans Neirynck, "Paul and the Sayings of Jesus," in Albert Vanhoye, ed., *L'Apôtre Paul: personnalité, style et conception du ministre.* Louvain: Peeters, 1986. Pp. 265-321.

1690 John C. O'Neill, "1 Corinthians 7,14 and Infant Baptism," in Albert Vanhoye, ed., *L'Apôtre Paul: personnalité, style et conception du ministre.* Louvain: Peeters, 1986. Pp. 357-61.

1691 Wolfgang Trilling, "Zum Thema: Ehe und Ehescheidung im Neuen Testament," in Joachim Rogge and Gottfried Schille, eds., *Theologische Versuche, 16.* Berlin: Evangelische Verlagsanstalt, 1986. Pp. 73-84.

1692 William A. Heth, "Unmarried 'for the Sake of the Kingdom' in the Early Church," *GTJ* 8 (1987): 55-88.

1693 Gerhard Dautzenburg, "Pheugete ten porneian (1 Kor 6,18): eine Fallstudie zur paulinischen Sexualethik in ihrem Verhältnis zur Sexualethik des Frühjudentums," in Helmut Merklein, ed., *Neues Testament und Ethik* (festschrift for Rudolf Schnackenburg). Freiburg: Herder, 1989. Pp. 271-98.

1694   Piet Farla, "The Two Shall Become One Flesh: Gen 1.27 and 2.24 in the New Testament Marriage Texts," trans. Richard Rosser in Sipke Draisma, ed., *Intertextuality in Biblical Writings* (festschrift for Bas van Iersel). Kampen: Kok, 1989. Pp. 67-82.

1695   Gregory W. Dawes, "But If You Can Gain Your Freedom (1 Corinthians 7:17-24)," *CBQ* 52 (1990): 681-97.

1696   Bruce N. Kaye, "One Flesh and Marriage," *CANZTR* 22 (1990): 46-57.

1697   Vincent L. Wimbush, "The Ascetic Impulse in Early Christianity: Methodological Challenges and Opportunities," in Elizabeth A. Livingstone, ed., *Studia Patristica, 25: Biblica et Arocrypha.* Louvain: Peeters, 1993. Pp. 462-78.

metaphor

1698   Michael Johnson, "Face to Face," *EGLMBS* 11 (1991): 222-37.

1699   K. Romaniuk, "... wie ein guter Baumeister ...." in J. J. Degenhardt, ed., *Die Freude an Gott - unsere Kraft* (festschrift for Otto B. Knoch). Stuttgart: Verlag Katholisches Bibelwerk, 1991. Pp. 164-69.

midrash

1700   Agustín del Agua Perez, "El papel de la 'escuela midrásica' en la configuración del Nuevo Testamento," *EB* 60 (1985): 333-49.

1701   L. Ann Jervis, " 'But I Want You to Know . . .': Paul's Midrashic Intertextual Response to the Corinthian Worshipers," *JBL* 112 (1993): 231-46.

ministry

1702   Ronald Y. K. Fung, "The Nature of the Ministry according to Paul," *EQ* 54/3 (1982): 129-46.

1703   C. W. Brister, "The Ministry in 1 Corinthians," *SouJT* 26/1 (1983): 18-31.

1704   Walter Radl, "Alle Mühe umsonst: Paulus und der Gottesknecht," in Albert Vanhoye, ed., *L'Apôtre Paul: personnalité, style et conception du ministre.* Louvain: Peeters, 1986. Pp. 144-49.

1705 George H. Gaston, "A Model for Leadership: Servant Stewardship Ministry," *SouJT* 29/2 (1987): 35-43.

1706 Daniel J. Harrington, "Paul and Collaborative Ministry," *NTheoR* 3/1 (1990): 62-71.

mishnah
1707 Charles A. Kennedy, "1 Corinthians 8 as a Mishnaic List," in Jacon Neusner, ed., *Religious Writings and Religious Systems: Systemic Analysis of Holy Books.* Vol. 2. Atlanta: Scholars Press, 1989. Pp. 17-24.

missions
1708 M. C. Griffths, "Today's Missionary, Yesterday's Apostle," *EMQ* 21/2 (1985): 154-65.

1709 Donald A. Carson, "Pauline Inconsistency: Reflections on 1 Corinthians 9:19-23 and Galatians 2:11-14," *Ch* 100 (1986): 6-45.

1710 Anne-Marie La Bonnardière, "Les deux vies: Marthe et Marie (Luc 10,38-42)," in A.-M. La Bonnardière, ed., *Saint Augustin et la Bible.* Paris: Editions Beauchesne, 1986. Pp. 411-25.

1711 Walter Radl, "Alle Mühe umsonst: Paulus und der Gottesknecht," in Albert Vanhoye, ed., *L'Apôtre Paul: personnalité, style et conception du ministre.* Louvain: Peeters, 1986. Pp. 144-49.

1712 Kenneth V. Neller, "1 Corinthians 9:19-23: A Model for Those Who Seek to Win Souls," *RQ* 29/3 (1987): 129-42.

1713 Walter Rebell, "Gemeinde als Missionsfaktor im Urchristentum: 1 Kor 14:24f, als Schlüsselsituation," *TZ* 44/2 (1988): 117-34.

1714 Jonathan J. Bonk, "Doing Mission out of Affluence: Reflections on Recruiting 'End of the Procession' Missionaries from 'Front of the Procession' Churches," *Miss* 17/4 (1989): 427-52.

1715 Richard B. Cunningham, "Wide Open Doors and Many Adversaries (1 Corinthians 16:9; Acts 19)," *RevExp* 89 (1992): 89-98.

misssionary work

1716 Richard B. Cook, "St. Paul—Preacher, Evangelist, or Organizer?" *ET* 93/6 (1982): 171-73.

music

1717 William W. Klein, "Noisy Gong or Acoustic Vase? A Note 1 Corinthians 13:1," *NTS* 32/2 (1986): 286-89.

mystery religions

1718 H. Wayne House, "Tongues and the Mystery Religions of Corinth," *BSac* 140 (1983): 134-50.

mysticism

1719 David Stanley, "The Apostle Paul as Saint," *SM* 35 (1986): 71-97.

Nag Hammadi

1720 Louis Painchard, "Le sommaire anthropogonique de (NH II, 117:38-118:2) à la lumiere de 1 Co 15:45-47," *VC* 44 (1990): 382-93.

narrative criticism

1721 Benoît Standaert, "La rhétorique ancienne dans saint Paul," in Albert Vanhoye, ed., *L'Apôtre Paul: personnalité, style et conception du ministre.* Louvain: Peeters, 1986. Pp. 78-92.

paraenesis

1722 T. Engberg-Pedersen, "The Gospel and Social Practice according to 1 Corinthians," *NTS* 33/4 (1987): 557-84.

1723 Carl R. Holladay, "1 Corinthians 13: Paul as Apostolic Paradigm," in David L. Balch, et al., eds., *Greeks, Romans, and Christians* (festschrift for Abraham J. Malherbe). Minneapolis: Fortress Press, 1990. Pp. 80-98.

passion

1724 Pasquale Colella, "Cristo nostra pasqua? 1 Cor 5:7," *BibO* 28 (1986): 197-217.

1725 Helmut Koester, "Jesu Leiden und Tod als Erzählung," in Rüdiger Bartelmus, et al., eds., *Konsequente Traditionsgeschichte* (festschrift for Klaus Baltzer). Fribourg: Universitätsverlag, 1993. Pp. 199-204.

pneumatikos
  1726 R. A. Horsley, "Pneumatikos vs. Psychikos: Distinctions of
            Spiritual Status among the Corinthians," *HTR* 69/3-4 (1976):
            269-88.

power
  1727 D. Sänger, "Die δυνατοι in 1 Kor 1:26," *ZNW* 76 (1985): 285-91.

  1728 E. A. Castelli, "Interpretations of Power in 1 Corinthians," *Semeia*
            54 (1991): 197-222.

prophecy
  1729 Thomas W. Gillespie, "Interpreting the Kerygma: Early Christian
            Prophecy according to 1 Corinthians 2:6-16," in James E.
            Goehring, et al., eds., *Gospel Origins andChristian Beginnings*.
            Sonoma CA: Polebridge Press, 1990, Pp. 151-66.

  1730 John F. Walvoord, "The Holy Spirit and Spiritual Gifts," *BSac*
            143 (1986): 109-22.

  1731 Thomas R. Schreiner, "Head Coverings, Prophecies and the
            Trinity: 1 Corinthians 11:2-16," in John Piper and Wayne Grudem,
            eds., *Recovering Biblical Manhood and Womanhood*. Wheaton IL:
            Crossway Books, 1991. Pp. 124-39, 485-87.

  1732 R. F. White, "Richard Gaffin and Wayne Grudem on 1 Cor 13:10:
            A Comparison of Cessationist and Noncessationist
            Argumentation," *JETS* 35/2 (1992): 173-81.

prophets
  1733 Walter Rebell, "Gemeinde als Missionsfaktor im Urchristentum: 1
            Kor 14:24f, als Schlüsselsituation," *TZ* 44/2 (1988): 117-34.

rabbinic literature
  1734 Mary Rose D'Angelo, "The Garden: Once and not Again:
            Traditional Interpretations of Genesis 1:26-27 in 1 Corinthians
            11:7-12," in G. A. Robbins, ed., *Genesis 1-3 in the History of
            Exegesis*. Lewiston NY: Mellen, 1988. Pp. 1-41.

  1735 Stanley E. Porter, "The Pauline Concept of Original Sin in Light
            of Rabbinic Background," *TynB* 41 (1990): 3-30.

racism

1736 William R. Herzog, "The New Testament and the Question of Racial Injustice," *ABQ* 5 (1986): 12-32.

recipients

1737 J. M. Ford, "The First Epistle to the Corinthians or the First Epistle to the Hebrews?" *CBQ* 28/4 (1966): 402-16.

redaction criticism

1738 Vincent P. Branick, "Source and Redaction Analysis of 1 Corinthians 1-3," *JBL* 101/2 (1982): 251-69.

relation to Judaism

1739 Robert T. Osborn, "The Christian Blasphemy," *JAAR* 53 (1985): 339-63.

1740 Gerard S. Sloyan, "Jewish Ritual of the 1st Century CE and Christian Sacramental Behavior," *BTB* 15 (1985): 98-103.

1741 Armando J. Levoratti, "Tú no has querido sacrificio ni oblación: Salmo 40:7; Hebreos 10:5; pt 1," *RevB* 48 (1986): 1-30.

1742 Charles A. Kennedy, "1 Corinthians 8 as a Mishnaic list," in Jacon Neusner, ed., *Religious Writings and Religious Systems: Systemic Analysis of Holy Books.* Vol. 2. Atlanta: Scholars Press, 1989. Pp. 17-24.

1743 Larry Kreitzer, "Christ and Second Adam in Paul," *CVia* 32 (1989): 55-101.

1744 Terrance Callan, "Paul and the Golden Calf," *EGLMBS* 10 (1990): 1-17.

1745 John R. Levison, "Did the Spirit Inspire Rhetoric? An Exploration of George Kennedy's Definition of Rarly Christian Rhetoric," in Duane F. Watson, ed., *Persuasive Artistry* (festschrift for George A. Kennedy). Sheffield: JSOT Press, 1991. Pp. 25-40.

1746 J. P. M. Sweet, "A House Not Made with Hands," in William Horbury, ed., *Templum Amicitiae: Essays on the Second Temple* (festschrift for Ernst Bammel). Sheffield: JSOT Press, 1991. Pp. 368-90.

1747 F. W. Horn, "Wandel im Geist: zur pneumatologischen Begründung der Ethik bei Paulus," *KD* 38 (1992): 149-70.

1748 F. Thielman, "The Coherence of Paul's View of the Law: The Evidence of First Corinthians," *NTS* 38/2 (1992): 235-53.

relation to Old Testament

1749 Arnold F. Nelson, "Some Principles of Paul's Quotations from the Old Testament as Reflected in First Corinthians," doctoral dissertation, New Orleans Baptist Theological Seminary, New Orleans LA, 1952.

1750 Agustín del Agua Perez, "El papel de la 'escuela midrásica' en la configuración del Nuevo Testamento," *EB* 60 (1985): 333-49.

1751 Mark W. Karlberg, "Legitimate Discontinuities between the Testaments," *JETS* 28 (1985): 9-20.

1752 Josef Blank, "Secundum Scripturas: Ursprung und Struktur der theologischen Hermeneutik im Neuen Testament," in Hans Küng and David Tracy, eds., *Das neue Paradigma von Theologie*. Zürich: Benzinger Verlag, 1986. Pp. 35-52.

1753 Armando J. Levoratti, "Tú no has querido sacrificio ni oblación: Salmo 40:7; Hebreos 10:5; pt 1," *RevB* 48 (1986): 1-30.

1754 Bertrand de Margerie, "Le troisième jour, selon les Ecritures, il est ressuscité: importance théologique d'une recherche exégétique," *RevSR* 60 (1986): 158-88.

1755 F. Pastor-Ramos, " 'Murió por nuestros pecados' (1 Cor 15,3; Gal 1,4). Observaciones sobre el origen de esta fórmula en Is 53," *EE* 61 (1986): 385-93.

1756 Otto Betz, "Der gekreuzigte Christus: Unsere Weisheit und Gerechtigkeit (der alttestamentliche Hintergrund von 1 Kor 1-2)," in Gerald F. Hawthorne and Otto Betz, eds., *Tradition and Interpretation in the New Testament* (festschrift for E. Earle Ellis). Grand Rapids: Eerdmans, 1987. Pp. 195-215.

1757 Charles H. Talbert, "Paul on the Covenant," *RevExp* 84 (1987): 299-313.

1758 Piet Farla, "The Two Shall Become One Flesh: Gen 1.27 and 2.24 in the New Testament Marriage Texts," trans. Richard Rosser in Sipke Draisma, ed., *Intertextuality in Biblical Writings* (festschrift for Bas van Iersel). Kampen: Kok, 1989. Pp. 67-82.

1759 Walter Harrelson, "Death and Victory in 1 Corinthians 15:51-57: The Transformation of a Prophetic Theme," in John T. Carroll, et al., eds., *Faith and History* (festschrift for Paul W. Meyer). Atlanta: Scholars Press, 1990. Pp. 149-59.

1760 G. R. O'Day, "Jeremiah 9:22-23 and 1 Corinthians 1:26-31: A Study in Intertextuality," *JBL* 109/2 (1990): 259-67.

1761 Martin Hengel, "Psalm 110 und die Erhöhung des Auferstandenen zur Rechten Gottes," in Cilliers Breytenbach and Henning Paulsen, eds., *Anfänge der Christologie* (festschrift for Ferdinand Hahn). Göttingen: Vandenhoeck & Ruprecht, 1991. Pp. 43-73.

1762 D. E. Lanier, "With Stammering Lips and Another Tongue: 1 Cor 14:20-22 and Isa 28:11-12," *CTR* 5/2 (1991): 259-85.

1763 Brian S. Rosner, "Moses Appointing Judges. An Antecedent to 1 Cor 6,1-6?" *ZNW* 82 (1991): 275-78.

1764 Beimund Bieringer, "Traditionsgeschichtlicher Ursprung und theologische Bedeutung der Hyper Aussagen im Neuen Testament," in Frans van Segbroeck, et al., eds.. *The Four Gospels 1992* (festschrift for Frans Neirynck). 2 vols. Louvain: Peeters, 1992. 1:219-48.

1765 Brian S. Rosner, " Ουσχι μᾶλλον ἐπενθήσατε': Corporate Responsibility in 1 Corinthians 5," *NTS* 38/3 (1992): 470-73.

1766 L. Ann Jervis, " 'But I Want You to Know . . .': Paul's Midrashic Intertextual Response to the Corinthian Worshipers," *JBL* 112 (1993): 231-46.

1767 John Proctor, "Fire in God's House: Influence of Malachi 3 in the NT," *JETS* 36 (1993): 9-14.

resurrection

1768   John W. Ousley, "Paul's Doctrine of the Resurrection," doctoral dissertation, Southwestern Baptist Theological Seminary, Fort Worth TX, 1948.

1769   William A. Lawson, "Historical and Exegetical Commentary on the Fifteenth Chapter of the First Epistle of Paul to the Corinthians," master's thesis, Midwestern Baptist Theological Seminary, Kansas City KN, 1955.

1770   Chalmer E. Faw, "Death and Resurrection in Paul's Letters," *JBR* 27 (1959): 291-98.

1771   William Dykstra, "1 Corinthians 15:20-28: An Essential Part of Paul's Argument against Those Who Deny the Resurrection," *CTJ* 4/2 (1969): 195-211.

1772   P. Seidemsticker, "The Resurrection Seen from Antioch," *TD* 17 (1969): 104-109.

1773   R. A. Horsley, "How Can Some of You Say That There is No Resurrection of the Dead? Spiritual Elitism in Corinth," *NovT* 20/3 (1978): 203-31.

1774   J. Kremer, "Auferstanded-Auferweckt," *BZ* 23/1 (1979): 97-98.

1775   A. J. M. Wedderburn, "The Problem of the Denial of the Resurrection in 1 Corinthians 15," *NovT* 23/3 (1981): 229-41.

1776   Gerald Borchert, "The Resurrection: 1 Corinthians 15," *RevExp* 80/3 (1983): 401-15.

1777   Robert Sloan, "Resurrection in 1 Corinthians," *SouJT* 26/1 (1983): 69-91.

1778   William L. Craig, "The Historicity of the Empty Tomb of Jesus," *NTS* 31 (1985): 39-67.

1779   Gordon Dalbey, "Does the Resurrection Happen?" *CC* 102 (1985): 319-20.

1780   Stephen T. Davis, "Was Jesus Raised Bodily," *CSR* 14/2 (1985): 140-52.

1781   Gary R. Habermas, "Knowing that Jesus' Resurrection Occurred," *FP* 2/3 (1985): 295-302.

1782   Luis F. Ladaria, "Presente y futuro en la escatología cristiana," *EE* 60 (1985): 351-59.

1783   M. Pamment, "Raised a Spiritual Body. Bodily Resurrection according to Paul," *NBlack* 66 (1985): 372-88.

1784   Vincenz Buchheit, "Resurrectio carnis bei Prudentius," *VC* 40 (1986): 261-85.

1785   Brendan Byrne, "Eschatologies of Resurrection and Destruction: The Ethical Significance of Paul's Dispute with the Corinthians," *DR* 104/357 (1986): 280-98.

1786   Ernst Haag, "Seele und Unsterblichkeit in biblischer Sicht," in Wilhelm Breuning, ed., *Seele: Problembegriff christlicher Eschatologie*. Freiburg: Herder, 1986. Pp. 31-93.

1787   Barnabas Lindars, "Jesus Risen: Bodily Resurrection but no Empty Tomb," *Theology* 89 (1986): 90-96.

1788   M. Mees, "Paulus, Origenes und Methodius über die Auferstehung der Toten," *Aug* 26 (1986): 103-13.

1789   Ben F. Meyer, "Did Paul's View of the Resurrection of the Dead Undergo Development?" *TS* 47 (1986): 363-87.

1790   G. M. M. Pelser, "Resurrection and Eschatology in Paul's Letters," *Neo* 20 (1986): 37-46.

1791   John V. Taylor, "Weep Not for Me: Meditations on the Cross and the Resurrection," *Risk* 27 (1986): 1-46.

1792   R. Trevijano Etcheverria, "Los que dicen que no hay resurrección (1 Cor 15,12)," *Salm* 33 (1986): 275-302.

1793   Gerhard Ebeling, "Des Todes Tod: Luthers Theologie der Konfrontation mit dem Tode," *ZTK* 84/2 (1987): 62-94.

1794   J. N. Vorster, "Resurrection Faith in 1 Corinthians 15," *Neo* 23/2 (1989): 287-307.

1795   Hermann Binder, "Zum geschichtlichen Hintergrund von 1 Kor 15,12," *TZ* 46/3 (1990): 193-201.

1796   Jens Christensen, "And That He Rose on the Third Day according to the Scriptures," *SJOT* 2 (1990): 101-13.

1797   Joël Delobel, "The Fate of the Dead according to 1 Thessalonians 4 and 1 Corinthians 15," in Raymond F. Collins, ed., *The Thessalonian Correspondence.* Louvain: Peeters, 1990. Pp. 340-47.

1798   Jacob Kremer, "Vor allem habe ich euch überliefert ...: bibeltheologische Erwägungen zum unverkürzten Verkünden von Gottes Wort," in J. J. Degenhardt, ed., *Die Freude an Gott - unsere Kraft* (festschrift for Otto B. Knoch). Stuttgart: Verlag Katholisches Bibelwerk, 1991. Pp. 176-82.

1799   Edgar M. Krentz, "Images of the Resurrection in the New Testament," *CTM* 18 (1991): 98-108.

1800   Gerhard Barth, "Zur Frage nach der in 1 Korinther 15 bekämpften Auferstehungsleugnung," *ZNW* 83/3-4 (1992): 187-201.

1801   Normand Bonneau, "The Logic of Paul's Argument on the Resurrection Body in 1 Cor 15:35-44a," *SE* 45 (1993): 79-92.

1802   Uta Heil, "Theologische Interpretation von 1 Kor 15,23-28," *ZNW* 84/1-2 (1993): 27-35.

1803   J. Lambrecht, "Line of Thought in 1 Cor 15,1-11," in *Pauline Studies: Collected Essays.* Louvain: Peeters, 1994. Pp. 109-24.

1804   C. E. Hill, "Paul's Understanding of Christ's Kingdom in 1 Corinthians 15:20-28," *NovT* 30/4 (1988): 297-320.

rhetoric/rhetorical criticism
1805   Kenneth E. Bailey, "Paul's Theological Foundation for Human Sexuality: (1 Cor 6:9-20) in the Light of Rhetorical Criticism," *TRev* 3/1 (1980): 27-41.

1806   Benjamin Fiore, " 'Covert Allusion' in 1 Corinthians 1-4," *CBQ* 47/1 (1985): 85-102.

1807 Jerome Hall, "Paul, the Lawyer, on Law," *JLR* 3/2 (1985): 331-79.

1808 Hans D. Betz, "The Problem of Rhetoric and Theology according to the Apostle Paul," in Albert Vanhoye, ed., *L'Apôtre Paul: personnalité, style et conception du ministre.* Louvain: Peeters, 1986. Pp. 16-48.

1809 C. Forbes, "Comparison, Self-Praise and Irony: Paul's Boasting and the Conventions of Hellenistic Rhetoric," *NTS* 32 (1986): 1-30.

1810 Mark Harding, "The Classical Rhetoric of Praise and the New Testament," *RTR* 45/3 (1986): 73-81.

1811 Andries H. Andries, "Remarks on the Stylistic Parallelisms in 1 Cor," in K. J. H. Petzer and Patrick Hartin, eds., *A South African Perspective on New Testament* (festschrift for Bruce Metgzer). Leiden: Brill, 1986. Pp. 202-13.

1812 Benoît Standaert, "La rhétorique ancienne dans saint Paul," in Albert Vanhoye, ed., *L'Apôtre Paul: personnalité, style et conception du ministre.* Louvain: Peeters, 1986. Pp. 78-92.

1813 Timothy H. Lim, "Not in Persuasive Words of Wisdom but in the Demonstration of the Spirit and Power," *NovT* 29/2 (1987): 137-49.

1814 Wilhelm Wuellner, "Where Is Rhetorical Criticism Taking Us?" *CBQ* 49 (1987): 448-63.

1815 J. Reiling, "Wisdom and the Spirit: An Exegesis of 1 Corinthians 2,6-16," in Tjitze Baarda, ed., *Text and Testimony: Essays on New Testament and Apocryphal Literature* (festschrift for A. F. J. Klijn). Kampen: Kok, 1988. Pp. 200-11.

1816 Duane F. Watson, "1 Corinthians 10:23-11:1 in the Light of Greco-Roman Rhetoric," *JBL* 108/2 (1989): 301-18.

1817 Carl R. Holladay, "1 Corinthians 13: Paul as Apostolic Paradigm," in David L. Balch, et al., eds., *Greeks, Romans, and Christians* (festschrift for Abraham J. Malherbe). Minneapolis: Fortress Press, 1990. Pp. 80-98.

1818   Peter Lampe, "Theological Wisdom and the 'Word about the Cross': The Rhetorical Scheme in 1 Corinthians 1-4," *Int* 44 (1990): 117-31.

1819   J. Smit, "The Genre of 1 Corinthians 13 in the Light of Classical Rhetoric," *NovT* 33/3 (1991): 193-216.

1820   Barth Campbell, "Flesh and Spirit in 1 Cor 5:5: An Exercise in Rhetorical Criticism of the New Testament," *JETS* 36 (1993): 331-42.

1821   M. M. Mitchell, *Paul and the Rhetoric of Reconciliation: An Exegetical Investigation of the Language and Composition of 1 Corinthians*. Louisville KY: Westminster/Knox, 1993.

1822   J. Smit, "Argument and Genre of 1 Corinthians 12-14," in Stanley E. Porter and Thomas H. Olbricht, eds., *Rhetoric and the New Testament: Essays from the 1992 Heidelberg Conference*. Sheffield: JSOT Press, 1993. Pp. 211-30.

1823   J. Smit, "Two Puzzles: 1 Corinthians 12:31 and 13:3: A Rhetorical Solution," *NTS* 39 (1993): 246-64.

1824   J. S. Vos, "Das Rätsel von 1 Kor 12:1-3," *NovT* 35 (1993): 251-69.

1825   Duane F. Watson, "Paul's Rhetorical Strategy in 1 Corinthians 15," in Stanley E. Porter and Thomas H. Olbricht, eds., *Rhetoric and the New Testament: Essays from the 1992 Heidelberg Conference*. Sheffield: JSOT Press, 1993. Pp. 231-49.

1826   D. Littin, *St. Paul's Theology of Proclarnation: 1 Corinthians 14 and Greco-Roman Rhetoric*. SNTSMS #79. Cambridge: University Press, 1994.

1827   J. G. Sigountos, "The Genre of 1 Connthians 13," *NTS* 40 (1994): 246-60.

righteousness
1828   Ulrich Luck, "Die Bekehrung des Paulus und das paulinische Evangelium: zur Frage der Evidenz in Botschaft und Theologie des Apostels," *ZNW* 76/3-4 (1985): 187-208.

1829   Robert J. Karris, "Pauline Literature," in John J. Collins and John Dominic Crossan, eds., *The Biblical Heritage in Modern Catholic Scholarship*. Wilmington: Glazier, 1986. Pp. 156-83.

1830   Otto Betz, "Der gekreuzigte Christus: Unsere Weisheit und Gerechtigkeit (der alttestamentliche Hintergrund von 1 Kor 1-2)," in Gerald F. Hawthorne and Otto Betz, eds., *Tradition and Interpretation in the New Testament* (festschrift for E. Earle Ellis). Grand Rapids: Eerdmans, 1987. Pp. 195-215.

sanctification

1831   Dale Clark, "Interpretation of the Pauline Concept of Sanctification in the Corinthian Correspondence," master's thesis, Southwestern Baptist Theological Seminary, Fort Worth TX, 1963.

1832   A. W. Pink, "The Doctrine of Sanctification," *BRR* 8/3 (1979): 5-11.

1833   Morna D. Hooker, "Interchange in Christ and Ethics," *JSNT* 25 (1985): 3-17.

1834   Donald Gee, "The Gifts and Fruit of the Spirit," *Para* 21 (1987): 21-26.

second Adam

1835   Egon Brandenburger, "Alter und neuer Mensch, erster und letzter Adam-Anthropos," in Walter Strolz, ed., *Vom alten zum neuen Adam*. Freiburg: Herder, 1986. Pp. 182-223.

sex

1836   M. L. Barré, "To Marry or to Burn: Purousthai in 1 Cor. 7:9," *CBQ* 36/2 (1974): 193-202.

1837   C. W. Brister, "The Ministry in 1 Corinthians," *SouJT* 26/1 (1983): 18-31.

1838   Paul D. Feinberg, "Homosexuality and the Bible," *FundJ* 4/3 (1985): 17-19.

1839   Randolph A. Nelson, "Homosexuality and Social Ethics," *WW* 5 (1985): 380-94.

1840   L. M. Russell, "Inclusive Language and Power," *REd* 80 (1985): 582-602.

1841   Terrance Callan, "Toward a Psychological Interpretation of Paul's Sexual Ethic," *EGLMBS* 6 (1986): 57-71.

1842   Richard B. Hays, "Relations Natural and Unnatural," *JREth* 14 (1986): 184-215.

1843   David Peterson, "The Ordination of Women: Balancing the Scriptural Evidence," *SMR* 125 (1986): 13-21.

1844   Timothy Radcliffe, " 'Glorify God in Your Bodies': 1 Corinthians 6:12-20 as a Sexual Ethic," *NBlack* 67 (1986): 306-14.

1845   Roy B. Ward, "Porneia and Paul," *EGLMBS* 6 (1986): 219-28.

1846   Angela West, "Sex and Salvation: A Christian Feminist Study of 1 Corinthians 6:12-7:39," *MC* 29/3 (1987): 17-24.

1847   Piet Farla, "The Two Shall Become One Flesh: Gen 1.27 and 2.24 in the New Testament Marriage Texts," trans. Richard Rosser in Sipke Draisma, ed., *Intertextuality in Biblical Writings* (festschrift for Bas van Iersel). Kampen: Kok, 1989. Pp. 67-82.

1848   W. E. Glenny, "1 Corinthians 7:29-31 and the Teaching of Continence in *The Acts of Paul and Thecla*," *GTJ* 11/1 (1990): 53-70.

1849   Bruce N. Kaye, "One Flesh and Marriage," *CANZTR* 22 (1990): 46-57.

1850   R. Trevijano Etchevrria, "A propósito del incestuoso (1 Cor 5-6)," *Salm* 38/2 (1991): 129-53.

1851   J.-J. Fauconnet, "La morale sexuelle chez Saint Paul: Analyse et commentaire de 1 Cor 6,12 à 7,40," *BullLittEccl* 93/4 (1992): 359-78.

sin

1852   I. L. Grohar, "El 'mundo' en los escritos juanicos: un ensayo de interpretación," *RevB* 47 (1985): 221-27.

1853   R. H. Allaway, "Fall or Fall-Short," *ET* 97 (1986): 108-10.

1854   Stanley E. Porter, "The Pauline Concept of Original Sin in Light of Rabbinic Background," *TynB* 41 (1990): 3-30.

slavery
1855   A. Callahan, "A Note on 1 Corinthians 7:21," *JITC* 17 (1989-1990): 110-14.

1856   Gregory W. Dawes, "But If You Can Gain Your Freedom (1 Corinthians 7:17-24)," *CBQ* 52 (1990): 681-97.

1857   L. Boston, "A Womanist Reflection on 1 Corinthians 7:21-24 and 1 Corinthians 14:33-35," *JWR* 9-10 (1990-1991): 81-89.

sociology
1858   Agustín del Agua Perez, "El papel de la 'escuela midrásica' en la configuración del Nuevo Testamento," *EB* 60 (1985): 333-49.

1859   J. D. G. Dunn, "Works of the Law and the Curse of the Law," *NTS* 31 (1985): 523-42.

1860   D. Sänger, "Die δυνατοι in 1 Kor 1:26," *ZNW* 76 (1985): 285-91.

1861   Jean-Noël Aletti, "L'autorité apostolique de Paul: théorie et pratique," in Albert Vanhoye, ed., *L'Apôtre Paul: personnalité, style et conception du ministre.* Louvain: Peeters, 1986. Pp. 229-46.

1862   Stephen C. Barton, "Paul's Sense of Place: An Anthropological Approach to Community Formation in Corinth," *NTS* 32/2 (1986): 225-46.

1863   Marlis Gielen, "Zur Interpretation der paulinischen Formel He kat' oikon ekklesia," *ZNW* 77 (1986): 109-25.

1864   Richard Oster, "When Men Wore Veils to Worship: The Historical Context of 1 Corinthians 11:4," *NTS* 34/4 (1988): 481-505.

1865   G. Harris, "The Beginnings of Church Discipline: 1 Corinthians 5," *NTS* 37/1 (1991): 1-21.

1866 Alan C. Mitchell, "Rich and Poor in the Courts of Corinth: Litigiousness and Status in 1 Corinthians 6:1-11," *NTS* 39 (1993): 562-86.

soteriology

1867 F. S. Parnham, "What Is the Christians' Expectation?" *EQ* 41/2 (1969): 113-15.

1868 Darrell Doughty, "The Presence and Future of Salvation in Corinth," *ZNW* 66/1-2 (1975): 61-90.

1869 Vincent P. Branick, "Apocalyptic Paul?" *CBQ* 47 (1985): 664-75.

1870 I. L. Grohar, "El 'mundo' en los escritos juanicos: un ensayo de interpretación," *RevB* 47 (1985): 221-27.

1871 Walter Kasper, "The Unity and Multiplicity of Aspects in the Eucharist," *CICR* 12 (1985): 115-38.

1872 François Refoulé, "Note sur Romains 9:30-33," *RB* 92 (1985): 161-86.

1873 Pasquale Colella, "Cristo nostra pasqua? 1 Cor 5:7," *BibO* 28 (1986): 197-217.

1874 Gerhard Ebeling, "Des Todes Tod: Luthers Theologie der Konfrontation mit dem Tode," *ZTK* 84/2 (1987): 62-94.

1875 J. K. Grider, "Predestination as Temporal only," *WTJ* 22 (1987): 56-64.

1876 J. R. Busto Saiz, "Se salvará como atravesando fuego? 1 Cor 3:15b reconsiderado," *EE* 68 (1993): 333-38.

soul

1877 Vincenz Buchheit, "Resurrectio carnis bei Prudentius," *VC* 40 (1986): 261-85.

1878 Ernst Haag, "Seele und Unsterblichkeit in biblischer Sicht," in Wilhelm Breuning, ed., *Seele: Problembegriff christlicher Eschatologie.* Freiburg: Herder, 1986. Pp. 31-93.

1879 James Benedict, "The Corinthian Problem of 1 Corinthians 5:1-8," *BLT* 32 (1987): 70-73.

1880 Jeanie Watson, "Seeing through the Glass: From Secular to Sacred Story," *ChrLit* 37/1 (1987): 45-53.

1881 N. George Joy, "Is the Body Really to be Destroyed?" *BT* 39/4 (1988): 429-36.

1882 Barth Campbell, "Flesh and Spirit in 1 Cor 5:5: An Exercise in Rhetorical Criticism of the New Testament," *JETS* 36 (1993): 331-42.

source criticism

1883 Vincent P. Branick, "Source and Redaction Analysis of 1 Corinthians 1-3," *JBL* 101/2 (1982): 251-69.

spirit

1884 E.-B. Allo, "Sagesse et Pneuma dans 1 Cor.," *RB* 43 (1934): 321-46.

1885 E. Earle Ellis, "Christ and Spirit in 1 Corinthians," *Prophecy and Hermeneutic in Early Christianity*. WUNT. Tübingen: Mohr, 1978. Pp. 63-71.

1886 J. Reiling, "Wisdom and the Spirit: An Exegesis of 1 Corinthians 2,6-16," in Tjitze Baarda, ed., *Text and Testimony: Essays on New Testament and Apocryphal Literature* (festschrift for A. F. J. Klijn). Kampen: Kok, 1988. Pp. 200-11.

1887 Justin S. Upkong, "Pluralism and the Problem of the Discernment of Spirits," *EcumRev* 41 (1989): 416-25.

1888 N. Nagel, "The Spirit's Gifts in the Confessions and in Corinth," *CJ* 18/3 (1992): 230-43.

spiritual gifts

1889 Robert H. Gundry, "Ecstatic Utterance (N.E.B.)?" *JTS* 17/2 (1966): 299-307.

1890 Stephen S. Smalley, "Spiritual Gifts and 1 Corinthians 12-16," *JBL* 87/4 (1968): 417-33.

1891 Walter J. Bartling, "The Congregation of Christ: A Charismatic Body: An Exegetical Study of 1 Corinthians 12," *CTM* 40/2 (1969): 68-80.

1892 Howard M. Ervin, "As The Spirit Gives Utterance," *CT* 13/14 (1969): 623-26.

1893 Stuart Fowler, "The Continuance of the Charismata," *EQ* 45/3 (1973): 172-83.

1894 David L. Baker, "The Interpretation of 1 Corinthians 12-14," *EQ* 46/4 (1974): 224-34.

1895 E. Earle Ellis, "Spiritual Gifts in the Pauline Community," *NTS* 20/2 (1974): 128-44.

1896 D. Moody Smith, "Glossolalia and Other Spiritual Gifts in a New Testament Perspective," *Int* 28/3 (1974): 307-20.

1897 James Davison, "The Spirit and Spiritual Gifts in the Apostolic Fathers," doctoral dissertation, University of Iowa, Iowa City IA 1981.

1898 Bert Dominy, "Paul and Spiritual Gifts: Reflections on 1 Corinthians 12-14," *SouJT* 26/1 (1983): 49-68.

1899 Andre Mehat, "L'Enseignement sur 'Les Choses de L'Esprit'," *RHPR* 63/4 (1983): 395-415.

1900 Charles H. Talbert, "Paul's Understanding of the Holy Spirit: The Evidence of 1 Corinthians 12-14," *PRS* 11/4 (1984): 95-108.

1901 Daniel J. Harrington, "Charism And Ministry: The Case of the Apostle Paul," *CS* 24/3 (1985): 245-57.

1902 Norbert Baumert, "Charisma und Amt bei Paulus," in Albert Vanhoye, ed., *L'Apôtre Paul: personnalité, style et conception du ministre*. Louvain: Peeters, 1986. Pp. 203-28.

1903 Dennis Ormseth, "Showing the Body: Reflections on 1 Corinthians 12-13 for Epiphany," *WW* 6 (1986): 97-103.

1904 Ronald Y. K. Fung, "Ministry in the New Testament," in Don A Carson, ed., *The Church in the Bible and the World.* Exeter: Paternoster Press, 1987. Pp. 154-212.

1905 Donald Gee, "The Gifts and Fruit of the Spirit," *Para* 21 (1987): 21-26.

1906 M. G. A. Haken, " 'A Sense of Awe in the Presence of the Ineffable:' 1 Cor. 2:11-12 in the Pneumatomachian Controversy of the Fourth Century," *SJT* 41/3 (1988): 341-57.

1907 Thomas A. Jackson, "Concerning Spiritual Gifts: A Study of 1 Corinthians 12," *FM* 7/1 (1989): 61-69.

1908 Andrew G. Hadden, "Gifts of the Spirit in Assemblies of God Writings," *Para* 24 (1990): 20-32.

1909 Randy Tate, "Christian Childishness and 'That Which is Perfect'," *Para* 24/1 (1990): 11-15.

1910 John J. Kilgallen, "Reflections on Charisma(ta) in the New Testament," *SM* 41 (1992): 289-323.

1911 David S. Lim, "Many Gifts, One Spirit," *Para* 26 (1992): 3-7.

1912 W. C. van Unnik, "The Meaning of 1 Corinthians 12:31," *NovT* 35 (1993): 142-59.

1913 J. S. Vos, "Das Rätsel von 1 Kor 12:1-3," *NovT* 35 (1993): 251-69.

1914 Arnold B. Lovell, "1 Corinthians 13," *Int* 48 (1994): 176-80.

1915 N. J. McEleney, "Gifts Serving Christ's Body," *BibTo* 33 (1995) 134-37.

syntax

1916 Juan Mateos, "Analisis de un campo lexematico: eulogia en el Nuevo Testamento," *FilN* 1 (1988): 5-25.

Temple

1917 Douglas R. de Lacey, "ohitines este Hymeis: The Function of a Metaphor in St. Paul," in William Horbury, ed., *Templum*

Amicitiae: Essays on the Second Temple (festschrift for Ernst Bammel). Sheffield: JSOT Press, 1991. Pp. 391-409

1918   K. Romaniuk, "... wie ein guter Baumeister ...." in J. J. Degenhardt, ed., *Die Freude an Gott - unsere Kraft* (festschrift for Otto B. Knoch). Stuttgart: Verlag Katholisches Bibelwerk, 1991. Pp. 164-69.

temptations
1919   D. M. Ciocchi, "Understanding Our Ability to Endure Temptation: A Theological Watershed," *JETS* 35/4 (1992): 463-79.

Testament of the Twelve Patriarchs
1920   Brian S. Rosner, "A Possible Quotation of Test. Reuben 5:5 in 1 Corinthians 6:18a," *JTS* 43/1 (1992): 123-27.

textual criticism
1921   Harold S. Murphy, "The Text of Romans and 1 Corinthians in Miniscule 93 and the Text of Pamphilius," *HTR* 52 (1958): 119-31.

1922   A. Penna, "La δυναμις θεου: reflessioni in margine a 1 Cor. 1:18-25," *RBib* 15 (1967): 281-94.

1923   E. G. Edwards, "On Using the Textual Apparatus of the UBS Greek New Testament," *BT* 28/1 (1977): 121-42.

1924   Roger L. Omanson, "Translations: Text and Interpretation," *EQ* 57 (1985): 195-210.

1925   Jerome Murphy-O'Connor, "Interpolations in 1 Corinthians," *CBQ* 48 (1986): 81-94.

1926   Gordon D. Fee, "Textual-Exegetical Observations on 1 Corinthians 1:2, 2:1, and 2:10," in David A. Black, ed., *Scribes and Scripture* (festschrift for J. Harold Greenlee). Winona Lake INL Eisenbrauns, 1993. Pp. 1-15

1927   J. H. Petzer, "Reconsidering the Silent Women of Corinth—A Note on 1 Corinthians 14:34-35," *ThEv* 26 (1993): 132-38.

1928   J. Smit, "Two Puzzles: 1 Corinthians 12:31 and 13:3: A Rhetorical Solution," *NTS* 39 (1993): 246-64.

tongues, speaking in

1929 Nat Tracy, "Speaking in Tongues," doctoral dissertation, New Orleans Baptist Theological Seminary, New Orleans LA, 1936.

1930 S. Lewis Johnson, "The Gift of Tongues and the Book of Acts," *BSac* 120 (1963): 309-11.

1931 Stanley D. Toussaint, "First Corinthians Thirteen and the Tongues Question," *BSac* 120 (1963): 311-16.

1932 Watson E. Mills, "A Theological Interpretation of Tongues in Acts and 1 Corinthians," doctoral dissertation, Southern Baptist Theological Seminary, Louisville KY, 1968.

1933 J. M. Ford, "Toward a Theology of 'Speaking in Tongues'," *TS* 32/1 (1971): 3-29.

1934 Gilbert B. Weaver, "Tongues Shall Cease," *GTJ* 14/1 (1973): 12-24.

1935 D. Moody Smith, "Glossolalia and Other Spiritual Gifts in a New Testament Perspective," *Int* 28/3 (1974): 307-20.

1936 Robert L. Thomas, " 'Tongues. . . Will Cease'," *JETS* 17/2 (1974): 81-89.

1937 Francis A. Sullivan, "Speaking In Tongues," *LV* 31/2 (1976): 145-70.

1938 Vern S. Poythress, "The Nature of Corinthian Glossolalia: Possible Options," *WTJ* 40/1 (1977): 130-35.

1939 A. C. Thiselton, "The Interpretation of Tongues: A New Suggestion in the Light of Greek Usage in Philo and Josephus," *JTS* 30/1 (1979): 15-36.

1940 H. Wayne House, "Tongues and the Mystery Religions of Corinth," *BSac* 140 (1983): 134-50.

1941 Charles H. Talbert, "Paul's Understanding of the Holy Spirit: The Evidence of 1 Corinthians 12-14," *PRS* 11/4 (1984): 95-108.

1942 G. L. Lasebikan, "Glossolalia: Its Relationship with Speech Disabilities and Personality Disorders," *AfTJ* 14/2 (1985): 111-20.

1943 W. E. Richardson, "Liturgical Order and Glossolalia: 1 Corinthians 14:26c-33a and Its Implications," *AUSS* 24 (1986): 47-48.

1944 John F. Walvoord, "The Holy Spirit and Spiritual Gifts," *BSac* 143 (1986): 109-22.

1945 R. K. Levang, "The Content of an Utterance in Tongues," *Para* 23/1 (1989): 14-20.

1946 D. E. Lanier, "With Stammering Lips and Another Tongue: 1 Cor 14:20-22 and Isa 28:11-12," *CTR* 5/2 (1991): 259-85.

1947 G. D. Fee, "Toward a Pauline Theology of Glossolalia," *Crux* 31 (1995): 22-23; 26-31.

torah

1948 Andreas Lindemann, "Die biblischen Toragebote und die paulinische Ethik," in Wolfgand Schrage *Studien zum Text und zur Ethik des Neuen Testaments* (festschrift for Heinrich Greeven). Berlin: de Gruyter, 1986. Pp. 242-65.

tradition criticism

1949 E. Earle Ellis, "Traditions in 1 Corinthians," *NTS* 32/4 (1986): 481-502.

1950 Beimund Bieringer, "Traditionsgeschichtlicher Ursprung und theologische Bedeutung der Hyper Aussagen im Neuen Testament," in Frans van Segbroeck, et al., eds.. *The Four Gospels 1992* (festschrift for Frans Neirynck). 2 vols. Louvain: Peeters, 1992. 1:219-48.

typology

1951 Larry Kreitzer, "Adam as Analogy: Help or Hindrance?" *KingsTR* 11 (1988): 59-62.

1952 Ingo Broer, "Darum: Wer da meint zu stehen, der sehe zu, dass er nicht falle: 1 Kor 10,12f im Kontext von 1 Kor 10,1-13," in Helmut Merklein, ed., *Neues Testament und Ethik* (festschrift for Rudolf Schnackenburg). Freiburg: Herder, 1989. Pp. 299-325.

1953   Giuseppe Barbaglio, "E tutti in Mosè sono stati battezzati nella nube e nel mare," in Pius Tragan, ed., *Alle origini del battesimo cristiano*. Rome: Pontificio Ateneo St. Anselmo, 1991. Pp. 167-91.

wealth

1954   William R. Herzog, "The New Testament and the Question of Racial Injustice," *ABQ* 5 (1986): 12-32.

wisdom

1955   William Baird, "Among the Mature: The Idea of Wisdom in 1 Corinthians 2:6," *Int* 13 (1959): 425-32.

1956   A. George, "Sagesse du Monde et Sagesse de Dieu," *BVC* 38 (1961): 16-24.

1957   M. M. Bourke, "The Eucharist and Wisdom in First Corinthians," in *Studiorum Paulinorum Congressus, 1961*. 2 vols. Rome: Pontifical Biblical Institute, 1963. 1:367-81.

1958   Earle McMillan, "An Aspect of Recent Wisdom Studies in the New Testament," *RQ* 10/4 (1967): 201-10.

1959   E. Earle Ellis, " 'Wisdom' and 'Knowledge' in 1 Corinthians," *TynB* 25 (1974): 82-98.

1960   R. A. Horsley, "Wisdom of Word and Words of Wisdom in Corinth," *CBQ* 39/2 (1977): 224-39.

1961   James M. Reese, "Paul Proclaims the Wisdom of the Cross: Scandal and Foolishness," *BTB* 9/4 (1979) 147-53.

1962   James M. Reese, "Christ as Wisdom Incarnate: Wiser than Solomon, Loftier than Lady Wisdom," *BTB* 11/2 (1980): 44-47.

1963   James L. Blevins, ""Wisdom" in Paul's Writings," *BI* 8/2 (1982): 15-17.

1964   Harry W. Lewis, "An Exegetical Study of the Pauline Concept of Sophia in 1 Corinthians," doctoral dissertation, Southwestern Baptist Theological Seminary, Fort Worth TX, 1982.

1965   Gerhard Sellin, "Das 'Beheimnis' der Weisheit und das Ratsel der 'Christtuspartei'," *ZNW* 73/1-2 (1982): 69-96.

1966 Gail P. Corrington, "Paul and the Two Wisdoms: 1 Corinthians 1:18-31 and the Hellenistic Mission," *EGLMBS* 6 (1986): 72-84.

1967 Eileen Kearney, "Scientia and Sapientia: Reading Sacred Scriptures at the Paraclete," in E. R. Elder, ed., *From Cloister to Classroom: Monastic and Scholastic Approaches to Truth.* Kalamazoo MI: Cistercian Publicatians, 1986. Pp. 111-29.

1968 Alan Padgett, "Feminism in First Corinthians: A Dialogue with Elisabeth Schüssler Fiorenza," *EQ* 58/2 (1986): 121-32.

1969 Otto Betz, "Der gekreuzigte Christus: Unsere Weisheit und Gerechtigkeit (der alttestamentliche Hintergrund von 1 Kor 1-2)," in Gerald F. Hawthorne and Otto Betz, eds., *Tradition and Interpretation in the New Testament* (festschrift for E. Earle Ellis). Grand Rapids: Eerdmans, 1987. Pp. 195-215.

1970 Peter Stuhlmacher, "The Hermeneutical Significance of 1 Cor 2:6-16," in Gerald F. Hawthorne and Otto Betz, eds., *Tradition and Interpretation in the New Testament* (festschrift for E. Earle Ellis). Grand Rapids: Eerdmans, 1987. Pp. 328-47.

1971 Settimio Ciproani, "Sapientia crucis e sapienza "umana" in Paolo," *RBib* 36 (1988): 343-61.

1972 J. Reiling, "Wisdom and the Spirit: An Exegesis of 1 Corinthians 2,6-16," in Tjitze Baarda, ed., *Text and Testimony: Essays on New Testament and Apocryphal Literature* (festschrift for A. F. J. Klijn). Kampen: Kok, 1988. Pp. 200-11.

1973 Ronald Byars, "Sectarian Division and the Wisdom of the Cross: Preaching from First Corinthians," *QR* 9/4 (1989): 65-97.

1974 Victor P. Furnish, "Theology in 1 Corinthians: Initial Soundings," *SBLSP* 28 (1989): 246-64.

1975 E. Elizabeth Johnson, "The wisdom of God as Apocalyptic Power," in John T. Carroll, et al., eds., *Faith and History* (festschrift for Paul W. Meyer). Atlanta: Scholars Press, 1990. Pp. 137-48.

1976 Peter Lampe, "Theological Wisdom and the 'Word about the Cross': The Rhetorical Scheme in 1 Corinthians 1-4," *Int* 44 (1990): 117-31.

1977 Stanley K. Stanley, "Paul on the Use and Abuse of Reason," in David L. Balch, et al., eds., *Greeks, Romans, and Christians* (festschrift for Abraham J. Malherbe). Minneapolis: Fortress Press, 1990. Pp. 253-86.

1978 Michael D. Goulder, "Σόφια in 1 Corinthians," *NTS* 37/4 (1991): 516-34.

1979 C. M. Tuckett, "Jewish Christian Wisdom in 1 Corinthians?" in S. E. Porter, et al., eds., *Crossing the Boundaries: Essays in Biblical Interpretation* (festschrift for Michael Goulder). Leiden: Brill, 1994. Pp. 219-24.

1980 J. D. G. Dunn, "In Search of Widsom," *EpRev* 22 (1995): 48-53.

women

1981 C. V. Beyler, "Meaning and Relevance of the Devotional Covering: A Study in the Interpretation of 1 Corinthians 11:2-16," master's thesis, Southern Baptist Theological Seminary, Louisville KY, 1954.

1982 Raymond T. Stamm, "The Status of Women Workers in the Church," *LQ* 10 (1958): 139-60.

1983 G. G. Blum, "Das Amt der Frau im Neuen Testament," *NovT* 7 (1964): 142-61.

1984 Madeleine Boucher, "Some Unexplored Parallels to 1 Corinthians 11:11-12 and Gal. 3:28: The NT on the Role of Women," *CBQ* 31/1 (1969): 50-58.

1985 Calvin Miller, "St. Paul and the Liberated Woman," *CT* 12/22 (1971): 999-1000.

1986 G. B. Caird, "Paul and Woman's Liberty," *BJRL* 54/2 (1972): 268-81.

1987 Noel Weeks, "Of Silence and Head Covering," *WTJ* 35/1 (1972): 21-27.

1988 A. Feuillet, "Le Signe de Puissance sur la Tête de la Femme: 1 Co 11, 10," *NRT* 95/9 (1973): 945-54.

1989 James B. Hurley, "Did Paul Require Veils or the Silence of Women? A Consideration of 1 Corinthians 11:2-16 and 1 Corinthians 14:33b-36," *WTJ* 35/2 (1973): 190-202.

1990 Elaine H. Pagels, "Paul and Women: A Response to Recent Discussion," *JAAR* 42/3 (1974): 538-49.

1991 William O. Walker, "1 Corinthians 11:2-16 and Paul's Views Regarding Women," *JBL* 94/1 (1975): 94-110.

1992 Neil R. Lightfoot, "The Role of Women in Religious Services," *RQ* 19/3 (1976): 129-36.

1993 Cindy Weber-Han, "Sexual Equality according to Paul: An Exegetical Study of 1 Corinthians 11:1-16 and Ephesians 5:21-33," *BLT* 22/3 (1977): 167-70.

1994 Gillian Clark, "The Women at Corinth," *Theology* 85 (1982): 256-62.

1995 James F. Bound, "Who Are The "Virgins" Discussed in 1 Corinthians 7:25-35?" *EvJ* 2/1 (1984): 3-15.

1996 Alan Padgett, "Paul on Women in the Church: The Contradictions of Coiffure in 1 Corinthians 11:2-16," *JSNT* 20 (1984): 69-86.

1997 Charles H. Talbert, "Paul's Understanding of the Holy Spirit: The Evidence of 1 Corinthians 12-14," *PRS* 11/4 (1984): 95-108.

1998 J. J. Buckley, "An Interpretation of Logion 114 in The Gospel of Thomas," *NovT* 27 (1985): 245-72.

1999 Jos Janssens, "Il cristiano di fronte al martirio imminente: testimonianze e dottrina nella chiesa antica," *Greg* 66/3 (1985): 405-27.

2000 Leonidas Kalugila, "Women in the Ministry of Priesthood in the Early Church: An Inquiry," *AfTJ* 14/1 (1985): 35-45.

2001 Pui Lan Kwok, "The Feminist Hermeneutics of Elisabeth Schüssler Fiorenza: An Asian Feminist Response," *EAJT* 3/2 (1985): 147-53.

2002 Jean Marc Laporte, "Kenosis and Koinonia: The Path Ahead for Anglican-Roman Catholic Dialogue," *OC* 21/2 (1985): 102-20.

2003 W. C. Linss, "St Paul and Women," *Dia* 24 (1985): 36-40.

2004 L. M. Russell, "Inclusive Language and Power," *REd* 80 (1985): 582-602.

2005 W. Stephen Sabom, "The Gnostic World of Anorexia Nervosa," *JPT* 13 (1985): 243-54.

2006 Lyle Vander Broek, "Women and the Church: Approaching Difficult Passages," *RR* 38 (1985): 225-31.

2007 Stephen C. Barton, "Paul's Sense of Place: An Anthropological Approach to Community Formation in Corinth," *NTS* 32/2 (1986): 225-46.

2008 Joël Delobel, "1 Cor 11,2-16: Towards a Coherent Interpretation," in Albert Vanhoye, ed., *L'Apôtre Paul: personnalité, style et conception du ministre*. Louvain: Peeters, 1986. Pp. 369-89.

2009 Paul S. Fiddes, "Woman's Head Is Man: A Doctrinal Reflection upon a Pauline Text," *BQ* 31 (1986): 370-83.

2010 Robert J. Karris, "Pauline Literature," in John J. Collins and John Dominic Crossan, eds., *The Biblical Heritage in Modern Catholic Scholarship*. Wilmington: Glazier, 1986. Pp. 156-83.

2011 Walter L. Liefeld, "Women, Submission and Ministry in 1 Corinthians," in Alvera Mickelsen, ed., *Women, Authority and the Bible*. Downers Grove IL: InterVarsity Press, 1986. Pp. 134-54.

2012 David K. Lowery, "The Head Covering and the Lord's Supper in 1 Corinthians 11:2-34," *BSac* 143 (1986): 155-63.

2013 Alan Padgett, "Feminism in First Corinthians: A Dialogue with Elisabeth Schüssler Fiorenza," *EQ* 58/2 (1986): 121-32.

2014 David Peterson, "The Ordination of Women: Balancing the Scriptural Evidence," *SMR* 125 (1986): 13-21.

2015 A. C. Wire, "Theological and Biblical Perspective: Liberation for Women Calls for a Liberated World," *ChS* 76 (1986): 7-17.

2016 David W. Odell-Scott, "In Defense of An Egalitarian Interpretation of 1 Cor 14:34-36," *BTB* 17 (1987): 100-103.

2017 David M. Scholer, "Feminist Hermeneutics and Evangelical Biblical Interpretation," *JETS* 30 (1987): 407-20.

2018 Thomas P. Shoemaker, "Unveiling of Equality: 1 Corinthians 11:2-16," *BTB* 17/2 (1987): 60-63.

2019 Charles H. Talbert, "Biblical Criticism's Role: The Pauline View of Women as a Case in Point," in Robison B. James, ed., *The Unfettered Word*. Waco TX: Word Books, 1987. Pp. 62-71.

2020 Angela West, "Sex and Salvation: A Christian Feminist Study of 1 Corinthians 6:12-7:39," *MC* 29/3 (1987): 17-24.

2021 Mary Rose D'Angelo, "The Garden: Once and not Again: Traditional Interpretations of Genesis 1:26-27 in 1 Corinthians 11:7-12," in G. A. Robbins, ed., *Genesis 1-3 in the History of Exegesis*. Lewiston NY: Mellen, 1988. Pp. 1-41.

2022 Ron Johnson, "The Theology of Gender," *JPsyC* 7 (1988): 39-49.

2023 Winsome Munro, "Women, Text and the Canon: The Strange Case of 1 Corinthians 14:35," *BTB* 18/1 (1988): 26-31.

2024 Linda M. Bridges, "Silencing the Corinthian Men, not the Women," in Anne Neil and Virginia Neely, eds., *The New Has Come*. Washington: Southern Baptist Alliance, 1989. Pp. 40-50.

2025 Susan A. Ross, "Then Honor God in Your Body: Feminist and Sacramental Theology on the Body," *Horizons* 16/1 (1989): 7-27.

2026 T. J. van Bavel, "Women as the Image of God in Augustine's De trinitate XII," in *Signum pietatis* (festschrift for Cornelius P. Mayer). Würzburg: Augustinus-Verlag, 1989. Pp. 267-88.

2027 W. E. Glenny, "1 Corinthians 7:29-31 and the Teaching of Continence in *The Acts of Paul and Thecla*," *GTJ* 11/1 (1990): 53-70.

2028 Wayne Grudem, "The Meaning of Kephale ('head'): A Response to Recent Studies," *TriJ* 11 (1990): 3-72.

2029 Margaret Y. MacDonald, "Women Holy in Body and Spirit: The Social Setting of 1 Corinthians 7," *NTS* 36/2 (1990): 161-81.

2030 Timothy Radcliffe, "Paul and Sexual Identity: 1 Corinthians 11:2-16," in J. M. Soskice, ed., *After Eve*. Basingstoke: Marshal Pickering, 1990. Pp. 62-72.

2031 A. Rowe, "Silence and the Christian Women of Corinth. An Examination of 1 Corinthians 14:33b-36," *CVia* 33/1-2 (1990): 41-84.

2032 L. Boston, "A Womanist Reflection on 1 Corinthians 7:21-24 and 1 Corinthians 14:33-35," *JWR* 9-10 (1990-1991): 81-89.

2033 Christine Amjad-Ali, "The Equality of Women: Form or Substance," in R. S. Sugirtharajah, ed., *Voices from the Margin: Interpreting the Bible in the Third World*. Maryknoll NY: Orbis, 1991. Pp. 205-13.

2034 Kari E. Borresen, "God's Image, Is Woman Excluded? Medieval Interpretation of Gen 1:27 and 1 Cor 11:7," in Karl E. Borresen, ed., *Image of God and Gender Models*. Oslo: Solum Forlag, 1991. Pp. 208-27.

2035 Donald A. Donald, "Silent in the Churches: On the Role of Women in 1 Corinthians 14:33b-36," in John Piper and Wayne Grudem, eds., *Recovering Biblical Manhood and Womanhood*. Wheaton IL: Crossway Books, 1991. Pp. 140-53, 487-90.

2036 Gail P. Corrington, "The 'Headless Woman': Paul and the Language of the Body in 1 Cor 11:2-16," *PRS* 18/3 (1991): 223-31.

2037 Lone Fatum, "Image of God and Glory of Man: Women in the Pauline Congregations," in Karl E. Borresen, ed., *Image of God and Gender Models*. Oslo: Solum Forlag, 1991. Pp. 56-137.

2038 M. Navarro Puerto, "La παρθενος: Un futuro significativo en el aquí y ahora de la comunidad (1 Cor 7,25-38)," *EB* 49/3 (1991): 353-87.

2039 A. Rowe, "Hermeneutics and 'Hard Passages' in the NT on the Role of Women in the Church: Issues from Recent Literature," *EpRev* 18 (1991): 82-88.

2040 K. T. Wilson, "Should Women Wear Headcoverings?" *BSac* 148/592 (1991): 442-62.

2041 Elsa Tamez, "Que la mujer no calle en la congregacion: Pautas hermenéuticas para comprender Gá 3.28 y 1 Co 14.23," *CrSoc* 30/3 (1992): 45-52.

2042 J. Winandy, "Un curieux *casus pendens:* 1 Corinthiens 11.10 et son interprétation," *NTS* 38/4 (1992): 621-29.

2043 J. H. Petzer, "Reconsidering the Silent Women of Corinth—A Note on 1 Corinthians 14:34-35," *ThEv* 26 (1993): 132-38.

2044 I. R. Reimer, "Da Memória à Novidade de Vida," *EstT* 33/3 (1993): 201-12.

2045 Wendy Cotter, "Women's Authority Roles in Paul's Churches: Countercultural or Conventional?" *NovT* 36 (1994): 350-72.

2046 J. M. Gundry-Volf, "Male and Female in Creation and New Creation: Interpretations of Galatians 3.28c in 1 Corinthians 7," in T. E. Schmidt and M. Silva, eds., *To Tell the Mystery: Essays on New Testament Eschatology* (festschrift for R. H. Gundry). Sheffield: JSOT Press, 1994. Pp. 95-121.

2047 Victor Hasler, "Die Gleichstellung der Gattin: Situationskritische Reflexionen zu 1 Kor 11.2-16," *TZ* 50 (1994): 189-200.

2048 D. J. Nadeau, "Le problème des femmes en 1 Cor 14:33-35," *ÉTR* 69 (1994): 63-65.

2049 A. C. Perriman, "The Head of a Woman: The Meaning of κεφαλη in 1 Cor. 11:3," *JTS* 45 (1994): 602-22.

2050 B. M. F. van Iersel, "Keep Quiet about Women in the Church (with Apologies to 1 Corinthians 14.34)," *Conci* 5 (1994): 137-39.

2051 L. A. Jervis, "1 Corinthians 14:34-35: A Reconsideration of Paul's Limitation of the Free Speech of Some Corinthian Women," *JSNT* 58 (1995): 51-74.

2052 C. Vander Stichele, "Is Silence Golden? Paul and Women's Speech in Corinth,' *LouvS* 20 (1995): 241-53.

word studies

2053 E. Peterson "Έργον in der Bedeutung 'Bau' bei Paulus," *Bib* 22 (1941): 439-41.

2054 George O. Evenson, "The Force of "Apo" in 1 Cor. 11:23," *LQ* 11 (1959): 244-46.

2055 Victor P. Furnish, " 'Fellow Workers in God's Service'," *JBL* 80 (1961): 364-70.

2056 Morna D. Hooker, "Authority on Her Head: An Examination of 1 Corinthians 11:10," *NTS* 10 (1964): 410-17.

2057 W. Harold Mare, "Prophet and Teacher in the New Testament Period," *JETS* 9/3 (1966): 139-48.

2058 Robin Croggs, "Paul: Sophos and Pneumatikos," *NTS* 14/1 (1967): 33-35.

2059 A. Penna, "La δυναμις θεου: reflessioni in margine a 1 Cor. 1:18-25," *RBib* 15 (1967): 281-94.

2060 Leslie C. Allen, "The Old Testament Background of (Pro)Orizein in the New Testament," *NTS* 17/1 (1970): 104-108.

2061 Gordon H. Clark, "Wisdom in First Corinthians," *JETS* 15/4 (1972): 197-205.

2062 Gene Miller, "Archontwn tou aiwnos toutou-A New Lokk at 1 Corinthians 2:6-8," *JBL* 91/4 (1972): 522-28.

2063 M. L. Barré, "To Marry or to Burn: Purousthai in 1 Cor. 7:9," *CBQ* 36/2 (1974): 193-202.

2064 E. Earle Ellis, " 'Wisdom' and 'Knowledge' in 1 Corinthians,"
TynB 25 (1974): 82-98.

2065 J. M. Ford, "You Are God's 'Sukkah'," *NTS* 21/1 (1974): 139-42.

2066 Gerd Theissen, "Soziale Schichtung in der Korinthischen
Gemeinde," *ZNW* 65/3-4 (1974): 232-72.

2067 Michael Hill, "Paul's Concept of Encrateia," *RTR* 36/3 (1977):
70-78.

2068 Brian Daines, "Paul's Use of the Analogy of the Body of Christ,"
EQ 50/2 (1978): 71-78.

2069 Jean Martucci, "Diakriseis Pneumaton," *EgT* 9/3 (1978): 465-71.

2070 Parker J. Palmer, "The Conversion of Knowledge," *REd* 74/6
(1979): 629-40.

2071 Gordon D. Fee, "Eidolothuta Once Again: An Interpretation of
1 Corinthians 8-10," *Bib* 61/2 (1980): 172-97.

2072 K. Romaniuk, "Exegese du Noveau Testament et Ponctuation,"
NovT 23/3 (1981): 195-209.

2073 D. Cohn-Sherbok, "A Jewish Note on to Poterion Tes Eulogias,"
NTS 27/5 (1981): 704-709.

2074 Paul J. Fedwick, "The Function of the Proestos in the Earliest
Christian Koinonia," *RTAM* 48 (1981): 5-13.

2075 James L. Blevins, ""Wisdom" in Paul's Writings," *BI* 8/2 (1982):
15-17.

2076 F. P. Chenderlin, "The Semantic and Conceptual Background and
Value of 'ANAMNHSIS in 1 Corinthians 11:24-25," doctoral
dissertation, Claremont Graduate School, Claremont CA, 1982.

2077 David Alan Black, "A Note on 'The Weak' in 1 Corinthians
9:22," *Bib* 64/2 (1983): 240-42.

2078 E. R. Rogers, "Epotisthemen Again," *NTS* 29/1 (1983): 139-42.

2079   Vincent P. Branick, "Apocalyptic Paul?" *CBQ* 47 (1985): 664-75.

2080   John Chryssavgis, "Soma - Sarx: The Body and the Flesh—An Insight into Patristic Anthropology," *Coll* 18/1 (1985): 61-66.

2081   Benjamin Fiore, " 'Covert Allusion' in 1 Corinthians 1-4," *CBQ* 47/1 (1985): 85-102.

2082   Bo Frid, "The Enigmatic ἀλλά in 1 Corinthians 2:9," *NTS* 31 (1985): 603-11.

2083   George W. Knight, "Two Offices and Two Orders of Elders: A New Testament Study," *Pres* 11/1 (1985): 1-12.

2084   Siegfried Kreuzer, "Der Zwang des Botenbeobachtungen zu Lk 14,23 und 1 Kor 9,16," *ZNW* 76(1/2) (1985); 123-28.

2085   Jean Marc Laporte, "Kenosis and Koinonia: The Path Ahead for Anglican-Roman Catholic Dialogue," *OC* 21/2 (1985): 102-20.

2086   H. von Lips, "Der Apostolat des Paulus - en Charisma: semantische Aspekte zu charis-charisma und anderen Wortpaaren im Sprachgebrauch des Paulus," *Bib* 66/3 (1985): 305-43.

2087   Dieter Lührmann, "Confesser sa foi à l'époque apostolique," *RTP* 117 (1985): 93-110.

2088   Sigfred Pedersen, "Theologische Uberlegungen zur Isagogik des Römerbriefs," *ZNW* 76/1-2 (1985): 47-67.

2089   D. Sänger, "Die δυνατοι in 1 Kor 1:26," *ZNW* 76 (1985): 285-91.

2090   Gerard S. Sloyan, "Jewish Ritual of the 1st Century CE and Christian Sacramental Behavior," *BTB* 15 (1985): 98-103.

2091   Galen W. Wiley, "A Study of 'Mystery' in the New Testament," *GTJ* 6/2 (1985): 349-60.

2092   Norbert Baumert, "Charisma und Amt bei Paulus," in Albert Vanhoye, ed., *L'Apôtre Paul: personnalité, style et conception du ministre.* Louvain: Peeters, 1986. Pp. 203-28.

2093   Arthur J. Dewey, "Paulos Pornographos: The Mapping of Sacred Space," *EGLMBS* 6 (1986): 104-13.

2094   Marlis Gielen, "Zur Interpretation der paulinischen Formel He kat' oikon ekklesia," *ZNW* 77 (1986): 109-25.

2095   L. D. Hurst, "Re-enter the Pre-existent Christ in Philippians 2:5-11," *NTS* 32 (1986): 449-57.

2096   William W. Klein, "Noisy Gong or Acoustic Vase? A Note 1 Corinthians 13:1," *NTS* 32/2 (1986): 286-89.

2097   Jerome Murphy-O'Connor, "Being at Home in the Body we are in Exile from the Lord," *RB* 93/2 (1986): 216-21.

2098   G. C. Nicholson, "Houses for Hospitality: 1 Cor 11:17-34," *CANZTR* 19 (1986): 1-6.

2099   G. W. E. Nickelsburg, "An ἐκτρώμη, Though Appointed from the Womb: Paul's Apostolic Self-Description in 1 Corinthians 15 and Galatians 1," *HTR* 79/1-3 (1986): 198-205.

2100   W. E. Richardson, "Liturgical Order and Glossolalia in 1 Corinthians 14.26c-33a," *NTS* 32 (1986): 144-53.

2101   John N. Suggit, "The Perils of Bible Translation: An Examination of the Latin Versions of the Words of Institution of the Eucharist," in K. J. H. Petzer and Patrick Hartin, eds., *A South African Perspective on New Testament* (festschrift for Bruce Metgzer). Leiden: Brill, 1986. Pp. 54-61.

2102   Roy B. Ward, "Porneia and Paul," *EGLMBS* 6 (1986): 219-28.

2103   Niels Hyldahl, "Meta to deipnesai, 1 Kor 11,25 (og Luk 22, 20)," *SEÅ* 51/52 (1986-1987): 100-107.

2104   Otto Betz, "Der gekreuzigte Christus: Unsere Weisheit und Gerechtigkeit (der alttestamentliche Hintergrund von 1 Kor 1-2)," in Gerald F. Hawthorne and Otto Betz, eds., *Tradition and Interpretation in the New Testament* (festschrift for E. Earle Ellis). Grand Rapids: Eerdmans, 1987. Pp. 195-215.

2105   Charles H. Cosgrove, "Justification in Paul: A Linguistic and Theological Reflection," *JBL* 106/4 (1987): 653-70.

2106   Ronald Y. K. Fung, "Ministry in the New Testament," in Don A Carson, ed., *The Church in the Bible and the World*. Exeter: Paternoster Press, 1987. Pp. 154-212.

2107   Paul W. Gooch, "Conscience in 1 Corinthians 8 and 10," *NTS* 33/2 (1987): 244-54.

2108   J. K. Grider, "Predestination as Temporal only," *WTJ* 22 (1987): 56-64.

2109   Charles A. Kennedy, "The Cult of the Dead in Corinth," in *Love and Death in the Ancient Near East* (festschrift for Marvin H. Pope). Guillford CN: Four Quarters Publishinh Company, 1987. Pp. 227-36.

2110   Robert Macina, "Pour éclairer le terme: digamoi," *RevSR* 61 (1987): 54-73.

2111   Oda Wischmeyer, "Theon agapan bei Paulus: eine traditionsgeschichtliche Miszelle," *ZNW* 78/1-2 (1987): 141-44.

2112   David F. Wright, "Translating Arsenokoitai," *VC* 41/4 (1987): 396-98.

2113   Norman H. Young, "Paidagogos: The Social Setting of a Pauline Metaphor," *NovT* 29 (1987): 150-76.

2114   J. C. de Moor, "O Death, Where Is Thy Sting?" in Lyle Eslinger and J. G. Taylor, eds., *Ascribe to the Lord* (festschrift for Peter C. Craigie). Sheffield: JSOTPress, 1988. Pp. 99-107.

2115   N. George Joy, "Is the Body Really to be Destroyed?" *BT* 39/4 (1988): 429-36.

2116   Juan Mateos, "Analisis de un campo lexematico: eulogia en el Nuevo Testamento," *FilN* 1 (1988): 5-25.

2117   Jay Shaynor, "Paul as Master Builder: Construction Terms in First Corinthians," *NTS* 34/3 (1988): 461-71.

2118 Gerhard Dautzenburg, "Pheugete ten porneian (1 Kor 6,18): eine Fallstudie zur paulinischen Sexualethik in ihrem Verhältnis zur Sexualethik des Frühjudentums," in Helmut Merklein, ed., *Neues Testament und Ethik* (festschrift for Rudolf Schnackenburg). Freiburg: Herder, 1989. Pp. 271-98.

2119 Bruce Fisk, "Eating Meat Offered to Idols: Corinthian Behavior and Pauline Response in 1 Corinthians 8-10," *TriJ* 10/1 (1989): 49-70.

2120 Otfried Hofius, "To soma to huper humon 1 Cor 11:24," *ZNW* 80/1-2 (1989): 80-88.

2121 George L. Klein, "Hosea 3:1-3—Background to 1 Cor 6:19b-20?" *CTR* 3 (1989): 373-75.

2122 Otto Merk, "Nachahmung Christi: zu ethischen Perspektiven in der paulinischen Theologie," in Helmut Merklein, ed., *Neues Testament und Ethik* (festschrift for Rudolf Schnackenburg). Freiburg: Herder, 1989. Pp. 172-206.

2123 A. Miranda, "L' 'uomo spirituale' nella Prima ai Corinzi," *RBib* 43 (1995): 485-519.

2124 Margaret Mitchell, "Concerning Peri De in 1 Corinthians," *NovT* 31/3 (1989): 229-56.

2125 J. H. Petzer, "Contextual Evidence in Favor of Kauchesomai in 1 Corinthians 13:3," *NTS* 35/2 (1989): 229-53.

2126 W. D. Spencer, "The Power in Paul's Teaching (1 Cor 4:9-20)," *JETS* 32/1 (1989): 51-61.

2127 Justin S. Upkong, "Pluralism and the Problem of the Discernment of Spirits," *EcumRev* 41 (1989): 416-25.

2128 William O. Walker, "The Vocabulary of 1 Corinthians 11:3-16: Pauline or Non-Pauline?" *JSNT* 35 (1989): 75-88.

2129 E. Earle Ellis, "Soma in First Corinthians," *Int* 44/2 (1990): 132-44.

2130 Wayne Grudem, "The Meaning of Kephale ('head'): A Response to Recent Studies," *TriJ* 11 (1990): 3-72.

2131 David R. Hall, "A Problem of Authority," *ET* 102 (1990): 39-42.

2132 Carl R. Holladay, "1 Corinthians 13: Paul as Apostolic Paradigm," in David L. Balch, et al., eds., *Greeks, Romans, and Christians* (festschrift for Abraham J. Malherbe). Minneapolis: Fortress Press, 1990. Pp. 80-98.

2133 Todd K. Sanders, "A New Approach to 1 Corinthians 13:1," *NTS* 36 (1990): 614-18.

2134 Michael D. Goulder, "Σόφια in 1 Corinthians," *NTS* 37/4 (1991): 516-34.

2135 M. Navarro Puerto, "La παρθενος: Un futuro significativo en el aquí y ahora de la comunidad (1 Cor 7,25-38)," *EB* 49/3 (1991): 353-87.

2136 T. Paige, "1 Corinthians 12.2: A Pagan *Pompe?*" *JSNT* 44 (1991): 57-65.

2137 S. E. Porter, "How Should ὁ κολλώμενος in 1 Cor 6,16.17 Be Translated?" *ETL* 67/1 (1991): 105-106.

2138 Edward B. Anderson, "Power on Her Head," *LO* 14 (1992): 19-22.

2139 Beimund Bieringer, "Traditionsgeschichtlicher Ursprung und theologische Bedeutung der Hyper Aussagen im Neuen Testament," in Frans van Segbroeck, et al., eds.. *The Four Gospels 1992* (festschrift for Frans Neirynck). 2 vols. Louvain: Peeters, 1992. 1:219-48.

2140 E. Borghi, "Il tema Σόφια in 1 Cor 1-4," *RivBib* 40/4 (1992): 421-58.

2141 James B. de Young, "The Source and NT Meaning of arsenokoitai, with Implications for Christian Ethics and Ministry," *MSJ* 3 (1992): 191-215.

2142   M. Lautenschlager, "Abschied vom Disputierer. Zur Bedeutung
        von συζητητὴς in Kor 1,20," *ZNW* 83/3-4 (1992): 276-85.   ·

2143   Peter D. Gooch, *Dangerous Food: 1 Corinthians 8-10 in Its
        Context*. Studies in Christianity and Judaism #5. New York: Edwin
        Mellen Press, 1993.

2144   James T. South, "A Critique of the 'Curse/Death' Interpretation of
        1 Corinthians 5:1-8," *NTS* 39 (1993): 539-61.

2145   Robert L. Thomas, "1 Cor 13:11 Revisited: An Exegetical
        Update," *MSJ* 4 (1993): 187-201.

2146   David R. Hall, "A Disguise for the Wise: μετεσχηματισμος in
        1 Corinthians 4.6," *NTS* 40 (1994): 143-49.

2147   Alan Padgett, "The Significance of ἀντί in 1 Corinthians 11:15,"
        TynB 45 (1994): 181-87.

worship
2148   Beverly R. Gaventa, " 'You Proclaim the Lord's Death':
        1 Corinthians 11:26 and Paul's Understanding of Worship,"
        RevExp 80/3 (1983): 377-87.

2149   Alan Padgett, "Feminism in First Corinthians: A Dialogue with
        Elisabeth Schüssler Fiorenza," *EQ* 58/2 (1986): 121-32.

2150   W. E. Richardson, "Liturgical Order and Glossolalia in
        1 Corinthians 14.26c-33a," *NTS* 32 (1986): 144-53. See *AUSS* 24
        (1986): 47-48.

PART THREE

Commentaries

2151 John Calvin, *The First Epistle of Paul to the Corinthians*, trans. J. W. Fraser. Calvin's New Testament Commentaries #9. Grand Rapids MI: Eerdmans, 1960. [1546]

2152 C. F. Kling, *The First Epistle of Paul to the Corinthians*, trans. Daniel W. Poor. New York: Scribner & Co., 1868.

2153 Charles Hodge, *An Exposition of the First Epistle to the Corinthians*. New York: Hodder & Stroughton, 1878.

2154 Joseph Beet, *A Commentary on St. Paul's Epistles to the Corinthians*. 6th ed. New York: Whittaker, 1882.

2155 T. C. Edwards, *A Commentary on the First Epistle to the Corinthians*. 2nd ed. London: Hodder & Stroughton, 1885.

2156 Frédéric Godet, *Commentary on the First Epistle to the Corinthians*, trans A. Cusin. Paris: Librairie Fischbacher, 1889.

2157 George W. Clark, *Romans and I and II Corinthians*. Philadelphia: American Baptist Publication Society, 1897.

2158 Marcus Dods, *The First Epistle to the Corinthians*. Expositor's Bible. New York: Funk & Wagnalls, 1900.

2159 S. Balke, *Erster Brief an die Korinther*. Hamburg: Agentur des Rauhen Hauses, 1908.

2160 S. C. Carpenter, *I and II Corinthians*. Cambridge: University Press, 1909.

2161 R. Nicoll, ed., *1 Corinthians. The Expositor's Greek Testament*. London: Hodder & Stroughton, 1910.

2162 Johannes Weiss, *Der erste Korintherbriefe*. Göttingen: Vandenhoeck & Ruprecht, 1910.

2163 A. T. Robertson and Alfred Plummer, *A Critical and Exegetical Commentary on the First Epistle of Paul to the Corinthians*. Edinburgh: T. & T. Clark, 1911.

2164 H. L. Goudge, *The First Epsitle to the Corinthians*. Westminsiter Commentaries. 4th ed. London: Methuen & Co., 1915.

2165 John Parry, *The First Epistle of Paul the Apostle to the Corinthians*. CBSC. Cambridge: University Press, 1916.

2166 Arthur S. Peake, "1 Corinthians," in Arthur S. Peake, ed., *A Commenatry on the Bible*. New York: Nelson, 1919. Pp. 832-48.

2167 E. F. Brown, *The First Epistle of Paul the Apostle to the Corinthians*. London: SPCK, 1923.

2168 C. R. Erdman, *The First Epistle of Paul to the Corinthians*. Philadelphia: Westminster Press, 1928.

2169 Ernest Evans, *The Epistles of Paul the Apostle to the Corinthians*. Oxford: Clarendon Press, 1930.

2170 Kenneth Grayson, "The Epistles to the Corinthians," in G. Henton Davies, ed., *The Twentieth Century Bible Commentary*. New York: Harper, 1932. Pp. 478-82.

2171 E.-B. Allo, *Première épître aux Corinthiens*. Paris: Gabalda, 1934.

2172 James Moffatt, *The First Epistle of Paul to the Corinthians*. Moffatt New Testament Commentary. New York: Harper, 1938.

2173 Werner Meyer, *Der erste Korintherbrief*. Zürich: Zwingli-Verlag, 1945.

2174 J. Huby, *Première épître aux Corinthiens*. Paris: Beauchesne, 1946.

2175 John Schmidt, *Letter to Corinth*. Phialdelphia: Muhlenberg Press, 1947.

2176 Hans Lietzmann, *An die Korinther 1-11*. Handbuch zum Neuen Testament, ed. W. G. Kümmel. Tübingen: Mohr, 1949.

2177 Adolf Schlatter, *Die Korintherbriefe*. Stuttgart: Calwer, 1950.

2178 W. Rees, "1 and 2 Corinthians," in Bernard Orchard, ed., *A Catholic Commenatry on Holy Scipture*. New York: Nelson, 1951. Pp. 1081-98.

2179 V. Jacono, *Le Epistole di S. Paolo ai Romani, ai Corinti e ai Galati*. La Sacra Bibbia. Rome: Marietti, 1952. Pp. 255-409.

2180 C. T. Craig, "First Corinthians," in George A. Buttrick, ed., *Interpreter's Bible*. Nashville: Abingdon Press, 1953. X:14-262.

2181 F. W. Grosheide, *Commentary on the First Epistle to the Corinthians*. Grand Rapids: Eerdmans, 1953.

2182 Günther Zuntz, *The Text of the Epistles*. London: Oxford University Press, 1953.

2183 Jean Héring, *La première épître de saint Paul aux Corinthiens*. Neuchâtel and Paris: Delachaux & Niestlé. ET, *The First Epistle of Paul to the Corinthians*. London: Epworth Press, 1955.

2184 William Barclay, *The Letters to the Corinthians*. London: Westminster Press, 1956.

2185 Leon Morris, *The First Epistle of Paul to the Corinthians*. Grand Rapids MI: Eerdmans, 1958.

2186 Gaston Deluz, *La sagesse de Dieu: explication de la 1re Epître aux Corinthiens*. Neuchatel: Delachaux & Niestlé, 1959.

2187 E. Osty, *Les épîtres de saint Paul aux Corinthiens*. Paris: Cerf, 1959.

2188 W. G. H. Simon, *The First Epistle to the Corinthians: Introduction and Commentary*. Torch Bible Commentaries. London: SCM, 1959.

2189 H.-D. Wendland, *Die Briefe an doe Korinther*. Das Neue Testament Deutsch #7. Göttingen: Vandenhoeck & Ruprecht, 1962.

2190 William Baird, *The Corinthian Church: A Biblical Guide to Urban Culture*. New York: Abingdon Press, 1964.

2191 Joseph Blenkinsop, *The Corinthian Mirror*. London: Sheed and Ward, 1964.

2192 Francis Baudraz, *Les épîtres aux Corinthiens*. Geneva: Labor et Fides, 1965.

2193 John C. Hurd, *The Origins of 1 Corinthians*. New York. Seabury Press, 1965.

2194 Margaret E. Thrall, *1 and 2 Corinthians*. The Cambridge Commentary on the New English Bible. Cambridge: University Press, 1965.

2195 C. K. Barrett, *The First Epistle to the Corinthians*. HNTC New York: Harper & Row, 1968.

2196   G. G. Findlay, "St. Paul's First Epistle to the Corinthians," in W. Margaret Avery, *Romans, 1 and 2 Corinthians, Galatians and Hebrews.* London: A. R. Mowbray, 1968.

2197   Raymond B. Brown, *1 Corinthians.* The Broadman Bible Commentary. Nashville: Broadman Press, 1970.

2198   F. F. Bruce, *1 and 2 Corinthians.* Grand Rapids MI: Eerdmans, 1971.

2199   Karl Maly, *Der erste Brief an die Korinther.* Düsseldorf: Patmos Verlag, 1971.

2200   J. Ruef, *Paul's First Letter to Corinth.* Pelican New Testament Commentaries. London: Penguin, 1971.

2201   Werner de Boor, *Der erste Brief des Paulus an die Korinther.* Wuppertal: Brockhaus, 1973.

2202   Hans Conzelmann, *1 Corinthians.* Trans. J. W. Leitch. Hermeneia. Philadelphia: Fortress, 1975.

2203   Erich Fascher, *Der erste Brief des Paulus an die Korinther.* Belin: Evangelische Verlaganstalt, 1975. THNT

2204   William D. Orr and James A. Walther, *1 Corinthians.* Anchor Bible #32. Garden City NY: Doubleday, 1975.

2205   Robert Gromacki, *Called to be Saints: An Exposition of 1 Corinthians.* Grand Rapids: Baker Book House, 1977.

2206   John Hargreaves, *A Guide to 1 Corinthians.* London: SPCK, 1978.

2207   Jerome Murphy-O'Connor, *1 Corinthians.* New Testament Message #10. Wilmington DL: Glazier, 1979.

2208   Christophe Senft, *La première épître de Saint-Paul aux Corinthiens.* Neuchatel: Delachaux & Niestlé, 1979.

2209   Robert G. Bratcher, *A Translator's Guide to Paul's First Letter to the Corinthians.* New York: United Bible Societies, 1982.

2210   H. A. W. Meyer, *Critical and Exegetical Handbook to the Epistles to the Corinthians,* trans. D. D. Bannerman [of the 6th ed., 1884]. Peabody MA: Hendrickson, 1983.

2211 Ralph Martin, *The Spirit and the Congregation. Studies in 1 Corinthians 12-15*. Grand Rapids MI: Eerdmans, 1984.

2212 David Prior, *The Message of 1 Corinthians*. The Bible Speaks Today. Downers Grove IL: Inter-Varsity Press, 1985.

2213 Gordon D. Fee, *The First Epistle to the Corinthians*. NICNT. Grand Rapids: Eerdmans, 1987.

2214 Roy A. Harrisville, *1 Corinthians*. Augsburg Commentary of the New Testament. Minneapolis: Augsburg, 1987.

2215 Norman Hillyer, "1 and 2 Corinthians," in Donald Guthrie, ed., *The Eerdmans Bible Commentary*. 3rd ed. Grand Rapids: Eerdmans, 1987. Pp. 1049-88.

2216 Charles Talbert, *Reading Corinthians: A Literary and Theological Commentary on 1 and 2 Corinthians*. New York: Crossroad, 1987.

2217 Jerome Murphy-O'Connor, "The First Letter to the Corinthians," in Raymond E. Brown, et al., eds., *The New Jerome Biblical Commentary*, Englewood Cliffs NJ: Prenetice Hall, 1988. Pp. 798-815.

2218 Richard Wilson, "Corinthian Correspondence," in Watson E. Mills, ed., *The Mercer Dictionary of the Bible*. Macon GA: Mercer University Press, 1990. Pp. 171-74

2219 James L. Price, "The First Letter of Paul to the Corinthians," in Charles M. Laymon, ed.. *The Interpreter's One-Volume Commentary on the Bible*, Nashville: Abingdon Press, 1991. Pp. 795-812.

2220 D. A. Carson, *The Cross and Christian Ministry: An Exposition of Passages from 1 Corinthians*. Grand Rapids: Baker, 1993.

2221 Simon J. Kistemaker, *Exposition of 1 Corinthians*. Grand Rapids: Baker, 1993.

Author Index

Hunt, Allen R., 0110, 0133, 0165, 0791, 0917
Hurd, J. C., 1570
Hurd, John C., 2193
Hurley, James B., 0623, 0937, 1989
Hurst, L. D., 0097, 0276, 0336, 0480, 0825, 2095
Hyldahl, Niels, 0017, 0753, 2103
Iber, Gerhard, 0837
Ireland, William J., 0379
Isaksson, A., 0659
Jackson, Thomas A., 0786, 1405, 1907
Jacono, V., 2179
Jansen, John F., 1086, 1205
Janssens, Jos, 0092, 1999
Jenson, Robert W., 1181
Jervis, L. A., 2051
Jervis, L. Ann, 0653, 1701, 1766
Jewett, Robert, 0320, 0440, 0482, 0525, 0544
Johanson, Bruce C., 0926
Johansson, Nils, 0859, 0906
Johnson, Barbara L., 1526
Johnson, E. Elizabeth, 0028, 1975
Johnson, Michael, 0897, 1672, 1698
Johnson, Ron, 0638, 2022
Johnson, S. Lewis, 1415, 1930
Johnson, Sherman E., 1535
Jones, Ivor H., 0871
Jones, P. R., 1038
Jones, Ray C., 0758, 1627
Joy, N. George, 0269, 1187, 1244, 1881, 2115
K., Ronald Y., 1904
Kaiser, Christopher B., 1554
Kaiser, W. C., 0123, 0513
Kalugila, Leonidas, 0616, 1279, 2000
Kamel, Bishoi, 0084, 0141
Kaplan, J., 1528
Karlberg, Mark W., 1078, 1121, 1593, 1751
Karrer, Martin, 0735, 1236, 1648
Karris, Robert J., 0543, 0939, 1829, 2010
Käsemann, Ernst, 0520
Kasper, Walter, 0593, 0731, 0881, 1337, 1494, 1620, 1871
Kaye, Bruce N., 0335, 1276, 1696, 1849
Kearney, Eileen, 0911, 1967
Kelly, Robert A., 0913, 1164, 1309
Kennedy, Charles A., 0467, 0477, 1445, 1707, 1742, 2109
Kent, Homer A., 0752, 1105

Kertelge, K., 0993
Kilgallen, John J., 0043, 0386, 0831, 0846, 0851, 1473, 1910
Kilmartin, E. J., 0723
Kirchhof, R., 0327
Kirchschläger, Walter, 0785, 1467
Kistemaker, Simon J., 0270, 1250, 2221
Klassen, William, 0220, 0284, 1587
Klauck, H.-J., 0699, 0727, 1229, 1628, 1642, 1660
Klein, George L., 0343, 2121
Klein, Gunter, 1222
Klein, William W., 0872, 1717, 2096
Kline, C. Benton, 0357
Kling, C. F., 2152
Kloppenborg, John, 1014
Knight, George A. F., 0763
Knight, George W., 0834, 1298, 2083
Kobayashi, N., 0754, 1658
Koester, Helmut, 1018, 1725
Kovacs, Judith L., 0129, 1349, 1439
Kreitzer, Larry, 0980, 0981, 1211, 1562, 1743, 1951
Kremer, J., 0966, 0992, 1774
Kremer, Jacob, 1010, 1798
Krentz, Edgar M., 0983, 1799
Kreuzer, Siegfried, 0526, 2084
Kruse, Colin G., 0248, 0549, 1245
Kubo, Sakae, 0413
Kuck, D., 0171
Kugelmann, R., 0449, 0751
Kümmel, Werner Georg, 0973
Kuyper, Lester J., 0407
Kwok, Pui Lan, 0910, 2001
La Bonnardière, Anne-Marie, 1095, 1342, 1710
la Serna, E. de, 1563
Lacan, M.-F., 0898
Ladaria, Luis F., 0071, 0149, 0235, 0273, 0445, 0845, 0895, 1082, 1338, 1782
Lambrecht, J., 0870, 0996, 1069, 1080, 1803
Lampe, Peter, 0007, 0709, 0736, 1449, 1451, 1652, 1654, 1662, 1818, 1976
Lance, Darrell H., 1487
Lane, William L., 1411
Laney, J. Carl, 0358
Langevin, P.-É., 0030
Langkammer, Hugolin, 0492
Lanier, D. E., 0927, 1431, 1762, 1946
Laporte, Jean Marc, 0053, 0475, 0529, 0878, 2002, 2085